LEADERSHIP AND MANAGEMENT

(TEXT, CASES AND EXERCISES)

Dr. A. CHANDRA MOHAN

Professor of Management Studies,
S.R.M. School of Management,
S.R.M. University,
Chennai - 603 203.

Formerly Head
Dept. of Business Studies,
IBRI College of Technology, Oman.

Himalaya Publishing House

ISO 9001 : 2015 CERTIFIED

First Edition : 2007
Reprint : 2009
Second Revised Edition : 2013
Reprint : 2022
Reprint : 2026

Published by : Mrs. Meena Pandey
for **HIMALAYA PUBLISHING HOUSE PVT. LTD.,**
Vishal Industrial Estate, 1st Floor, Office No. 63/64,
Bhandup Village Road, Subhash Nagar (Opp. CEAT Tyres),
Nahur (W), Mumbai - 400 078. **Phone:** 022-35131464/65/66/67
E-mail: himpub@bharatmail.co.in; **Website:** www.himpub.com

Branch Offices :

New Delhi : "Pooja Apartments", 4-B, Murari Lal Street, Ansari Road, Darya Ganj, New Delhi - 110 002. Phone: 011-23270392, 23278631; Fax: 011-23256286

Nagpur : Kundanlal Chandak Industrial Estate, Ghat Road, Nagpur - 440 018. Mobile: 09325409992, 09325908881

Bengaluru : Plot No. 91-33, 2nd Main Road, Seshadripuram, Behind Nataraja Theatre, Bengaluru - 560 020. Phone: 080-41138821; Mobile: 09379847017, 09379847005

Hyderabad : No. 3-4-184, Lingampally, Besides Raghavendra Swamy Matham, Kachiguda, Hyderabad - 500 027. Phone: 040-27560041, 27550139

Chennai : No. 34/44, Motilal Street, T. Nagar, Chennai - 600 017. Mobile: 09380460419

Pune : "Laksha" Apartment, First Floor, No. 527, Mehunpura, Shaniwarpeth (Near Prabhat Theatre), Pune - 411 030. Phone: 020-24496323, 24496333; Mobile: 09370579333

Cuttack : Plot No. 5F-755/4, Sector-9, CDA Markat Nagar, Cuttack - 753 014, Odisha. Mobile: 09338746007

Kolkata : 3, S.M. Bose Road, Near Gate No. 5, Agarpara Railway Station, North 24 Parganas, West Bengal - 700 109. Mobile: 09674536325

DTP by : **Sunanda**

Printed at : Trinity Academy, Mumbai. On behalf of HPH.

PREFACE TO THE SECOND EDITION

There has been continuous demand for this book since its publication in 2007 and to sustain the flow of supply it has been reprinted several times. The overwhelming response from the students of Management Studies, Leaders and Managers in the Corporate World, Research Schools, Professor of Management Studies of B-Schools and Universities in India and abroad for the first edition of my book on **"Leadership and Management – Text, Cases and Exercises"**, inspired me to modify it more effectively.

The present issue has been prepared with a student-friendly approach,wide coverage and exercises to understand the concepts. The feedbacks received from users of this book using as text books for MBA and PGDM Programs of Universities and B-Schools and also for different training and Management Development Programs have inspired me to revise its contents. While revising, I have also kept in mind the changes made in the syllabus of MBA and PGDM programs of several Universities and B-Schools. These changes are directed towards development of Communication, Leadership Skills which are most important for the success of any business and advancement of all professionals. Many case studies and exercises have been added. The new chapters and appendices added are as follows:

Chapters

- Employee Morale, Attitude and Job Satisfaction.
- Teams and Teamwork
- Personality and Perception
- Human Resource Development

Appendices

- Profile of Successful Leaders
- How to Analyse Case Study

Besides making relevent changes in several Chapters, Case studies, Exercises have also been added at appropriate places to understand the concept. I hope that with these changes, this issue would be better able to cater to the needs and requirements of Students, Scholars, Professors of Management Studies and also Managers in the Corporate World.

Prof. A. Chandra Mohan
Professor of Management,
SRM University.

PREFACE TO THE FIRST EDITION

Leadership and management are related terms but they are not same. A person can be an effective manager, a leader or both. This is due to the fact that leadership is different from management. In this book, it has been clearly specified. The practice of management is different from organization to organization. Practical knowledge is different from what business schools taught the management students. Therefore, this book provides more practical examples in view of the present changing business scenario. In the organizations, there are differences of social, cultural, political, legal and economic variables. All the variables may act as constraints and limiting options for managers and leaders in an organizational environment. They may provide opportunities to achieve success. A successful manager or leader must be sensitive to the environment where he is working and directing the people. He/she must learn to make decisions from time-to-time and organize all activities in the environmental perspective of his own organization. This book provides perspectives to the management students, research scholars, academicians and practicing managers. Books written by other authors are obviously different to this text.

This text book presents clear-cut picture on management and leadership. It provides in-depth explanation with relevant case studies and exercises. Some real-life situations have been specified in each chapter to understand very clearly. All the practical examples will help the young management aspirants. As such, it is designed for management graduates, postgraduate training and development for leadership and management development programs at all levels. It is a suitable book for HRM and OB courses in MBA, M.Com. and other management courses of different B-Schools. This text is immensely useful for both continuing and distance education of different universities and institutions.

— Author

ACKNOWLEDGEMENTS

I am grateful to Teachers and Managers who provided the comments for upgrading this book particularly I would like to express my gratitude to Mr. Niraj Pandey and Mr. Vijay Pandey, Nimisha, Sunanda, Sangeetha and other editorial team members of Himalaya Publishing House Pvt. Ltd. for their continuous support and follow-up in bringing out this revised edition.

I would like to express my gratitude to my Ph.D. Guide Dr. CNK Naik, Professor and Dean of BOS of Management, SK University, Ananthapur, Andhra Pradesh. I would like to express my thanks to my wife Mrs. A. Anantha Lakshmi and also to Sri. A. Seshagiri Rao (Tahsildar) and N. Varakumar Boja for their encouragement.

I express my special thanks to Mrs. Poonguzhali, P., Assistant Professor, SRM School of Management, SRM University for assistance given in typing material during the period of revising the second edition. I am also thankful to Dr. Jayshree Suresh, Dean and my colleagues Dr. V.M. Ponniah, Prof. S. Sundarajan, Dr. R. Krishna Raj, Prof. B.V.S. Prasad, SRM School of Management, SRM University, Chennai for their inspiring words and encouragement.

Dr. A. Chandra Mohan

Professor of Management

CONTENTS

DETAILED CONTENTS

CHAPTER 1

The Concept of Leadership

Introduction – Meaning and Definitions – Concepts and Significance – Importance of Leadership–Leader vs. Managers – Qualities of Leadership – Difference between Leadership and Management – Formal and Informal Leadership – Leadership Trait Questionnaire (LTQ) – Case Study – Exercise.

Learning Objectives of this Chapter are:

- To know the meaning and definitions of leadership.
- To understand the concept and significance of leadership.
- To identify the importance of leadership.
- To study the Leader vs. Manager.
- To study the characteristics of leadership.
- To identify the various studies on leadership characteristics.
- To explain the difference between the leadership and management.
- To know the difference formal and informal leadership.

INTRODUCTION

Human beings are the most precious part of the organisation. In the organisation, effective utilization of the capacity of human resources depends upon management. Management can get the results from the people in the organisation in two ways: (i) by exercising authority (ii) by winning support of the people. Out of these, the second method is better as it has a lasting effect over the people's motivation. However, it is only possible when a manager becomes their leader, in the real sense to influence their behaviour in desired direction. This leadership is an essential ingredient for successful organisation. It is an integral part of Management and play a vital role in managerial operations. Success of any organisation depends upon the dynamic and effective leadership.

MEANING AND DEFINITION OF LEADERSHIP

Leadership is an influencing process. It is an important element of directing process. To get things done by subordinates, the manager has to lead and guide their activities. Leadership is a study of influencing the behaviour of subordinates. By influencing the working behaviour of subordinates, the manager directs it towards the accomplishment of organizational objectives. Leadership is required in every organisation, the success or failure of an organisation to the great extent depends on the quality of leadership particularly on the part of top management. It is true that the manager can manage without having qualities of leadership but if he has leadership qualities he can manage efficiently. In this regard Peter Drucker has rightly pointed out that "the managers or business leaders are the basic and scarce resource of any business enterprise and most of the failure of the business establishment has been attributed to ineffective leadership". It is because by using leadership qualities the manager develops vision about organisation and directs the activities of members in that direction. The managers at every level or organisation are expected to be leaders of work group so that subordinates may carry out their instruction and accept their guidance[1]. Thus, leadership is the study of leader's influenced over the thoughts, feelings, opinions, beliefs, attitudes and action of the followers.

Many authors have defined the term leadership and some of the important definitions are given hereunder:[2]

Box 1.1

Leadership is "influencing people to follow the achievement of common goals. It is the ability to exert interpersonal influence by means of communication towards the achievement of goals" - *Koontz O'Donnell*.

"Is a process of interpersonal influence by which executive or manager influences the activities of others in choosing and attaining given goals". - *McFarland*.

Leadership is "the ability of influencing people to strive willingly for mutual objectives". - *Terry*.

"Leadership is the relation function between an individual and a group around some common interest and behaving in a manner directed or determined by them". - *Encyclopaedia of Social Science*.

Managerial leadership "is a process of directing and influencing the task related activities of group members." - *Ralph M. Stogdill*.

A more recent definition of leadership is as follows:

"Leadership is the process of influencing and supporting others to work enthusiastically towards achieving objectives".

An analysis of these definition brings certain features of leadership, which are as follows :[3]

1. Leadership is a continuous process of behaviour; it is not one-shot activity.
2. Leadership may be seen in terms of relationship between a leader and his followers, individuals as well as groups functioning for common goals.

3. By exercising his leadership, the leader tries to influence the behaviour of individuals or group of individuals around him to achieve common goals.
4. The followers work willingly and enthusiastically to achieve those goals. Thus, there is no coercive force, which induces the followers to work.
5. Leadership gives an experience of help to followers to attain common goals. It happens when the leader feels thc importance of individuals, gives them recognition, and conveys them about the importance of activities performed by them.
6. Leadership is exercised in a particular situation, at a given point of time, and under specific set of circumstances. It implies that leadership styles may be different under different situations.

CONCEPT AND SIGNIFICANCE OF LEADERSHIP

The concept of leadership has undergone a sea change from the concept of 'born-leader- to 'situation-leader' and to effective leader. Views, assumptions and theories of leadership have changed significantly in recent years. Business and industry have set managers more as leaders to achieve the challenges. The quality of leadership provided by the managers determines the degree of success of business. Some people are born leaders and need little training or development. But many managers do not born with qualitative leadership skills. They need training and development to develop leadership skills. However, born leaders can be more efficient with little training. [4]

For example, Mahatma Gandhi, Jawarharlal Nehru, Indira Gandhi Jamshedji Tata and Dheerubhai Ambani belong to the born leaders category whereas Vikram Singh of Hindustan Aluminum, N.R.Narayana Murthy of Infosys Technology and Parthasaradhi of Hindustan Lever belong to the 'made leaders' category.

Leadership is an important part of managing process. The manager becomes more effective and efficient if he is a good leader. Without having the qualities of a good leader he may find it difficult to direct the activities of subordinates for achieving organizational objectives. More so, the success, development and growth of an organisation depends on the leadership qualities of its managers. Significance of leadership can be understood on the following grounds: [5]

1. **Directing and motivating the subordinates:** Leadership helps in motivating the members of the group to work for the accomplishment of objectives. Leadership may be regarded as an important factor in directing and channelising all energies of the employees in this direction. The leader created an urge among the employees for higher performance. In the words of George Terry "the will to do is triggered by leadership and lukewarm desires for achievement and transformed into a burning passion for successful accomplishment by the skilful use of leadership". Thus, it is only with the help of effective leadership a sense of belongingness, loyalty and commitment can be created among the employees working in an organisation.

2. **Getting cooperation of employees:** Managers can secure high-level co-operation of employees for achieving objectives, when they are good leaders, as a leader manager persuades his subordinates to work more enthusiastically. To seek maximum co-operation from the followers, he modifies their working behaviour and makes it more comfortable and meaningful for achieving organizational goals.

3. **Creating confidence among employees:** By providing guidelines and support to his employees he creates confidence among the employees. He provides psychological support and spirit of enthusiasm among the followers so that they can realize their capabilities and potentialities.

4. **Creating conducive work environment:** Leadership, primarily aims at creating congenial and proper environment in work setting so that the employees can make maximum contribution for seeking the objectives of the organisation. The leader maintains rapport with the followers and has reciprocal relation with them which helps in creating an environment of mutual help and trust.

5. **Introducing change:** Leadership also helps in introducing change in the organisation. The managers who has the qualities of leadership finds it easy to convince the employees about the positive effects of change to be introduced and thereby reduces their resistance to change. He takes them into confidence and seeks their full cooperation for implementing the change. Thus, the leader may be regarded as change facilitating agent in the organisation.

6. **Following discipline among members:** An effective leader has qualities to get his orders and instruction followed by the members. He always attempts to produce goal-directed working behaviour among members and forces them to work in a disciplined manner. He does not exercise an authority but shows exemplary character to maintain discipline, ultimately to achieve the common goals.

7. **Representing the members:** The leader is a representative of members to lead the people. Although, he makes all efforts for directing the behaviour of members towards the accomplishment of group goals, but he also takes care of personal interest of the members. He attempts to protect and promote their interest and integrates it with that of common interest.

8. **Providing satisfaction to the members:** One of the important characteristics of leader is to provide satisfaction. Characteristics of a leader is to provide satisfaction to his members. The real and effective leader is capable of satisfying personal needs and wants of the members in order to motivate and maintain team spirit of members. Thus, leader has capacity to solve the problems and difficulties of the members.

IMPORTANCE OF LEADERSHIP

Leadership is an important element in the process of direction in any organisation. It is a continuous effort of the leader to influence his employees. It is an essential ingredient for successful organisation. Throughout the history, it has been recognised that the difference between success and failure, whether in a war, a political movement, a business, or a team game can be attributed largely to leadership. The success, development and growth of organisation depends on the leadership qualities of its managers. The importance of good leadership can be discussed as follows:

1. Motivating and guiding subordinates.
2. Securing co-operation of the employees.
3. Creating confidence among the employees.
4. Maintaining discipline among the employees.
5. Developing morale among the employees.
6. Implementing change.
7. Representing the employees.
8. Developing the morale and job satisfaction.

Motivating and guiding subordinates

Leadership helps in motivating the members of the group to work for the accomplishment of the objectives. Leadership may be regarded as an important factor in directing and channelising all energies of the members in this direction. The leader creates an urge among the employees for higher performance. With the help of an effective leadership, a sense of belongingness, loyalty and commitment can be created among the employees working in an organisation.

Securing co-operation of the employees

Manager can secure wholehearted co-operation of employees for achieving objectives, when he is a good leader. As a leader the manager persuades his subordinates to work enthusiastically.

Creating confidence among employees

By providing ready help, guidance and support, the leader successfully creates confidence and zeal among the employees.

Maintaining discipline among employees

Leadership primarily aims at creating congenial and proper environment in work setting, so that the employees can make maximum contribution for seeking the objectives of an organisation.

Developing morale among the employees

An effective leader has qualities to get his orders and instruction followed by the employees. He always attempts to produce goal-directed working behaviour among them and forces them to work in a disciplined manner. He does so, not by exercising an authority but by showing exemplary character and maintaining self-discipline and self-restraint.

Implementing change

Leadership process provides proper mechanism for bringing about and implementing changes in the group. Leader uses his skill, innovativeness and creativity for discovering changes and takes the members into confidence for implementing them. Thus, the leader may be regarded as "change facilitating agent" in the organisation.

Representing the employees

The leader is a representative of employees led by him. He also takes care of personal interest of the employees. He attempts to protect and promote their interest and integrates it with that of common interest. Thus, good leadership is essential in all aspects of managerial functions, whether it be motivation, communication or direction. Good leadership ensures success in the organisation, and unsatisfactory human performance in any organisation can be attributed to poor leadership.

Developing morale of the employee

The leader will help the employees to increase the morale and job satisfaction among the employees. He creates job satisfaction among the employees based on the effective guidelines and directions. Leader also helps to solve the various problems of employees. Leader will interact frequently to know the satisfaction and dissatisfaction about their jobs.

LEADER vs. MANAGER

The leader in the new millennium like Mr. Bill Gates of Microsoft, Dheerubai Ambani of Reliance Petrochemicals have created new external environment in the competitive corporate world but the managers in the past like Mr. Krishna Murthy of Maruti Udyog Limited ran the business under the relatively stable environmental factors.

As Bennig put it, "To survive in the twenty-first century, we are going to need a new generation of leaders – leaders, not managers. The distinction is an important one. Leaders conqueror the context – the volatile, turbulent, ambiguous surroundings that sometimes seem to conspire against us and will surely suffocate us if we let them while managers surrender to it."[6]

Thus, managers surrender to the external environment, while leaders fight with the environment and create new environment. Theorists and practitioners are differentiating the leaders from managers only in recent years. This is more so, particularly after globalization and liberalization of world economies. Abraham Zalenznik argues that leaders and managers are very different kinds of people. They differ in motivation, personal history, etc. Managers tend to be impersonal towards goals while leaders take active and personal attitude towards goals.[7]

- Managers tend to view work as an enabling process while leaders work from high task positions, seek out risk and danger when opportunity and reward appear high.
- Managers work with people while leaders relate ideas to people in more intuitive and empathetic ways.

- Managers cope up with change, whereas leaders bring change. Leaders develop a vision and direction for the future. [8]
- Managers have to refer all the functions of management like planning, organizing, directing and controlling. Leader does not require to refer all the functions of the management. Leader only influences the people.[9] The difference between Manager and Leaders can be presented in Exhibit 1.1.

Exhibit – 1.1 The Difference Between Leader and Manager

Manager	Leader
Administers	Innovates
A copy	Orginal
Maintains	Develops
Focuses on systems and structures	Focuses on people
Relies on control	Inspires trust
Short-range view	Long-range perspective
Asks how and when	Asks what and why
Eye on the bottom line	Eye on the horizon
Imitates	Originates
Accepts the status quo	Challenges the status quo
Classic good soldier	Own person
Does things right	Does the right thing.

Source: Warren G. Bennig, "Managing the Dream: Leadership in the 21st Century," Journal of Organisational Change Management, Vol.2., No.1. 1989.

QUALITIES OF A LEADER

A leader has certain inherent qualities and traits, which assists him in directing and guiding role to influence the people. Some of these traits according to Stogdill are as given below:[10]

1. Physical Features
2. Intelligence
3. Emotional Stability
4. Human Relations
5. Empathy
6. Objectivity

7. Motivating Skills
8. Technical Skills
9. Communication Skills
10. Social Skills

1. Physical Features

Physical feature of a man determined by heredity factor. It is the transmission of the qualities from ancestor to descendant physical features of man includes height, weight, physique, health and appearance. To some extent these are important for leadership.

2. Intelligence

High level of intelligence is required for an effective and successful leader. It is expressed in terms of mental ability and natural quality, which is related to brain. It can be increased through various training programmes.

3. Emotional Stability

A leader should be free from bias. He is consistent in action, and retrains from anger. He shouled be well-adjusted without having anti-social attitudes. He is self-confident to solve the problems based on the situations. Thus, a leader should have high level of emotional stability.

4. Human Relations

A leader has to maintain good human relations to influence the people according to his objectives. The leader also requires understanding the behaviour and knowledge of the people and satisfy their needs. The leader has to maintain good human relations with all the employees working in the organization for the success of his leadership.

5. Empathy

Empathy is understanding the things and situations from others' point of view. A leader has to observe the things from others' point of view for the success of his leadership. Empathy requires respect for the other persons, and their rights, beliefs, values and feelings. Thus, empathy is essential for the leader.

6. Objectivity

Objectivity relates to relevant facts and information. The leader has to assess these without any basis or prejudice. Objectivity should be based on his relationship. Thus, a leader has to make clear objectives is for the success of his leadership.

7. Motivating Skills

A leader should require qualities to motivate his followers. Motivation of employees will help to improve the performance for better results. Motivation may be financial or non-financial. Thus, leader has to motivate his employees to do work effectively and efficiently for the success of his leadership.

Box 1.2 Studies on Leadership Characteristics

Stogdill (1948)	*Mann (1959)*	*Stogdill (1974)*	*Lord, Devader, and Alliger (1986)*	*Kirkpatrick and Locke (1991)*	*AC MOHAN (2005)*
Intelligence	Intelligence	Achievement	Intelligence	Drive	Physical Features
Alertness	Masculinity	Persistence	Masculinity	Motivation	Intelligence
Insight	Adjustment	Insight	Dominance	Integrity	Emotional Stability
Responsibility	Dominance	Initiative		Confidence	Human Relations
Initiative	Extroversion	Self-Confidence		Cognitive ability	Empathy
Persistence	Conservation	Responsibility		Task	Objectivity
Self-Confidence		Co-operativeness		Knowledge	Motivating Skills
Sociability		Tolerance			Technical Skills
		Influence			Communication Skills
		Sociability			Social Skills

(***Source:*** Modified Version from Peter G. Norshouse, *Leadership (Theory & Practice)*)

8. Technical Skills

A successful leader should have the ability to plan, organize, delegate, analyse, seek advice, make decision control and co-operation. All these will help to compete leadership.

9. Communication Skills

A successful leader should know how to communicate the ideas effectively to his followers. A leader has to send the message skillfully and in stimulating process for the success of his leadership.

10. Social Skills

A leader has to understand the strength and weaknesses of his people. He has the ability to co-operate the people to do the work. Thus, successful leader requires social skills.

Though all these qualities contribute to the success of leadership. Successful leader in equal quality may not possess them. The above list of qualities may be suggestive and not comprehensive.

The above traits are not universal in nature, nor all the leaders have all these traits. Not all these traits work all the time. Some of these characteristics are different from leader to leader. The leadership behaviour is directly related to individual and group work activity, loyalty of the group, absence, turnovers and employee morale. These are some of the indicators, which to some degree reflect the effectiveness of leadership behaviour. Thus, all these qualities may be suggestive and not comprehensive.

DIFFERENCE BETWEEN LEADERSHIP AND MANAGEMENT

Leadership and management are related but they are not the same. A person can be an effective manager, a leader, both, or neither. This is due to the fact that leadership differs from management on some aspects. Many researchers have studied, both the leadership and management concepts. They have concluded that leadership differs from management in terms of the emphasis that is put on four activities – creating an agenda, developing a human network for achieving the agenda, executing plans, and outcomes of activities. While leadership emphasizes change in these activities, management believes in status quo. Stephen Covey, a consultant on developing leadership, has emphasized the difference between leadership and management as follows. [11] (See box 1.3,1.4 and 1.5).

Leadership is a process that is similar to management in many ways. Leadership involves influence, as does management. Leadership requires working with people, which management requires as well. Leadership is concerned with effective goal accomplishment and so is management. In general, many of the functions of management are activities that are consistent with the definition of leadership we set forth in the beginning of this chapter. But leadership is also different from management. While the study of leadership can be tracked back to Aristotle, management emerged around the turn of the 20th Century with the advent of industrialized society. Management was created as a way to reduce chaos in organisations and to make them run more effectively and efficiently. The primary functions of management, first identified by Fayol (1916), were planning, organizing, staffing, and controlling. These functions are still representatives of the field of management today.

Box 1.3

1. Leadership deals with vision – keeping the mission in sight – and with effectiveness and results. Management deals with establishing structure and systems to get those results.
2. Leadership focuses on the top line; management focuses on the bottom line. Leadership derives its power from values and correct principles, whereas Management organizes resources to serve selected objectives to produce the bottom line.
3. Leadership inspires and motivates people to work together with a common vision and purpose. Management involves controlling and monitoring results against plans, identifying deviations, and then planning and organizing to solve the problems.
4. Leadership emphasizes transformation aspect and, therefore, transformational leadership emerge. On the other hand management focuses on transactional aspect and, therefore, transactional leadership emerges.

Box 1.4

MANAGEMENT

"Produces order and consistency"

Planning/Budgeting

- Establish agendas
- Set time-tables
- Allocate resources

Organizing/Staffing

- Provide structure
- Make job placements
- Establish rules and procedures

Controlling/Problem Solving

- Develop incentives
- Generate creative solutions
- Take corrective action

LEADERSHIP

"Produces change and movement"

Establishing Direction

- Create a vision
- Clarify big picture
- Set strategies

Aligning People

- Communicate goals
- Seek commitment
- Build teams and coalitions

Motivating and Inspiring

- Inspire and energize
- Empower subordinates
- Satisfy unmet needs

Source: Adapted from, *A Force for Change: How Leadership Differs From Management* by John P. Kotter, 1990, New York: Free Press.

In a book that compared the functions of management with the functions of leadership, Kotter (1990) argued that the functions of the two are quite dissimilar (Box 1.3). The overriding function of management is to provide order and consistency to organisations, whereas the primary function of leadership is to produce change and movement. Management is about seeking order and stability; leadership is about seeking adaptive and constructive change. As illustrated in Box 1.3, the major activities of management get played differently than the activities of leadership. While different in scope, Kotter (1990) contended that both management and leadership are essential if an organisation is to prosper. For example, if an organisation has strong management without leadership, the outcome can be stifling and bureaucratic. Conversely, if an organisation has strong leadership without management, the outcome can be meaningless or misdirected change for change's sake. To be effective, organisations need to nourish both competent management and skilled leadership.

Box 1.5 Differences between Leadership and Management

Sl. No.	*Factors*	*Leadership*	*Management*
1.	Source of power	Personal abilities	Authority delegated
2.	Focus	Vision and purpose	Operating results
3.	Approach	Transformational	Transactional
4.	Process	Inspiration & influencing	Directing and controlling
5.	Emphasis	Collectivity	Individualism
6.	Futurity	Proactive	Reactive
7.	Type	Formal and informal	Formal
8.	Progress	Innovating	Planning & organizing

FORMAL AND INFORMAL LEADERSHIP

Leadership is broadly divided into two types: 1. Formal Leaders, 2. Informal Leaders. The formal leaders are appointed or elected based on official authority. For example, anyone who is appointed to the job of a manager is also given the authority to exercise formal leadership in relationship to his subordinates. Similarly, a formally elected leader of a country or a state acquires the authority of leadership and in giving directions to the country or state. Informal leaders are exercised the power based on their interpersonal influence. They are not designated any authority or power. They emerge in certain situations because of their intelligence, skills and knowledge. Informal leaders generally influence the people based on the influencing capacity.

The informal leaders use interpersonal influences in a group without designated authority or power. These leaders are not officially elected. These leaders emerge in certain situations because of their charm, intelligence, skills or other traits and to whom other people turn to for advice, direction and guidance. Religious and civic leaders fit into this category. Successful managers who exercise their given authority in a formal way are also capable to exercising informal leadership relationships with people both within as well as outside the organisation.

LEADERSHIP TRAIT QUESTIONNAIRE (LTQ)

Instructions : Thc purpose of this questionnaire is to measure personal characteristics of leadership. The questionnaire should be completed by the leader and five individuals who are familiar with the leader.

For each adjectives listed below indicate the degree to which you think the adjective describes the leader. Please select one of thc following responses to indicate the strength of your opinion.

Key: 5 = Strongly agree 4 = Agree 3 = Neutral 2 = Disagree 1 = Strongly disagree

1. Articulate – Communicates effectively with others. 1 2 3 4 5
2. Perceptive – Discerning and insightful. 1 2 3 4 5
3. Self-confident – Believes in oneself and one's ability. 1 2 3 4 5
4. Self-assured – Secure with self, free of doubts. 1 2 3 4 5
5. Persistent – Stays fixed on the goals(s), despite interference. 1 2 3 4 5
6. Determined – Takes a firm stand, acts with certainty. 1 2 3 4 5
7. Trustworthy – Acts believable, inspires confidence. 1 2 3 4 5
8. Dependable – Is consistent and reliable. 1 2 3 4 5
9. Friendly – Shows kindness and warmth. 1 2 3 4 5
10. Outgoing – Talks freely, get along well with others. 1 2 3 4 5

Scoring Interpretation

The scores you received on the LTQ provide information about how you see yourself and how others see you as a leader. The chart allows you to see where your perceptions are the same as others and where they differ from others.

	R1	*R2*	*R3*	*R4*	*R5*	*AVE*	*SELF*	*DIF*
1. Articulate	4	3	5	2	5	3.8	5	-1.2
2. Perceptive	3	5	5	5	4	4.4	3	+1.4
3. Self-confident	4	4	5	4	4	4.2	4	+0.2
4. Self-assured								
5. Persistent								
6. Determined								
7. Trustworthy								
8. Dependable								
9. Friendly								
10. Outgoing								
Total								

Source: Peter G. Northouse, *Leadership Theory and Practice,* Response Books, New Delhi, 2003.

The example above provides ratings for the first three characteristics, which help explain how the questionnaire can be used. For example, on the characteristic. Articulate, the leader rated himself or herself significantly higher than the observers. On the second characteristic, Perceptive, the leader rated himself or herself substantially lower than others. On the self- confident characteristics, the leader was quite close to others' ratings of his or her leadership.

There are no best ratings on this questionnaire. The purpose of the instrument is to give you a way to assess your strengths and weaknesses and to evaluate areas where your perceptions are congruent with others and where there are discrepancies.

CASE STUDY ON LEADERSHIP CHARACTERISTICS

A Remarkable Turnaround

Carol Baines was married for 20 years to the owner of the Baines company until he lost his life in a tragic car accident. After his death, Carol decided not to sell the business but to try to run it herself. Before the accident, her only involvement in the business was in informal discussions with her husband over dinner, although she has a college degree in business, with a major in management.

Baines company was one of three office suppliers in a city with a population of 200,000 people. The other two stores were owned by national chains. Baines company had stable sales of about $200,000 a year, serving mostly the smaller companies in the city. The firm had not grown in a number of years and was beginning to feel the pressure of the advertising and lower prices of the national chains.

For the first 6 months, Carol spent her time familiarizing herself with the employees and the operations of the company. Next, she did a citywide analysis of those companies that had reason to purchase office supplies. Based on her understanding of Baines's capabilities and her assessment of the potential market for their products and services, Carol developed a specific set of short-term and long-range goals for the company. Behind all of her planning, Carol had a vision that Baines could be a viable, healthy, and competitive company. She wanted to carry on the business that her husband had started, but more that that, she wanted it to grow.

Over the first 5 years, Carol invested significant amounts of money in advertising, sales, and services. These efforts were well spent because the company began to show rapid growth immediately. Because of the growth, another 20 individuals were hired at Baines.

The expansion at Baines was particularly remarkable because of another major hardship Carol had to confront. Carol was diagnosed with breast cancer a year after her husband died. The treatment for her cancer included 2 months of radiation therapy and 6 months of strong chemotherapy. Although the side effects included losing her hair and being very tired, Carol continued to manage the company throughout the ordeal. In spite of her difficulties, Carol was successful. Under the strength of her leadership, the growth at Baines continued for 10 consecutive years.

Interviews with new and old employees at Baines revealed much about Carol's leadership. Employees said that Carol was a very solid person. She cared deeply about others and was fair and considerate. They said she created a family-like atmosphere at Baines. Few employees had quit Baines since Carol took over. Carol was devoted to all the employees and she supported their interests. For example, the company has a softball team in the summer and a basketball team in the winter, and both are sponsored by Baines. Others described Carol as a strong individual. Even though she had cancer, she continued to be positive and interested in them. She did not get depressed with the cancer and its side effects, even though is was difficult. Employees said she was a model of strength, goodness, and quality.

At the age of 55, Carol turned the business over to her two sons. She continues to act as the president but does nor supervise the day-to-day operations. The company is presently doing more than $3.1 million in sales, and it outpaces both of the other two chain stores in the city.

Questions

1. How would you describe Carol Baines's leadership traits?
2. How big a part did Carol's traits play in the expansion of the company?
3. Would Carol be a leader in other business contexts?

EXERCISE ON LEADERSHIP ROLES

INTSTRUCTIONS: Indicate the following scale:

1- disagree strongly; 2- disagree; 3- neutral; 4- agree; 5- agree strongly

1. Many people imitate my ideas.

   1 2 3 4 5

2. Building team spirit is important to me.

   1 2 3 4 5

3. I would enjoy coaching other members of the team.

   1 2 3 4 5

4. It is important to me to recognize others for their accomplishments.

   1 2 3 4 5

5. I would enjoy entertaining visitors to my firm even if it interfered with my completing a report.

   1 2 3 4 5

6. It would be fun for me to represent my team at gathering outside our department.

   1 2 3 4 5

7. What my team accomplishes is more important than my personal glory.

   1 2 3 4 5

8. I like to cheer people up even when my own spirits are down.

   1 2 3 4 5

9. It's easy for me to compliment others.

   1 2 3 4 5

10. It's a good practice to ask people provocative questions about their work.

    1 2 3 4 5

11. It would be accurate to say that I have inspired other people.

    1 2 3 4 5

12. It is enjoyable to have people count on me for ideas and suggestions.

    1 2 3 4 5

13. The problems of my teammates are my teammates are my problems too.

    1 2 3 4 5

14. Resolving conflict is an activity I enjoy.

    1 2 3 4 5

15. I would cooperate with another unit in the organization even if I disagreed with the position taken by its members.

    1 2 3 4 5

16. Team members liten to me when I speak.

    1 2 3 4 5

17. I am an idea generator in the job.

    1 2 3 4 5

18. It is fun for me to bargain whenever I have the opportunity.

    1 2 3 4 5

Total score: ____________

For Answer Email: dracmohan_mannava@yahoo.com

REFERENCES

1. G.K. Puri "Principles and Practice of Management for All", IIMS Publications, New Delhi, 1993. p. 271.
2. B.S. Moshal "Management Theory and Practice", Galgotia Publishing Company, New Delhi 2000, pp.269 – 270.
3. L.M. Prasad "Principles and Practice of Management", Sultan Chand & Sons, New Delhi, 2001, pp. 631-632.
4. P.Subba Rao "Personnel and Human Resource Management", Text and Cases, Himalaya Publishing House, Mumbai, 2002, p. 300.
5. B.S.Moshal "Management Theory and Practice", Galgotia Publishing Company, New Delhi 2000, pp. 271-275.
6. Warren, G. Bennig, Managing the Dream Leadership in the 21st Century,"Journal of Organisational Change Management", p. 7.
7. Abraham Zeleznik, "Managers and Leaders, are they different? Harvard Business Review" , 1999, March – April, pp. 126-135.
8. J.P. Kotter, "What Leaders Really Do" Harvard Business Review" May, 1990, June, pp. 103-111.
9. L.M. Prasad, "Principles and Practices of Management", Sultan Chand & Sons, New Delhi, 2001, p. 633.
10. Ralph M. Stogdill, Personal Factors Associated with Leadership: A Survey of Literature, Journal of Psychology, January 1948, pp. 35-71.
11. Stephen Corey, "Yin or Yang", *The Economic Times*, April 21, 2000, pp. 1-2 (Supplement).
12. JIT S. Chandran 'Organizational Behaviour' , Vikas Publishing House, New Delhi, 1997, pp. 339-340.
13. Aswathappa, K., "Organizational Behaviour", Himalaya Publishing House, 2000, pp. 345-346.
14. Peter G. Northhouse, "Leadership Theory and Practice", Response Books, New Delhi, 2003.
15. P.C. Tripathi & P.N. Reddy, "Principles of Management", Tata McGraw Hill, New Delhi, 2006.
16. Anjali Ghanekar "Organizational Behaviour" Everest Publishing House, Pune, 2002.

CHAPTER

2

Theories of Leadership

Classification of Leadership – Trait Theory – Behavioural Theory – Situation Theory – Path-goal Theory of Leadership – Fielder's Contingency Theory – McGregor's Theory X and Theory Y – Charismatic Leadership Theory – Transformational Leadership Theory – Exercise – Case Study – Exercise.

Learning Objectives of this Chapter are:

- To know the classification of leadership.
- To identify the different theories of leadership.
- To examine the difference among the various theories.
- To analyze the various theories practiced by the managers based on the situation.
- To understand the theories and interrelated styles of leadership.
- To examine the difference between charismatic leadership theory and transformation leadership theory.

Many of the Research studies have been conducted by the behavioural Scientists on leadership to find out the answer to the question, what makes a leader effective? Is leadership successful due to his personality or, his behaviour, or the types of followers he has or the situation in which he works, or a combination of all these? These researchers, however, could not give a satisfactory answer of the question. These researchers have been presented various theories or approaches on leadership. The understanding of the various theories of leadership will provide guidelines to judge as how a leader emerges. Leadership theories are broadly classified into eight types including some of the famous theories classified by great men. Theory of Leadership it is also called as Charismatic Leadership Theory.

CLASSIFICATION OF LEADERSHIP THEORIES

Leadership Theories can be classified into various types by many Authors. The important theories can be classified into the following are:

1. Trait Theory
2. Behavioural Theory
3. Situational Approach
4. Path-Goal Theory of Leadership
5. Fielder's Contingency Theories
6. McGregor's Theory X and Theory Y
7. Charismatic Leadership Theory
8. Transformational Leadership Theory

TRAIT THEORY

Trait is defined as relatively enduring quality of an individual. The trait approach seeks to determine 'what makes a successful leader' from the leader's own personal characters. Trait approach leadership studies were quite popular between 1930 and 1950. The method of study was to select leaders of eminence and characteristics were studied. It was the hypothesis that the persons having certain traits could be successful leaders. A number of research studies were conducted during the last 50 years. The cumulative findings of these studies conclude that some traits increase the likelihood of success as a leader, but more of the traits guarantee success.

Trait theories of leadership sought personality, social, physical or intellectual traits those differentiated leaders from non-leaders. Traits theorists refer the people like Mahatma Gandhi, Indira Gandhi, Marget Thatcher, Nelson Mandela, N.T. Rama Rao and describe them in terms of charismatic, enthusiastic and courageous. Thus, trait theories assume that leaders are born, made. The research studies focus on personal traits or characteristics that distinguish the leaders from the followers and a successful leader from an unsuccessful leader. The characteristics of successful leaders can be presented in the following exhibit.

Stogdill has presented a review of various research studies. According to him various trait theories have suggested these traits in a successful leader. The following are the major innate qualities in a successful leader:

1. Physical features
2. Intelligence
3. Emotional stability
4. Human relations
5. Empathy

6. Objectivity
7. Motivating skills
8. Technical skills
9. Communication skills
10. Social skills

Exhibit 2.1 Characteristics of Successful Leaders

Trait/Characteristic	Description
Drive	Desire for achievement, ambition, and high energy, tenacity, initiative
Honesty and Integrity	Trustworthy, reliable, open
Leadership Motivation	Desire to exercise influence over others to reach their goals.
Self-confidence	Trust in own abilities
Cognitive Ability	Intelligence, ability to integrate and interpret large amounts of information
Knowledge of the business	Knowlede of industry, relevant technical matters
Creativity	Originality
Flexibility	Ability to adapt to need of followers and requirements of the situation

Source: Jerald Greenberg and Robert A.Bazron, "Behaviour in Organisation," Prentice-Hall of India, 1999, p. 501.

Though all these qualities contribute to the success of leadership, but it cannot be said for certain about the relative contributions of these qualities. Motivation, it is not necessary that successful leader in equal quantity possesses all these qualities. The list of qualities may be only suggestive and not comprehensive.

Evaluation of Trait Theory

The Trait theory is very simple. However, this fails to produce clear-cut results. It does not consider the whole environment of leadership of which trait may be only one factor. Moreover, no generation can be drawn about various traits for leadership, as there were considerable variations in traits established by various researchers. Jennings has concluded, 50 years of study has failed to produce one personality trait or set of qualities that can be used to discriminate leaders and non-leaders. In brief, this approach presents the following problems:

1. There cannot be generation of traits for a successful leader. This was evident by various researches conducted on leadership traits.

2. No evidence has been given about the degree of various traits because people have various traits with different degrees.
3. There is a problem of measuring traits. Though there are various tests to measure the personality traits, however no definite conclusion can be drawn.
4. There have been many people with the traits specified for leader's but they were not good leaders.

However, this approach gives indication that leaders should have certain personal characteristics. This helps management to develop such qualities through training and development programmes.

BEHAVIOURAL THEORY

This approach emphasizes that strong leadership is the result of effective role Behaviour. Leadership is shown by a person's acts more than by his traits. Though trait influence acts, followers, goals and the environment in which these occur also affect. Thus, there are four basic elements in this approach, such as leaders, followers, goals, and environment, which affect each other in determining suitable behaviour. Leadership acts may be viewed in two ways. Some acts are functional (favourable) to leadership and some are disfunctional (unfavourable). These dysfunctional acts are also important in leadership because they de-motivate employees to work together. As such a leader will not act in this way. The dysfunctional acts are inability to accept subordinates' ideas, display of emotional immaturity, poor human relations and poor communication. This approach uses three skills by a leader, such as technical, human and conceptual skill to lead his followers. A technical skill refers to a person's knowledge and proficiency; human skill is ability to interact effectively with people and to build teamwork. Conceptual skills deal with the ideas and enables managers to deal successfully with abstraction, to set up models and devise plans. Behaviour of a manager in a particular direction will make him good leader while opposite of this would discard him as a leader. Setting goals, motivating employees for achieving goals, raising the level of morale, building teamwork, effective communication, etc., are the functional behaviour for a successful leader.

Critical Evaluation of Behavioural Theory

The basic difference between the trait approach and behavioural approach is that former emphasizes some particular trait to the leader, while latter emphasizes particular behaviour by the leader. It is true that favourable behaviour provides greater satisfaction to the followers and the person can be recognized as a leader. However, this approach suffers from one weakness i.e., a particular Behaviour at a time may be effective, while at other times may not be effective. This means that time factor becomes a vital element, which has not been considered here.

SITUATIONAL APPROACH

The prime attention in this approach is given to the situation in which leadership is exercised. Since 1945, much emphasis in leadership research is being given to the situations that surround the exercise of leadership. For the first time, this approach was applied in 1920 in armed forces of Germany with the objective to get good Generals under the different situations. Winston Churchill was treated to be the most efficient Prime Minister during the Second World War. However, he was a flop afterwards when the situation changed. Ohio State University research has given four situational variables that effect performance of leadership. These are.

1. The cultural environment
2. Difference between individuals
3. Difference between jobs
4. Difference between organizations.

1. The cultural environment: Culture is a man made social system of belief, faith and value. Culture has a significant influence upon behaviour and any understanding of employee's behaviour requires the understanding of culture in which he lives. Culture may interfere with rational production efficiency by requiring action unnecessary or unrealistic from a national point of view, but necessary from culture point of view. Thus, leadership should be directed to influence behaviour of followers in the context of culture.

2. Difference between individuals: Human Behaviour is caused by some combination of antecedent factors. Besides for any given aspect of behaviour, there may be many contributing factors, not causative in nature. There are a variety of such factors which affect behaviour in different ways such as aptitudes, personality characteristics, physical characteristics, interest and motivation, age, sex, experience, etc., within this framework, individuals in the leadership process may be classified as leaders and followers. The individual characters affect the leadership process. Thus, some persons may perceive particular leadership style suitable while others may have different perceptions.

3. Difference between jobs: People are performing different types of jobs in the organisation. The importance of placing individuals in jobs which they can perform at satisfactory level stems from four different considerations such as economic, legal, personal and social. Different conditions also influence leadership behaviour differently. It is because of the fact that demands of jobs almost inevitably force a leader into certain kinds of activities. Such requirements do much to set the framework within which the leader must operate.

4. Difference between the organisations: Various organisations differ on the basis of their size, ownership pattern, objective, complexity, managerial pattern, organizational structure, leadership pattern and cultural environment, etc. In different types of organizations, leadership process tends to differ. For example, in military or Government administration, leadership behaviour will be different as compared to business organisation.

Critical Analysis of Situational Approach

The situational theory of leadership gives the analysis how leadership behaviour differs with situational variables. Thus the question, why a manager in particular situation is successful while in the other situation is unsuccessful, is answered by this theory. However, this approach is not free from certain limitations such as this theory emphasis leadership ability of an individual in a given situation, organizational factor's become helpful or constraints to a great extent to an individual leader in exercising the leadership and theory does not emphasize the process by which good leaders can be made in the organization. Thus, it puts a constraint over leadership development process.

PATH-GOAL THEORY OF LEADERSHIP: (PGT)

One of the most respected approaches to the study of leadership currently is discussed in the path-goal theory developed by Robert House. The essence of the theory is that the leader's job is to use structure, support, and rewards to create work environment that helps employees reach the organizational goals. According to this theory the leader must clarify goals for the followers and clear the path for achieving the goals. The theory is called Path-Goal because its major concern is how the leader influences the follower's perception of their work goals, personal goals and paths to goal attainment. This theory suggests that a leader's behaviour is motivating or satisfying to the degree that the behaviour increases follower's goal attainment and clarifies the path to these goals. The path goal theory is closely related to the Expectancy theory of motivation. This theory helps us in understanding and predicting effectiveness of leadership in different situations.

The path-goal theory focuses on how leaders might influence by increasing the availability and attractiveness of rewards and by strengthening expectancies that effort can result in performance and performance in rewards. As mentioned earlier, the path-goal theory is one of the contingency models. The leader's effectiveness, according to the path-goal theory, in influencing rewards and expectancies depends on the characteristics of the environment and the characteristics of the followers. Ultimate effect of leadership behaviour on motivation and satisfaction is contingent upon the characteristics of environment and of the subordinates.

As figure PGT show four kinds of leader behaviour and two categories of contingency variables together, the behaviours and contingencies influence the motivation for task performance and satisfaction of employees. The four dimensions of leader behaviour are directive, supportive, achievement oriented and participative. The true meaning of these dimensions as they would be reflected in actual leader behaviour is analyzed in Behavioural theories. These four dimensions include, and go beyond the task and relationship orientations used in Fiedler's approach. The contingency variables include subordinate attributes and work setting. Important subordinate attributes are locus of control and perceived ability. Characteristics of work setting include task structure, authority system and work group.

Critical Evolution of the Path-Goal Theory

On the plus side it may be stated that the path-goal theory is an improvement over Fiedler's model in as much as the former takes into account the personality characteristic of subordinates as well as situational variables. On the minus side, it can be mentioned that it is a posthoc theory and is yet to be extensively tested.

FIELDER'S CONTINGENCY THEORY

Contingency approach of leadership states that management leadership styles that best contributes to the achievement of organizational goals might vary in different types of situations or circumstances. Fred Fiedler developed theory of leadership after having conducted extensive research on leadership for thirty years. This theory is known as Contingency Theory of leadership. Fielder developed a model to predict work group effectiveness by taking into consideration the 'fit' or match among (i) The leader's style (task/relationship oriented); (ii) The leader – member relations; (iii) Task – Structure; and (iv) The position power of the leader. This theory is presented in the following figure.

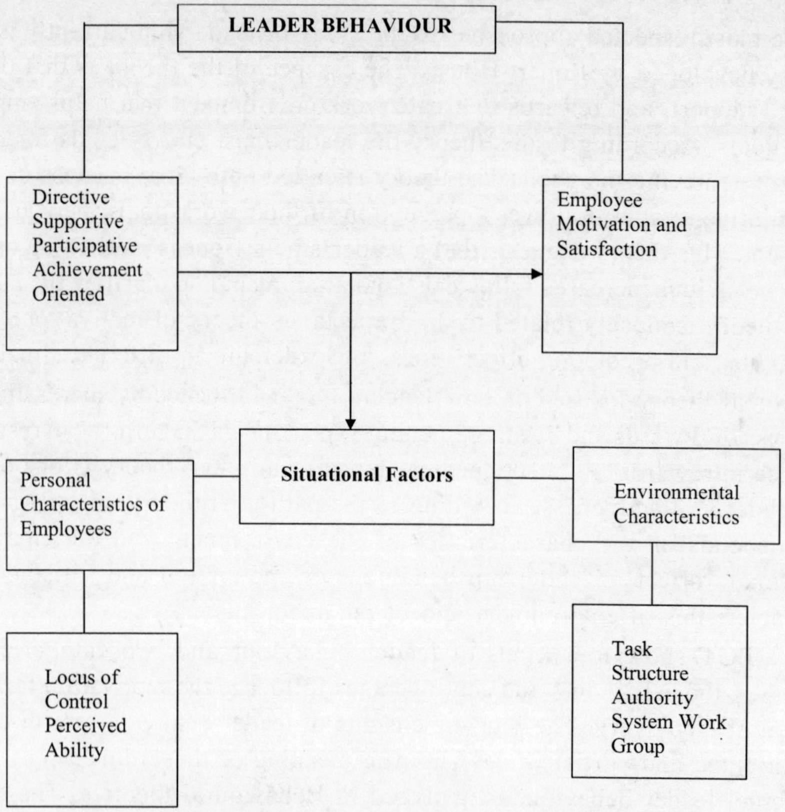

Fig. 2.1: The Path-goal Theory of Leadership

Situation Characteristics

Leader-member Reations	Good	Good	Good	Good	Poor	Poor	Poor	Poor
Task-Structure	High	High	Low	Low	High	High	Low	Low
Position–Power	Strong	Weak	Strong	Weak	Weak	Strong	Strong	Weak

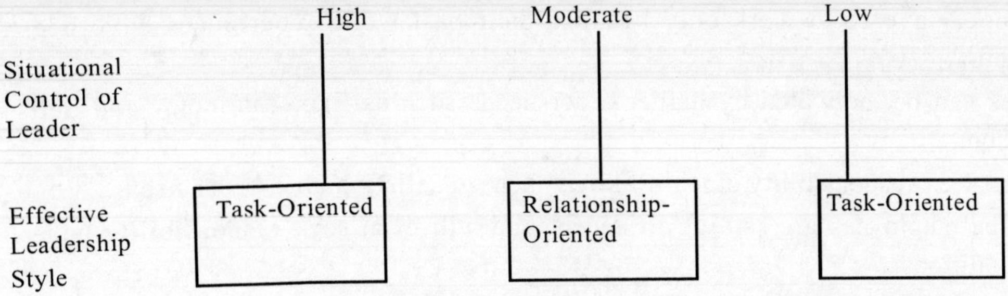

Source: P.Subba Rao "Personnel and Human Research Management" Himalaya Publishing House, 2000.

MCGREGOR'S THEORY X AND THEORY Y

Douglas McGregor classified the leadership theory under the terms of theory X and theory Y in his book "The Human Side of Enterprise". Theory X which fits strikingly with the rational, and economic concepts of the man and theory Y which leads to a social self-actualizing concept of a man. McGregor's Theory X and Theory Y is probably most widely known of all the theories, having been discussed much in text books, journals and management training programmes. It is difficult to determine whether theory X and theory Y are leadership theories or theories of motivation. We include the theories in discussion because of the assumptions a leader makes about his subordinates. It should not, however be forgotten that the theories have applications for employee motivation.

McGregor argued that traditional manager behaviour was inappropriate since it was based on some questionable assumptions about employees. Theory X has the following assumptions:

1. Employees are inherently lazy and will avoid work unless forced to do it.
2. Employees have no ambition or desire for responsibility. They prefer to be directed or controlled.
3. Employees have no motivation to achieve organizational objectives.
4. Employees are only motivated by psychological and safety needs.
5. Most of the employees seek security and want to avoid responsibility. Therefore they are willing to accept the direction of the managers.

McGregor contended that many managerial practices were based on Theory X assumptions and pointed to such examples as hierarchical models of organizations where one person controls another or on small scale, a quality control inspector who checks on the behaviour of the others. He further believed that theory X assumptions were out-dated and that employees would contribute far more to the organization if a completely different set of assumptions, which he called Theory Y were guiding force behind managerial behaviour. Theory Y has the following assumptions:

1. Employees find work as natural as play if organizational conditions are appropriate. People appear averse to work only because their past work experiences have been unsatisfactory.
2. Employees can be motivated by higher order needs such as Ego, Autonomy and Self-actualization.
3. Employees seek responsibility since it allows them to satisfy higher order needs.
4. Most of the employees are willing to accept and will even seek responsibility under proper conditions.
5. Most of the employees are capable of demonstrating more of both creativity and intellectual ability than they do in many organizational settings.

It is clear that the above set of assumptions has quiet different implications for leadership. If it is assumed that man has the potential for development, the capacity for assuming responsibility and the readiness to direct his own behaviour towards organizational goals, it follows that the manager has to act more as a sympathizer and supporter than as a director and controller. Thus, he is likely to have a democratic style with an occasional touch of *laissez faire*. In others words, Theory Y relies heavily on self-control and self-direction of an employee as opposed to the reliance on external control of his behaviour in Theory X.

Modern Theories of Leadership

The modern theories of leadership can be classified into Two types; they are:

1. Charismatic leadership theory
2. Transformational leadership theory.

CHARISMATIC LEADERSHIP THEORY

According to House, the characters of the charismatic leaders include: self-confidence, confidence in subordinates, high expectations for subordinates, ideological vision, and use of personal example. The characters of the followers of the charismatic leaders include: identification with the leader's mission, exhibit extreme loyalty to and confidence in the leader, emulate the leader's values, behaviours and derive self-esteem from their relationship with the leader. It is also called as Great Theory of Leadership.

Mahatma Gandhi's character of self-confidence, ideological vision and personal example made him as a charismatic leader. Mr. Dheerubhai Ambani's character of self-confidence, Mr. Ramalinga Raju's (of Satyam Computers) character of confidence in subordinates and high expectation for subordinates made them charismatic leaders. These characters of Ramalinga Raju resulted in performance of the followers beyond the expectations. Similarly, Mr. Kurian's ideological vision resulted in the success of 'white resolution'. Dr. N.T.Rama Rao's unconventional behaviour made as Chief Minister of Andhra Pradesh. (Exhibit 2.2).

Exhibit 2.2 Key Characteristics of Charismatic Leaders

1. Self-confidence. They have complete confidence in their judgement and ability.
2. A vision. This is an idealized goal that proposes a future better than the status quo. The greater the disparity between this idealized goal and the status quo, the more likely that followers will attribute extraordinary vision to the leader.
3. Ability to articulate the vision. They are able to clarify and state the vision in terms understandable to others. This articulation demonstrates on understanding of the follower's needs and, hence, acts as a motivating force.
4. Strong conviction about the vision. Charismatic leaders are perceived as being strongly committed, and willing to take on high personal risk, incurs high cost, and engage in self-sacrifice to achieve their vision..
5. Behaviour that is out of the ordinary. Those with charisma engage in behaviour that is perceived as being, none, unconventional, and counter to norms. When successful, these behaviours evoke surprise and admiration in followers.
6. Perceived as being a change agent. Charismatic leaders are perceived as agents of radical change rather than as caretakers of the status quo.
7. Environment sensitivity. These leaders are able to make realistic assessments of the environmental constraints and resource needed to bring about change.

Source: Based on J.A.Conger and R.N.Kanungo, "Behavioural Dimensions of Charismatic Leadership," in J.A.Conger and R.N.Kanungo, Charismatic Leadership (San Francisco: Jossey – Boss, 1988), p.91.

Exhibit 2.3 Ethical and Unethical Characteristics of Charismatic Leaders

Ethical Charismatic Leader	Unethical Charismatic Leader
• Uses power to serve others.	• Uses power only for personal gain or impact.
• Align vision with followers needs and aspiration	• Promotes own personal vision.
• Considers and learns from criticism.	• Censures critical or opposing views.
• Stimulates followers to think independently and to question the leader's view.	• Demands own decision be accepted without questions.
• Open, two way communication.	• One-way communication.
• Coaches, develops, and supports Followers; shares recognition with others.	• Insensitive to follower's needs.
• Relies on internal moral standards to satisfy organizational and societal interests.	• Relies on convenient, external Moral standards to satisfy self-interests.

Source: Academy of Management, Executive, May, 1992.

Chaismatic leaders, thus, lure and motivate the subordinates towards performance beyond expectations, innovations, creations, and create the work culture among the followers. Charismatic leaders tend to be portrayed as wonderful heroes. However, there can also be unethical characters associated with these leaders. (Exhibit 2.3). Behavioural components of charismatic and non charismatic leaders are presented in Exhibit 2.4.

Exhibit 2.4 Behavioural Components of Charismatic and Non Charismatic Leaders

Charismatic Leaders	Non Charismatic Leaders	Charismatic Leaders
Relation to *Status Quo*	Essentially agrees with *status quo* and strives to maintain it.	Essentially opposed to *status quo* and strives to change it.
Future Goal	Goal not too discrepant from *status quo*.	Idealized vision which is highly discrepant from *status quo*.
Likableness	Shared perspective makes him/ her likable.	Shared perspective and idealized vision makes him/her a likable and Honourbale hero, worthy of identification and imitation.
Trust-Worthiness	Disinterested advocacy in persuasion attempts.	Disinterested advocacy by incurring great personal risk and cost.
Expertise	Expert in using available means to achieve goals within the framework of the existing order.	Expert in using unconventional means to transcend the existing order.
Behaviour	Conventional, conforming to existing norms.	Unconventional or counter normative.
Environmental Sensitiivity	Low needs for environmental sensitivity to maintain *status quo*.	High need for environmental sensitivity for changing the *status quo*.
Articulation	Weak articulation of goals and motivation to lead.	Strong articulation of future vision and motivation to lead.
Power Base	Position power and personal power (based on reward, expertise and liking for a friend who is a similar other).	Personal power (based on expertise, respect, and admiration for a unique hero).
Leader Follower	Egalitarian, consensus seeking, or directive. Nudges or orders people to share his/her views.	Elitist, entrepreneur and exemplar. Transforms people to the radical changes advocated.

Source: Richard M. Hodgetts, *Organisational Behaviour,* p. 234.

TRANSFORMATIONAL LEADERSHIP THEORY

Mr. Nair of Roorkela Steel Plant of SAIL, Mr. G. Subba Rao of Andhra Pradesh Paper Mills Limited, and Mr. Krishna Kumar of Tata Tea and Prof. M. Rama Mohana Rao of Indian Institute of Management, Bangalore transformed their organisations from loss-making/less performed into highly profit making/highly performed companies/organisations. Mr. Anji Reddy of Dr. Reddy Labs made his company as one of the leading Pharmaceutical companies with R & D base.

Transformational leadership theory conceptualizes such developments.

Two types of political leadership *viz.*, transactional and transformational are identified. Transactional leadership involves an exchange relationship between leaders and followers. Whereas, transformational leadership is based on leaders' shifting the values, beliefs and needs of the followers. The characteristics of transformational leaders include identifying themselves as a change agents, courageous, belief in people, value driven, lifelong learners, have the ability to deal with complexity and visionaries Exhibit 2.5 presents the characteristics of transactional and transformational leaders.

Exhibit 2.5 Transformational Leadership in South Korea

In 1989, When Lee Hun–Jo became Chief Executive of the once-successful Korean electrical appliance and electronics company Goldstar, the company was headed for ruin. Global and domestic share was slipping, quality was declining and even rank – and – file employees realized that if things did not change, bankruptcy was imminent. Less than 10 years after Hun – Jo took over, Goldstar (renamed LG Electronics Co. In 1994) recovered its spot as the top producer of washing machines, refrigerators and colour Tvs in Korea. LG Electronics is also gaining ground globally in the areas of liquid – crystal displays and semiconductors.

Hun–Jo realized from the start that nothing short of a major transformation was necessary to turn around LG Electronic's fortunes. As he put it, "You have to transform human beings. If you can't change your people, you can't change your organization. If you can't do that, you can't reach your goal."

Hun-Jo's vision for LG Electronics included its being a top performer domestically and globally. He also envisioned dramatic changes for the organization's structure and culture. Like many Korean companies, LG Electronics had a relatively rigid hierarchy with decision making centralized at the top and a culture that respected authority and tradition. Hun–Jo's vision included decentralization of decision making and a culture supportive of efficiency, effectiveness and innovation. In numerous face-to-face meetings, Hun–Jo enthusiastically communicated his vision throughout LG Electronics, made many changes to support it and even has taken symbolic steps to communicate that things are changing. Rather than wearing the conservative neckties favoured by Korean top managers, Hun–Jo wears radiantly coloured ties and refuses to sit in the traditionally honoured spots reserved for the Chief Executive in meetings with managers.

Hun-Jo intellectually stimulates his subordinates in multiple ways. He has opened new paths to communication between non-managerial employees and managers and has openly shared the company's problem with employees and made them feel responsible for helping to solve them. Decision making has been decentralized and all employees are encouraged to feel responsible for coming up with improvements, ideas for new products and ways to increase quality. LG Electronics traditionally took products developed by foreign competitors, such as the Japanese and tried to copy and customize them for the Korean market place. Part of Hun-Jo's vision is for LG Electronics to come up with its own innovative products. He made product development engineers feel responsible for doing this and sent them out to talk to LG Electronic's customers to see what they really wanted. As a result of this intellectual stimulation, LG Electronics now has an innovative and best-selling product on its hands – a refrigerator specially designed to keep kimchi (Korea's national dish of pickled and fermented cabbage and radishes) fresh tasting and smelling for much longer than is possible in a conventional refrigerator.

Hun-Jo also engages in developmental consideration. He has taken dramatic steps to improve management relations with the union and not only has shared information with union leaders but also encouraged them to meet with him whenever they wanted to determine how to improve things at LG Electronics. He wants his employees to reach their full potential and is doing whatever he can think of to help them do that. Hun–Jo also reads extensively about the latest advances in management thought and practice in the United States and other countries to help himself be an effective manager and leader. All in all, Hun-Jo seems to be just the kind of leader LG Electronics needed to regain its position as a top–performing global organization-a transformational leader.

(***Source:*** Gareth R. Jones, et. al., *Management*, Irwin McGraw-Hill, 1998, p.422)

Exhibit 2.6 Characteristics of Transactional and Transformational Leaders

Transactional Leader

Contingent Reward: Contracts exchange of rewards for effort, promises rewards for good performance, recognizes accomplishments .

Management by Exception (active): Watches and searches for deviations from rules and standards, takes corrective action.

Management by Exception (Passive): Intervenes only if standards are not met.

Laissez-Faire: abdicates responsibilities, avoids making decisions.

Transformational Leader

Charisma: Provides vision and sense of mission, instills pride, gains respect and trust.

Inspiration: Communicates high expectations, uses symbols to focus, expresses important purposes in simple ways.

Intellectual Stimulation: Promotes intelligence, rationality, and careful problem solving.

Individualized Consideration: Gives personal attention, treats each employee individually, coaches, and advises.

Source: B.M.Boss, "From Transactional to Transformational Leadership: Learning to Share the vision" , Organizational Dynamics, Winter 1990, p. 22).

Exercise on Least Preferred Co-worker (LPC) Measure

Instruction: Think of the person with whom you can work least well. He or she may be someone you work with now or someone you knew in the past. He or she does not have to be the person you like but should be the person with whom you had the most difficulty in getting a job done. Describe this person as he or she appears to you.

										Scoring
Pleasant	8	7	6	5	4	3	2	1	Unpleasant	____
Friendly	8	7	6	5	4	3	2	1	Unfriendly	____
Rejecting	8	7	6	5	4	3	2	1	Accepting	____
Tense	8	7	6	5	4	3	2	1	Relaxed	____
Distant	8	7	6	5	4	3	2	1	Close	____
Cold	8	7	6	5	4	3	2	1	Warm	____
Supportive	8	7	6	5	4	3	2	1	Hostile	____
Boring	8	7	6	5	4	3	2	1	Interesting	____
Quarrelsome	8	7	6	5	4	3	2	1	Harmonious	____
Gloomy	8	7	6	5	4	3	2	1	Cheerful	____
Open	8	7	6	5	4	3	2	1	Closed	____
Backbiting	8	7	6	5	4	3	2	1	Loyal	____
Untrustworthy	8	7	6	5	4	3	2	1	Trustworthy	____
Considerate	8	7	6	5	4	3	2	1	Inconsiderable	____
Nasty	8	7	6	5	4	3	2	1	Nice	____
Agreeable	8	7	6	5	4	3	2	1	Disagreeable	____
Insincere	8	7	6	5	4	3	2	1	Sincere	____
Kind	8	7	6	5	4	3	2	1	Unkind	____

Scoring Interpretation

Your final LPC score is determined by adding up the numbers you circled on all of the 18 scales.

If your score is 57 or below, you are a low LPC, which suggests that you are task motivated. If your score is within the range of 58 to 63, you are a middle LPC, which means you are independent. Individuals who score 64 or above are called high LPCs, and they are thought to be more relationship motivated.

Because the LPC is a personality measure, the score you get on the LPC scale is believed to be quite stable over time and not easily changed. Low LPCs tend to remain low, moderate LPCs tend to remain moderate, and high LPCs tend to remain high. As was pointed out earlier in the chapter, research shows that the test-retest reliability of the LPC is very strong (Fiedler & Garcia, 1987)

Source: Adapted from Improving Leadership Effectiveness: The Leader Match Concept (2nd ed.). By F.E.Fiedler and M.M.Chemers, 1984, New York: John Wiley. Copyright 1984. Reprinted by permission of John Wiley & Sons, Inc.

EXERCISE ON PATH-GOAL LEADERSHIP QUESTIONNAIRE

Instruction: This questionnaire contains questions about different styles of path-goal leadership. Indicate how often each statement is true of your own bahaviour.

Key: 1 = Never 2 = Hardly ever 3 = Seldom 4 = Occasionally 5 = Often 6 = Usually 7 = Always

______ 1. I let subordinates know what is expected of them.

______ 2. I maintain a friendly working relationship with subordinates.

______ 3. I consult with subordinates when facing a problem.

______ 4. I listen receptively to subordinates' ideas and suggestions.

______ 5. I inform subordinates about what needs to be done and how it needs to be done.

______ 6. I let subordinates know that I expect them to perform at their highest level.

______ 7. I act without consulting my subordinates.

______ 8. I do little things to make it pleasant to be a member of the group.

______ 9. I ask subordinates to follow standard rules and regulations.

______ 10. I set goals for subordinates' performance that are quite challenging.

______ 11. I say things that hurt subordinates' personal feelings.

______ 12. I ask for suggestions from subordinates concerning how to carry out assignments.

______ 13. I encourage continual improvement in subordinates' performance.

______ 14. I explain the level of performance that is expected of subordinates.

______ 15. I help subordinates overcome problems that stop them from carrying out their tasks.

_____16. I show that I have doubts about subordinates' ability to meet most objectives.

_____17. I ask subordinates for suggestions on what assignments should be made.

_____18. I give vague explanations of what is expected of subordinates on the job.

_____19. I consistently set challenging goals for subordinates to attain.

_____20. I behave in a manner that is thoughtful of subordinates' personal needs.

Source: Adapted from A Path-Goal Theory Investigation of Superior Subordinate Relationships, by J. Indvik, unpublished doctoral dissertation, University of Wisconsin-Madison, 1985, and Indvik (1983). Based on the work of House and Dessler (1974) and House (1976) cited in Fulk and Wendler (1982). Used by permission.

CASE STUDY ON TRANSFORMATIONAL LEADERSHIP THEORY

Students Dig it

Every year, Dr. Cook, a college professor, leads a group of 25 college students to the Middle East on an archaeological dig that usually lasts about 8 weeks. The participants, who come from big and small colleges throughout the country, usually have little knowledge or background in what takes place during an excavation. Dr. Cook enjoys leading these expeditions because he likes teaching students about archaeology and because the outcomes of the digs actually advance his own scholarly work.

While planning for his annual summer excavation, Dr. Cook told the following story:

This summer will be interesting because I have 10 people returning from last year. Last year was quite a dig. During the first couple of weeks everything was very disjointed. Team members seemed lost, unmotivated, and tired. In fact, there was one time early on when it seemed as if nearly half the students were either physically ill or mentally exhausted. Students seemed lost and uncertain about the meaning of the entire project.

For example, it is our tradition to get up every morning at 4:30 a.m. to depart for the excavation site at 5:00 a.m. However, during the first weeks of the dig, few people were ever ready at 5, even after several reminders.

Every year it takes some time for people to learn where they fit with each other and with the purposes of the dig. The students all come from such different backgrounds. Some are from small, private, religious schools, and others are from large state universities. Each comes with a different agenda, with different skills, and with different work habits. One person may be a good photographer, another a good drawer, and another a good surveyor. It is my job to complete the excavation with the resources available to us.

At the end of week 2, I called a meeting to assess how things were going. We talked about a lot of things including personal things, how our work was progressing, and what we needed to change. The students seemed to appreciate the chance to talk at this meeting. Each of them described their special circumstances and their hopes for the summer.

I told the students several stories about past digs; some were humourous and others highlighted accomplishments. I shared my particular interests in this project and how I thought we as a group could accomplish the work that needed to be done at this important historical site. In particular, I stressed two points: (a) that they shared the responsibility for the successful outcome of the venture and (b) that they had independent authority to design, schedule, and carry out the details of their respective assignments, with the director and other senior staff available at all times as advisers and resource persons. In regard to the departure time issue, I told the participants that the standard departure time on digs was 5:00 a.m.

Well, shortly after our meeting I observed a real shift in the group attitude and atmosphere. People seemed to become more involved in the work, there was less sickness, and there was more comradery. All assignments were completed without constant prodding and in a spirit of mutual support. Each morning at 5:00 a.m. everyone was ready to go.

I find that each year my groups are different. It's almost as if each of them has a unique personality. Perhaps that is why I find it so challenging. I try to listen to the students and utilize their particular strengths. It really is quite amazing how these students can develop in 8 weeks. They really become good at archaeology and they accomplish a great deal.

This coming year will again be different because of the 10 returning "veterans".

Questions

1. How is this an example of transformational leadership?
2. Where are Dr. Cook's strengths on the full range of leadership model?
3. Where is the vision Dr. Cook has for the archaeology excavations?

EXPERIENTIAL LEARNING ON LEADERSHIP TRAITS

Do you have positive opinion on your abilities and experience when you are directing your people and for team work. This exercise tells about how you are doing and building self esteem.

Time : 30 minutes

Procedure : Rank 1-4 individually and add your scores and analyse each statement

1. Rarely 2. Sometimes 3. Often 4. Usually

1. I cannot perform my job upto the mark	1	2	3	4
2. I get into conflict with others.	1	2	3	4
3. I am easily bored.	1	2	3	4
4. I don't like to do work	1	2	3	4
5. I cannot communicate with strain	1	2	3	4
6. I am forgetful	1	2	3	4

7. I lack energy and enthusiasm 1 2 3 4
8. I am late to show-up for appointments too often. 1 2 3 4
9. I get into conflict with other people. 1 2 3 4
10. I am not conscientious about my developments 1 2 3 4

For Answer Email: dracmohan_mannava@yahoo.com

EXERCISE ON LEADERSHIP QUALITIES

This exercise has been designed to understand your Leadership Qualities by using 5 point scale. After you have evaluated thro all the points. It helps to improve some of the qualities for further development.

Time: 1 hour

Procedure: Everyone has to explain two to three minutes of each statement after adding your scores. He/She has to specify the priorities of his score.

1. I encourage and support the rights of others. 1 2 3 4 5
2. I always communicate in understandable manner. 1 2 3 4 5
3. I am confident and competent leader. 1 2 3 4 5
4. I am honest and open minded. 1 2 3 4 5
5. I am comfortable to give good judgement and making decisions. 1 2 3 4 5
6. I am willing to introduce changing trends of the business. 1 2 3 4 5
7. I like to take risks to develop team work. 1 2 3 4 5
8. I am good in motivating and influencing my team members. 1 2 3 4 5
9. I believe that hardwork is the secret of success of leadership styles. 1 2 3 4 5
10. I am willing to share knowledge to my team member. 1 2 3 4 5

For Answer Email: dracmohan_mannava@yahoo.com

REFERENCES

1. L.M.Prasad, "Principle and Practice of Management" Sultan Chand and Sons Educational Publishers 2001.
2. P.Subba Rao, "Personnel and Human Resource Management" Himalaya Publishing House, 2001.
3. K.Aswathappa, "Organizational Behaviour" Himalaya Publishing House, 2000.

4. Robert J.House, A., 1976. "Theory of Charismatic Leadership, in JG Hunt and Larson Leadership, The cutting edge."
5. Peter G. Northhouse, "Leadership Theory and Practice", Response Books, New Delhi, 2003.
6. P.C.Tripathi & P. N. Reddy, "Principles of Management", Tata McGraw Hill, New Delhi, 2006.
7. Anjali Gnanekar, "Organizational Behaviour" Everest Publishing House, Pune, 2002.
8. Korman, Abraham, K., "Organizational Behaviour", Prentice–Hall, 1978. pp.175–178.
9. Byrne, D. and Nelson, D., "Attraction as a linear function of proportion of position of positive reinforcements", *Journal of Personality and Social Psychology*, 1965, 1., pp. 659 – 663.
10. Based on inputs from Thought Leaders by Srinivas Pandit, Tata McGraw-Hill, 2002, pp.3-21.
11. Ralph M. StogLill, "Handbook of Leadership", New York, The Free Press, 1974.
12. Keith Davis and J.W.Newstrom, "Human Behaviour At Work", New York, McGraw-Hill, 1989,
13. G.A.Yukl, Leadership in Organisation, New Jersey, Prentice Hall, 1981.
14. J.L.Gray and F.A. Starke, "Organisational Behaviour – Concepts and Application", Colombus, Merril Publishing Co., 1988,
15. George R.Terry and S.G.Franklin, "Principles of Management", Illinois, Richard D.Irwin, 1987.
16. Chung and L.C.Megginson, "Organisational Behaviour – Developing Managerial Skills", New York, Harper.
17. John Kotter, "What Leaders Do", *Harward Business Review*, May-June 1990.
18. D.C.Feldman and H.J.Arnold, "Managing Individual and Group Behaviour in Organisations", New York, McGraw-Hill, 1983.

CHAPTER 3

Leadership Styles of Indian Managers

Meaning and Definitions of Leadership Styles – Styles based on Behavioral Theories – Styles based on Situational Theories – Styles based on Modern Theories – The Effective Leadership Styles of Indian Managers – Case Study – MLQ – Exercises.

Learning Objectives of this Chapter are:

- To know the meaning and definitions of leadership styles.
- To understand the different leadership styles of the managers.
- To study leadership styles of Indian managers.
- To explain the managerial grid style.
- To study the path goal leadership style.
- To study the Likert's systems of Management Leadership.
- To identify the effective leadership styles of Indian managers.

MEANING AND DEFINITIONS OF LEADERSHIP STYLE

Leadership styles are the patterns of behaviour used by the leader in influencing the behaviour of his subordinates in the organizational context. The styles practiced by leader may be positive or negative. These patterns are different from one leader to another leader. The patterns are also different from manager to manager. Managers have followed various styles in influencing the followers to do the work basing on the situation and attitudes, belief, values of people in the organization. The pattern is also depending upon the leader's role and his objectives. The patterns, which are followed by leaders also depends upon the nature of the leader and the organization structure. Various researchers have proposed different leadership styles based on the different theories and these can be classified as given below:

- Styles based on the behavioural theories
- Situational Theories
- Modern theories

Styles Based on the Behavioural Theories

- Power orientation
- Leadership as a continuum
- Employee production orientation
- Likert's management system
- Managerial grid
- Tri-dimensional grid

Styles Based on Situational Theories

- Fiedler's contingency model
- Hursey and Blanchard's structural model
- Path goal model

Styles Based Modern Theories

- Envisioning
- Energizing
- Enabling

STYLES BASED ON BEHAVIOURAL THEORIES

Power Orientation: Leadership styles are classified into three types based on the power orientation. These styles are based on the power and authority used by leader in influencing the behaviour of his subordinates. These can be analyzed as given below:

Autocratic Leadership Style

This style is also called as authoritarian or directing leadership style. Autocratic is defined as manager centred decision–making power in him. He prepares the rules and regulations for the employees, what they have to do or follow. Followers should do the work according to the guidelines and direction given by the leader. Here, the leader may be negative because followers are insecured and afraid of the leaders authority. There are three categories of autocratic leaders. They are (1) Strict Autocratic, (2) Benevolent Autocratic, (3) Incompetent Autocratic.

1. Strict Autocratic

Leader or Manager follows autocratic leadership styles in a very strict way. Method of influencing the behaviour of the subordinates is through negative motivation. Penalties and punishments are imposed by the leaders through this approach.

2. Benevolent Autocratic

In this approach, leader also centralize the decision making power, but his motivational style is positive. Some degree of participation may be allowed based on the situation. He can be effective in getting efficiency in many situations. Some people may be willing to work under strong authoritative structure followed by the leader. Thus, this style may be provided satisfaction through the positive motivation.

3. Incompetent Autocratic

Sometimes, leaders may adopt autocratic styles just to hide their incompetence. Other styles may be exposed before the subordinates. However, incompetent autocratic leadership styles cannot be used for a long time to achieve the long run objectives of the organisation.

Advantages of Autocratic Leadership Styles

- Most of the subordinates may be preferred to work under the strict rules, regulations and strict discipline. Hence, they get satisfaction from this style.
- This style provides strong motivation and rewards to a manager.
- This style also permits the manager to take immediate decision by the single person/ Manager.
- Less competent subordinates also have scope to work effectively and efficiently under the strict conditions.

Disadvantages of Autocratic Leadership Styles

- Most of the people in the organisation dislike strict rules and regulations without having proper motivation.
- Subordinates lack of motivation, frustrations, low morale and conflict develop in organization jeopardizing the organizational efficiency.
- Autocratic leadership style cannot help the subordinator to develop the leadership skills based on more dependence and less individuality in organisation.

Participative Leadership Style

This style is also known as Democratic, consultative or ideographic. Participation is defined as mental and emotional involvement of people to contribute the goals and share responsibility among the group members. A participative manager takes decisions based on the consultation and participation of his subordinates. By the suggestions and ideas given by subordinates, the manager can achieve the objectives of the individuals and organisation. There is positive motivation of employees working in the group. Employees also increase the morale and job satisfaction through the leader's participation approach. The participation is either real or pseudo. There are various advantages in real participative style of leadership. These are as follows:

- The participative styles is highly motivating technique to employees based on the preference given for the suggestions and ideas of employees.
- This style also helps to increase the productivity of employees based on their wholehearted involvement.
- There is a scope for sharing of responsibilities between the leader and followers and this ultimately help the followers to develop leadership skills.

- This style provides organizational stability by raising morale and favourable attitude of employees in the working environment.

This approach is suitable for organizational success based on the effective participation, suggestion programmes and multiple management. However, this style has some limitations, which are as follows:

- Some of the employees may not be able to understand the complex nature of the organization, its structure and rigid policies etc. Here participation is not meaningful. Some people in the organization want minimum interaction with their managers or superiors or leaders. Thus, a participation technique is discouraging for them instead of encouraging.

Free Rein

This style is also called as *Laissez–faire* technique. It means giving complete freedom to employee/ leader once he determines policies, programmes, plans and limitations for action and entire process is left to subordinates to perform everything. Leader is nominally elected or appointed in this approach. Everyone can take decisions and implement the policies according to opinions and ideas. This type of style is suitable for some situations. This will help the subordinates to develop their leadership qualities and skills. This style is not practiced in business organisations and institutions because people cannot be controlled and manager participation or contribution is almost nil.

Leadership as a Continuum

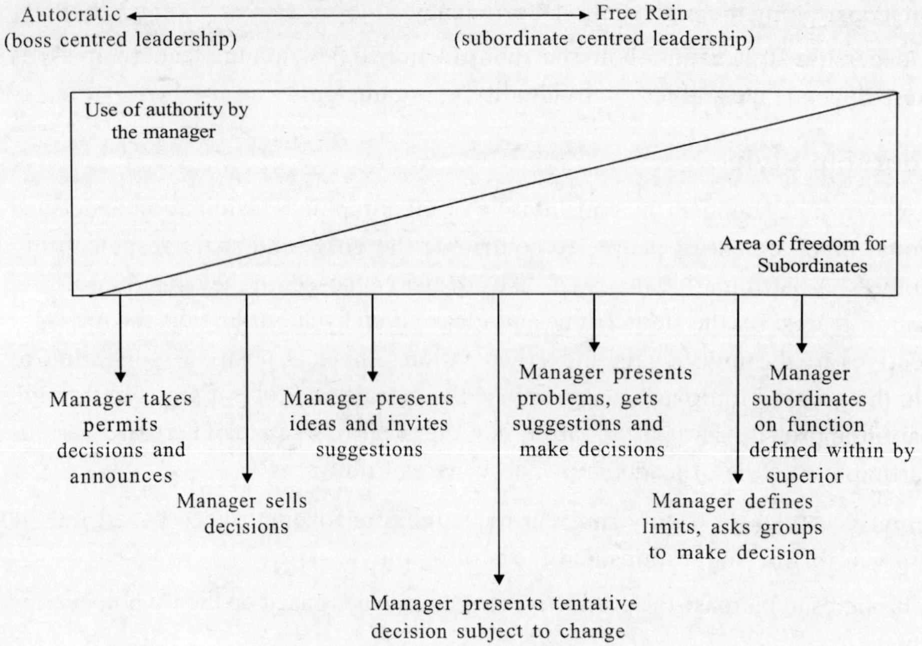

Fig. 3.1: Leadership as a Continuum

Source: L.M.Prasad, *Principles and Practice of Management*, 2001.

Tannebaum and Schmidit identified a broad range of styles on a continuum moving from authoritarian leadership behaviour to free rein behaviour. In fact, these style, all variety of patterns used by leader are based on the autocratic and free rein. This style can be presented in Fig 3.1. The figure presents a range of leadership behaviour used by the management. These styles represent the degree of authority used by leader and degree of freedom enjoyed by this subordinates. The left side shows that the manager controls people and right side shows that manager has given full freedom to his subordinates.

Employee – Production Orientation

A study was conducted by survey research centre at the University of Michigan, USA. This research was made to study the leadership behaviour by locating clusters of characteristics, which are related to each other and various indicators of effectiveness. This study identified two concepts such as the employee orientation and production orientation. This is called Employee- production oriented style. The employee orientation stressed the relationship aspect of employee's job. This style in similar to the democratic style. On the other hand, production orientation emphasized production and technical aspects of jobs and employees for accomplishing the tasks. This is similar to the authoritarian style of leadership behaviour.

At the same time Bureau of Research at Ohio State University to identify the various dimensions of leader behaviour conducted another study. This study has identified two dimensions, such as initiative structure and consideration. The research studies concluded that these two are separate dimensions. Initiative structure refers patterns, methods and procedures determined by the leader, on the other hand consideration refers friendship and mutual trust between the leader and members. This is similar to the participative syles of leadership. This can be presented in Figure 3.2.

The Ohio State Leadership Dimension

High Consideration and Low Structure	High Structure and High Consideration
Low Structure and Low Consideration	High Structure and Low Consideration

Managerial Grid

This is also called as leadership grid. This is one of the well-known leadership styles developed by Blake and Mouton. It consist of two factors such as task oriented and relation oriented behaviour. This style is related to concern for people and concern for production, concern for people includes the degree of personal commitment, maintaining self-esteem of workers, responsibility, interpersonal relationship etc., towards goal achievement. Concern for production means the attitude of supervisor / leader, quality of decisions, work efficiency, volume of output, quality of staff services, etc. The managerial grid has identified five styles based on two factors. This can be presented in the Fig. 3.3.

1. The style 1.1 is impoverished management – low concern for both people and production. This is similar to *Laissez-faire* leadership style.
2. This style 1.9 is country club management – high concern for employees, but low concern for production.
3. The style 9.1 is task oriented – high concern for production and low concern for employees.
4. The style 5.5 is middle of the road of Management, both production and employees concern, a medium which mean intermediate stage.
5. The style 9.9 is team management – both production and employees are the highest concern. This is similar to democratic style. Blake and Mouton strongly argued that 9.9 style is effective leadership style. Hence, management may use this style for effective goal attainment.

1.9 (Country Club) Thoughtful attention to needs of people leads to a friendly and comfortable organizational atmosphere and work tempo.	(Team 9.9) Work accomplished from committed people with interdependence through a common stake in organization purpose and with trust and respect.
Adequate performance through balance of work 5.5 (Middle Road) Requirements and Maintaining satisfactory morale	
Exertion of minimum effort is Required to get work done and sustain organization morale. 1.1 (impoverished)	Efficiency results for arranging work, in such a way human elements have little effect. (Task) 9.1

Figure. 3.3: The Managerial Grid Style

Likert's Management System

Rensis Likert and his associates have studied the patterns and styles of managers for three decades at University of Michigan, USA. They have developed some important concepts and approaches to understand the behaviour of leadership. He has presented a continuum of four systems. He has selected seven variables of different management systems, such as leadership, motivation, communication, interaction influence, decision making process, goal setting and control process. Likert's four systems may be selected as autocratic, benevolent autocratic participative and democratic styles. This study has been presented in Exhibit 3.1.

Exhibit 3.1: Likert's Systems of Management Leadership

Leadership variable	*System 1*	*System 2*	*System 3*	*System 4*
Trust and confidence in subordinates	Has no trust and confidence in subordinates	Has condescending confidence and trust in subordinates, such as master has to a servant	Substantial but not complete confidence and trust; still wishes to keep control of decisions	Complete confidence and trust in all matters
Subordinates feeling of freedom	Subordinates do not feel at all free to discuss things about the job with their superior	Subordinates do not feel very free to discuss things about job with their superior	Subordinates feel rather free to discuss things about the job with their superior	Subordinates feel completely free to discuss things about the job with their superior
Superior seeking involvement with subordinates.	Seldom gets ideas and opinions of subordinates in solving job problems.	Sometimes gets ideas and opinions of subordinates in solving job problems.	Usually get ideas and opinions and usually tries to make constructive use of them.	Always gets ideas and opinion and always tries to make constructive use of them.

Source: Adapted from Rensis Likert, *The Human Organization*, New York: McGraw-Hill, 1967.

Three-Dimensional

W.J. Reddin identified this style. He has presented three dimensions, such as task orientation, relationship orientation and effectiveness. Reddin has integrated the concept of leadership styles with the situational demand of a specific environment. This style is also called three dimensional grid or 3D management. This style is used by leaders as a combination of task orientation and result orientation. Planning, organizing and controlling characterize task orientation. Relation orientation is characterized by mutual trust, respect for subordinates' ideas and suggestions. Leader is used for basic styles. They represent four basic types of behaviour. Each of these styles has a less effective as well as more effective equivalent. Thus, the four basic styles result into eight styles. These eight styles result from the eight possible combinations of task orientation, relationship orientation and effectiveness. This can be presented in Figures 3.4, 3.5 and 3.6. Each of these styles has a less effective as well as more effective equivalent.

High	Related	Integrated
Relationship Orientation	Separated	Dedicated
Low	Low	High
	Task Orientation	

Fig. 3.4: Task and Relationship Orientation

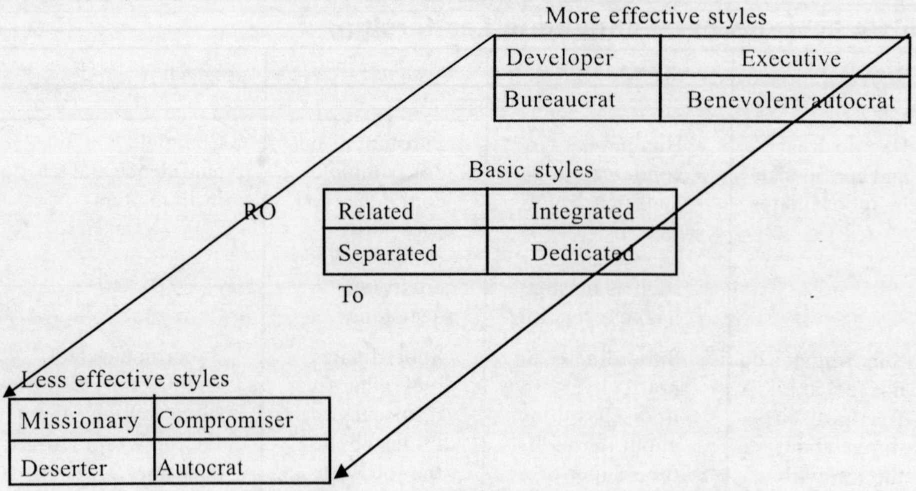

Fig. 3.5: Three-Dimensional Grid

Basic Style	Less effective Style	More effective style
Integrated	Compromiser	Executive
Dedicated	Autocrat	Benevolent Autocrat
Related	Missionary	Developer
Separated	Deserter	Bureaucrat

Fig. 3.6: More and Less Effective Styles

STYLES BASED ON SITUATIONAL THEORIES

Fiedler's Contingency Style: Fiedler has identified leadership styles on two dimensions such as Task directed and Human relations oriented. Task directed style is primarily concerned with the achievement of the task performance. Human relations style is concerned with achieving good interpersonal relations and achieving personal position. Fiedler used two types of scores to measure the style adopted by a leader. They are least preferred co-worker end scores on assumed similarly between opposites. Rating on least preferred co-worker in based on liking and disliking of an individual and measured on sixteen items such as pleasant – unpleasant, accepting, rejecting, trendy, untrendy and so on. Fiedler also identified three critical dimensions of a leader's most effective style. They are leader's position power, task structure and leader member relations. This has been presented in Figure 3.7.

Leader-member Relations	Good	Good	Good	Good	Poor	Poor	Poor	Poor
Task-Structure	High	High	Low	Low	High	High	Low	Low
Position–Power	Strong	Weak	Strong	Weak	Weak	Strong	Strong	Weak

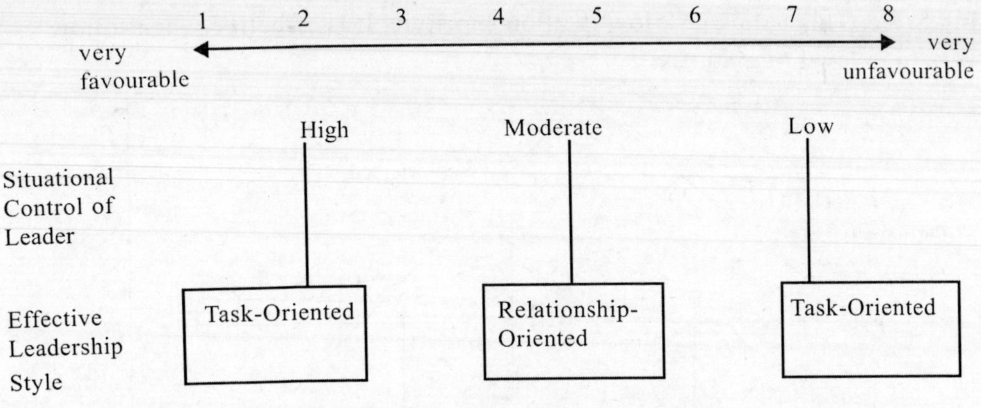

Fig. 3.7: More and Less Effective Styles

Hersey-Blanchard's Situational Model

Paul Hersey and Kennet H. Blanchard have classified the leadership into four categories based on the combination of relationship behaviour and task behaviour. Relationship behaviour is socio-emotional support provided by the leader. Task behaviour is the amount of guidance and direction provided by the leader. They have identified four styles based on two dimensions which has been presented in Fig. 3.8.

High Relationship	High relationship and low task	High relationship and high task
Behaviour Low	Low relationship and low task	Low relationship and high task
	Low	High
	Task Behaviour	

Fig. 3.8: Hersey-Blanchard's Four Style Models

Combination of Leadership Styles with Maturity

There are four leadership styles, each being appropriate to specific level of maturity. They are selling, telling, participating and delegating. The four styles of leadership is presented in Fig 3.9.

1. **Telling Style:** This is a high task, low relationship style. It is effective when followers are at a very level of maturity.
2. **Selling Style:** This is a high task high relationship style. It is effective when followers are on the low side of maturity.
3. **Participative Style:** This is low task, high relationship style. It is effective when followers are on the high side of maturity.

4. **Delegating Style:** This is low task low relationship style. It is effective when followers are at a very high level of maturity.

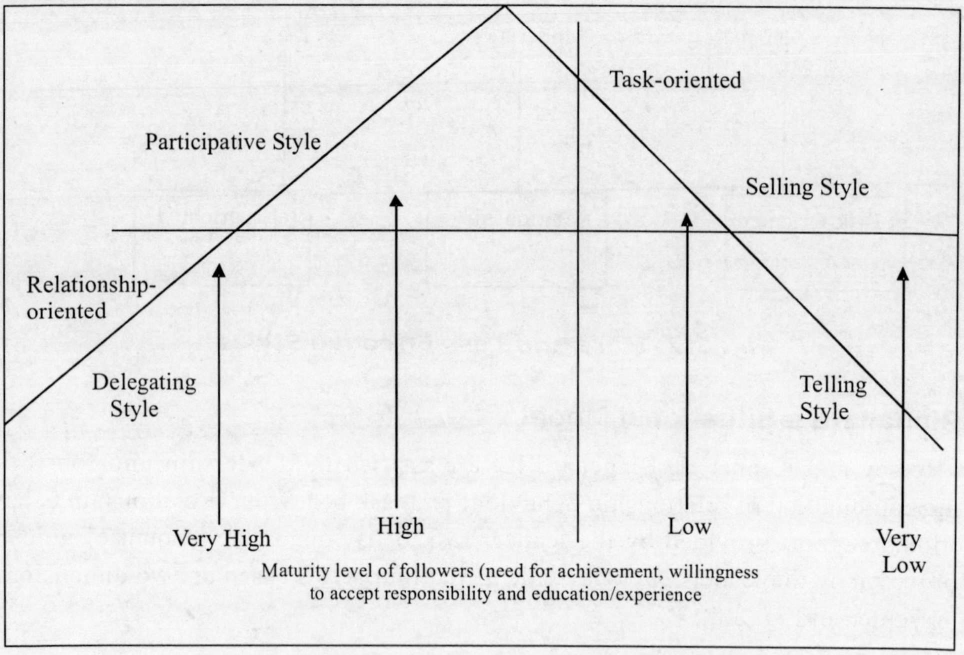

Fig. 3.9: More and Less Effective Styles

Source: Paul Hersey and Kenneth Blanchard, *Management of Organizational Behaviour: Utilization of Human Resources*, Prentice Hall, Englewood Cliffs N.J., 1977.

Path Goal Leadership Styles

Robert House and his association have studied the Path Goal styles of leadership based on the path goal theory. It was developed by Evans in 1957. They have identified the four styles based on the situation. They are directive, supportive participative and achievement orientation. These styles are based on the two situational variables – characteristics of subordinates and work environment. These are analyzed below. Various situational variables and styles have been presented in Exhibit 3.2.

Directive: The leader gives subordinates specific orders and makes it clear what is expected of them; his focus is on planning, organizing, coordinating and controlling the activities of the subordinates.

Supportive: The leaders show friendly behaviour to the employees; he shows his concern for their needs and welfare; creates pleasant organizational climate.

Participative: The leader makes the decisions with active participation of the employees; shares information with them and seeks suggestions from them.

Achievement-oriented: The leader sets challenging goals, seeks improvement of performance by displaying confidence in the abilities of the subordinates.

Exhibit 3.2: Path Goal Leadership Style Variables

Leadership Styles	Situation in which it is appropriate
Directive	Positive effect on satisfaction and expectancies of subordinates working on unstructured task.
Supportive	Positive effect on satisfaction of subordinates working on dissatisfying, stressful or frustrating task.
Participative	Positive effect on satisfaction of subordinates who are ego-involved with non-repetitive task.
Achievement	Positive effect on the confidence that the efforts will lead to effective performance of subordinates working on ambiguous and non-repetitive task.

Source: P. Subba Rao, *PHRM*, Millenium Edition, HPH, 2000.

These styles are also presented in the below given Figure 3.10:

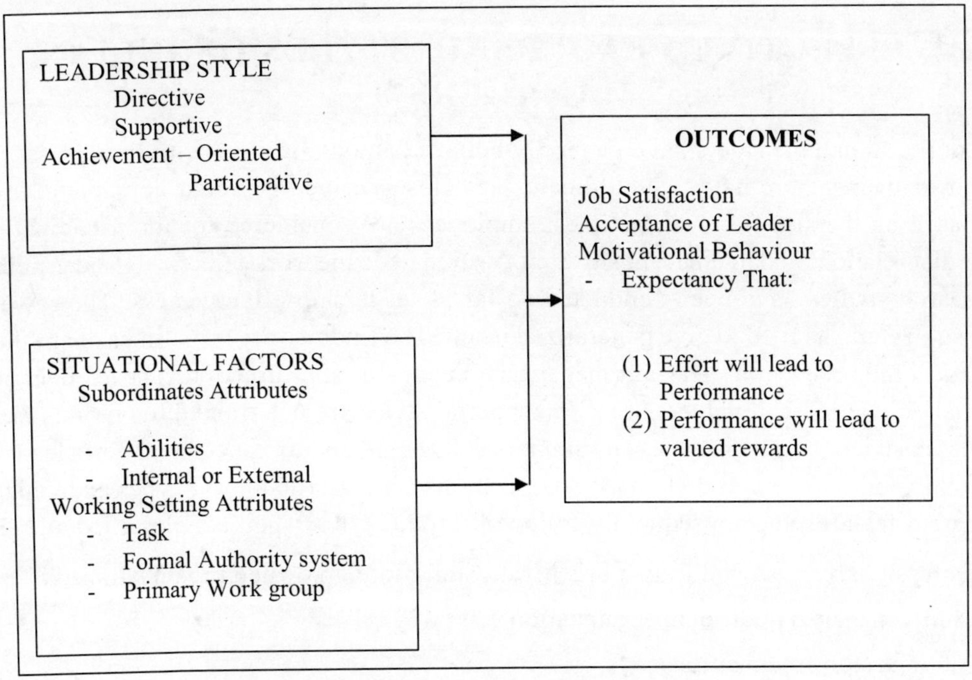

Fig. 3.10: Path Goal Leadership Style

Source: P.Subba Rao, *Personnel and Human Resources Management*, Millennium Edition, 2000.

STYLES BASED ON MODERN THEORIES

Mr. Kulkarni of Larsen and Turbo leads the company with clear vision. He has emphasized on quality comprehensive outlook, perfectness in work, creation and diversification into related areas. He sets high goals by consulting the managers, employees and followers of the company. He has encouraged and motivated the employees for working efficiently and effectively.

Modern leaders generally use high technology and competitive organizations exhibit inspirational style with vision and perform the work effectively. They do the right things, these styles are based on the charismatic and transformational theories. These styles can be classified into three types they are: Envisioning, Energizing and Enabling. These can be presented as follows:

Envisioning: This style includes creating a picture of the future or a desired future state with which people can identify. Envisaging generates excitement. Thus, this style emphasizes on articulating a compelling vision and setting high goals and expectations.

Energizing: The leader in this style directs the generating of energy, the motivation to act among the organizational employees. This style also includes demonstrating personal excitement and confidence seeking, finding and using success.

Enabling: The leader helps the followers psychologically to act or perform, this style includes empowering, expressing personal support and empathizing.

THE EFFECTIVE LEADERSHIP STYLES OF INDIAN MANAGERS

Most of the Indian managers have generally believed autocratic style with limited degree of participation to their subordinates. Subordinates are closely supervised and appreciated by the managers based on the situations. Sometimes, employees are considered for the participation to main the cordial relations and to create positive motivation to do the work effectively and efficiently. Various research studies have been conducted so far as leadership effectiveness. The review of various research studies failed to give generalized result. The findings are sometimes contradictory which indicates the absence of clear-cut managerial behaviour and direction. They reflect a lack of managerial conviction and values. Since, managerial styles are determined by various factors, such as forces in superiors, subordinates and situations, it is unlikely to expect the uniform leadership style. From this point of view, Indian work organizations are classified into 3 types and which are having different features and consequently follow different styles. They are classified as below.

1. Professionally managed Indian organization and foreign owned organisations.
2. Family managed traditional organizations.
3. Public sector organizations.

Managers working in family-managed traditional organizations; they follow autocratic style. Today, sons and great grandsons of the entrepreneurs are automatically promoted without having minimum educational background and knowledge, etc. Inheritance or management involves these people by chromosomes without any consideration to efficiency and suitability. They are highly centralized in their organizational structure and authorization in their approach.

Head of the family members manages most of the family managed organizations. They have the attitude of being highly paternalistic oriented, the same paternalistic attitude can be developed in influencing their employees in the organisations. At the initial stage; authoritarian style is more suitable for these organisations. This style has been inherited by sucessors with appreciable change of modification. On the other side, there are many private sectors organized and owned by Indian or multinationals. They have the attitude of consideration and participative to encourage their employees. The manager working in private sectors generally used practical participative style or democratic style. Managers have applied modern technique in using their styles to motivate the employees based on the modern approach of management. Thus, there is a greater participation of employees in such organisations.

The third category organisations are in public sector. The present study is also related to public sector managers at different levels and areas. At the initial state most of the public sector Civil servants who brought bureaucratic culture with their people managed organizations. Entire organizational processes are governed by bureaucratic approach. This is against the participative style. In the recent years, it has been changed to participative approach, based on changes made by government in the economic structure, and global competitive world.

The Right Style

What is the right and appropriate style for Indian manager is a difficult question to be answered. There are numerous variables, which are to be affected on leadership style. Thus, what is the effective style for one manager, may not be equally appropriate to others. The style is followed based on the situations and important variables in the different variables through some light upon the adoption of the right and appropriate style.

Indian Society

Indian society is considered as a traditional one. Power and authority is an important characteristic of the society and it is highly considered. Indian society is based on 3 important aspects such as joint family, caste system and ritualism. In a joint family, elders are having the authority and responsibilities. Respect for power and authority is followed by the family members from the beginning of childhood. Head of the family member exercises the authority on the entire family members. This respect for authority spreads through every type of social system including working organizations. Similarly, caste system is also emphasized so much which creates conflicts among the different castes. Besides, there are many rituals in the Indian society which reduces the anxiety. Rituals help the people for smooth functioning of an organization and also reduce the tension and anxiety.

There are many changes in social attitudes and cultural life of the people based on the industrialization. Manager has to identify the rituals, which are developed by the society based on the situations. Thus, participative style is more suitable based on the changing business environment, and changing situations.

Indian Managers

There is no uniformity in the attitude; personality, educational qualifications and experiences of Indian managers. Most of the top managers are also just Graduates along with the fully qualified professional manager. The former groups of managers are all self-developed and self contained. As such they present very little scope for participation, on the other hand young professionals have applied more interdependence and integrated approach. Hence, they have generally followed more democratic approach. The satisfaction of such managerial class depends upon the degree of responsibility and trust. Based on the survey some available research data on the value systems of Indian managers, have identified the following characteristics. Most of the Indian managers show autocratic style of management.

- Indian managers evaluate higher status positions more positively.
- Most of the Indian managers have ethics and morals to accomplish a task.
- Indian managers have been feeling powerless to the influence of political decision-making.
- Indian managers have the sense of dependence on external environments.

Considering the above different variables, the effective leadership style is participative. It is of general description to be of practical use in both Private and Public Enterprises. The participative leadership style attaches high importance to boot work and people.This style improves job satisfaction and morale of employees. This style helps in gaining services from a more satisfied and cohesive group. In fact, no managers can perform effectively over an extended period of time without some degree of employees participation. Sometimes, Authoritarian leadership style is also effective in case of firms using mass production technology such as autos, foods and clothing etc, Here the product is standardized and market for the product also exists. The leader has to apply unity of command for efficient operation of duties and responsibilities of his workers but this is not suitable in all situations. Finally, the researcher can conclude that most of the profit making public and private enterprises in our country have been results oriented. Thus, participative style is more effective, it is considerable for the success of an enterprises objects. Most of the reputed and enlightened company's have been following participative style.

Most of the highest profits making public and private sector in India have been following participated leadership style. Authoritarian or autocratic style in practiced by some of the company's based on the situation. They may be only 10 to 20 per cent. Thus most of the managers, near about 90% follow participative style. However, it should not be taken granted in all circumstances. This may be changed based on the future changes in the work culture and its environment. The styles followed by some of the professional Indian managers and top industrialists have been presented in exhibit 3.3 and 3.4.

Exhibit 3.3: Leadership Styles of some Industrialists and Chief Executives

Dheerubhai Ambani, Chariman of Reliance: First generation entrepreneur has built the largest company in the private sector, believes in entrepreneurial style with propensity to high risk taking, creative, innovative, keeps watch on the environment continuously, a great collector of managerial talents.

Ratan Tata, Chief Tata group: Inherited large industrial empire, believes in consolidation, though not very creative, delegates authority to the lowest possible levels, has democratic temperament.

Keki Dadiseth, former Chairman of Hindustan Lever: Highly professional, believes in consolidation, averse to taking big risks, a number cruncher by temperament, 'how to attract and maintain talents' is always on top on his mind.

Rahul Bajaj, Chairman of Bajaj Auto: Inherited industrial group, further developed and consolidated, quite friendly and philosophical approach, always making sure for level-playing, can't take things lying down, slightly resistant to change.

N.R.Narayana Murthy, Chairman of Infosys Technologies: Great computer technocrat turned as industrialist, believes in simple living and high thinking, supporter of middle class culture, is never ever satisfied, constantly aspires for more, believes is doing great things but takes care of others, highly creative and innovative.

Source : Aruna Vaidyanadhan "The Corporate India XI, *The Economic Times* June 4th 1999.

Front: Ganesh Ayyar CEO Hewlett-Packard (India)

People used to think of a manager as the person who knew the domain better than others. The relationship between a manager and his team was that of a superior and his subordinates. But in today's organisation, can you find, for instance, someone who has 15 years of experience on the Net?

Today, a manager's role is increasingly becoming that of an enabler and facilitator. The organisation is now a network where the manager focuses on providing an environment where people can have fun and excel at whatever they do. An environment where people can invent and be innovative.

It comes to the same thing finally: technology will keep changing. Hence, the roles people play will also keep changing. And the success of an organization will depend on people: People who have the drive; people who have that X-factor that makes them different. Everyone can create a strategic plan; few can implement one.

For a manager to be successful in today's world, first, he should be prepared to do things himself. Two, he should always be willing to listen to his people. Three, he should be open to ideas that he is not comfortable with. And finally, a manager must realize that his success is dependent on the performance of individuals.

To some extent, it is important for a manager to be a good leader. When you're a facilitator, you are a catalyst. But at the same time, you need to have conviction too. You can't just not add value to your team. Someone once said "A leader is a dispenser of hope, whereas a manager is a dispenser of caution." In today's world, since we are dealing with things hitherto unknown, the word hope carries a lot of weight. To that extent, leadership is a must. Inspiration will not arise from caution.

Exhibit 3.4: Leadership Development at Wipro

The main business of Wipro is information technology, which is a knowledge-based industry. Wipro has about 9,000 employees with majority of them being IT professionals. The company relies on filling the higher-level positions through promotions. Therefore, it emphasizes on developing people for these positions. The importance given to leadership development at Wipro can be gauged by the statement given by its CEO, Azeem Premji, " creating leaders has a personal pay-off."

That is what Wipro does through its development programmes known as Wipro Leaders Programme (WLP)/ Through WLPs which started in 1988, leaders are developed with seven qualities: vision, high energy, aggressive commitment, ownership, self-confidence, commitment to excellence, and building star performers and teams. Each year, about 30-50 middle-management employees are chosen to take part in this week-long programme, which starts off with the Chairman outlining his vision for the group. This gives participants a sense of focus.

This is followed by what is called 'outward bound' training where the group is packed off to a camp on the outskirts of Bangalore. Physical limits are tested at this level, with the seemingly shy ones emerging as quiet but dependable leaders. The togetherness of two-day camp brings people from different departments close, and team spirit is enhanced. Back in Bangalore, there are mind exercises, meditation, introspection and group efforts to solve imaginary problems in creative ways. Efforts are made to:

1. Create awareness and understanding of Wipro Leader's (WL) qualities.
2. Inculcate the relevance and significance of WL qualities.
3. Enable participants to assess their current status *and* qualities;
4. Provides inputs to guide participants for continuous development in WL qualities.

WLPs has been able to develop personnel in the company and many participants have researched the level of chief executive in their business units.

Source: Alistar Robertson "Leadership Development" , No Smoke and Mirror, *The Economic Times* March 31st 2000.

1. CASE STUDY

A Defining Year for Corporate Leadership

The year 2002 will surely be remembered as the *anus horribilis* of business. It was a time of tumult and reassessment, high drama and low comedy. Corporate crime and greed were spectacularly exposed in companies that had once been prasied, run by executives who had once been trusted. It was the year Enron set new vots in corporate ethics, while World Com broke records for the size of its bankruptcy. It was also the year we learned the Rigas family may have defrauded Adelphia Communications of some $1 billion, Bernie Ebbers borrowed $ 408 million from World Com, and Samuel Waksal urged his daughter and father to trade on inside information he gave them about ImClone Systems Inc. Andrew Fastow, ex-chief financial offer at Enron faces no fewer than 78 felony charges. The outside auditors and the supposedly independent directors, they pleaded ignorance.

Chief executives seemed startled by the ridicule, distrust, and outright contempt they faced. At the same time, they had to contend with an economy that edged ever-so-slowly toward a recovery but kept falling short. If ever there was a year to examine the many ways in which managers succeed- and fail-this was it.

The best executives responded by providing more information about company operations to dispel suspicions and they got back to work. Some – Andrea Jung at Avon, A.G.Laftley at Procter & Gamble, and Robert Tillman at Lowe's – even managed to excel, despite the extremely trying conditions. Others, however, such as Jack Greenberg, the abruptly replaced head of McDonald's, and Jean-Maried Messier, the ex-chief of Vivendi Universal, were unable to outrun their problems. They were not alone: We've included more than a dozen new executives who have taken over major companies in 2002.

In a year as turbulent as this one, we decided to take a new approach to our annual wrap-up of the year's best managers. Along with the best, we've also looked closely at the worst executives, the fallen, the indicted (and those under fire), and managers to watch in the year to come. Many of the names are familiar. Last year, for example, we called Dennis Kozlowski one of the best managers of 2001, citing his ability to lead Tyco International through a recession that flattened most of its counterparts. What we didn't see was that the company was struggling to keep up appearances as investigators were eyeing Kozlowski. Now you can find him in the section called Perp Walk. Two years ago we praised Sandy Weill at Citigroup for making the huge financial firm his own, elbowing out his co-chief executive and installing his number-obsessed loyalists in key positions. With Citi enmeshed in almost every scandal to hit Walt Street in 2002, we named Weill one of the worst.

Business Week surveyed its staff of some 144 writers and editors in New York and in 21 areas around the world to decide whose performance should be lauded and who deserved a different kind of renown.

1. If you were to select the "Best" and the "Worst" corporate leaders, what would be some objective criteria that you would use in this selection process?
2. Choosing one of the traditional theories of leadership, what criteria would you use in the selection process?
3. Why is this such a defining time for assessing corporate leadership? Which leadership theory would be most relevant and applicable to understanding and developing effective corporate leaders in today's environment? Why?

2. CASE STUDY

Mention the word leadership in reference to CEOs and it often conjures up the names of people such as Carly Fiorina of HP or some other chief executive of one of America's most admired firms. However, there are many effective leaders who are not well known but are considered extremely effective. A good example is Steve Wynn, whose face is known to millions from his television advertising appearances but otherwise goes unrecognized.

Steven Wynn is head of Mirage Resorts Inc., an empire that consists mainly of upscale resort hotels in Las Vegas and, over the next few years, other cities in Nevada, New Jersey, and Mississippi. To most people who are familiar with his face, he is an advertising pitchman who urges viewers to come out to one of his casinos. However, Wynn is a lot more than this. He has taken bold risks to build his casino empire and has always been an astute risk taker. During the 1980s he linked up with the infamous "junk bond king" Michael Milken and used junk bonds to finance his rise in the casino business. Then , when interest rates subsided, he replaced the troubled bonds with lower-interest securities.

At the same time Wynn has shown that he can be very effective in managing in-house operations. One of the key areas on which he focuses a great deal of attention is employee relations. He contends that "you can never go wrong indulging your employees. "Throughout the company, personnel are given "Gotcha Awards, " which usually entail an extra day off or a gift certificate. These awards are given simply for doing their jobs in a highly competent manner. As Wynn's director of human resoures at the Las Vegas Mirage puts it, "We reward the ordinary, not just the extraordinary." In addition, employees at the Mirage are given fresh, free meals in the hotel's gleaming new cafeteria, which is in sharp contrast to employees at other hotels, who are typically fed with leftovers from the guest buffet. Moreover, Employees and Supervisors of the Year are treated to Hawaiian vacations and a lavish banquet that costs upward of $400,000.

Wynn's winning approach also extends to day-to-day work activities. His hotels operate under a system that uses "planned insubordination." This unusual approach requires supervisors to explain to subordinates why a task should be accomplished. And if the workers find that the explanation is unsatisfactory, they are not required to do that job. Do the personnel like this idea? They might be given than turnover at Wynn's operations runs around 12 percent annually, whereas it is twice this for the industry at large. In addition, jobs at the Mirage are so coveted that employees are willing to work there for pay that is at or below market rates. And although 40 percent of the workers belong to unions, not a single grievance has been filed against the company in more than four years.

On the other side of the coin, some people complain that Wynn's leadership style can be offensive. He has been accused of erupting into anger and launching verbal assaults at subordinates over minor matters such as a burned-out lightbulb or a dirty ash-tray. He explains these behaviours by noting, "I've always been emotional and passionate. I guess it's a fear that I'll become isolated and not know what's going on." Outsiders who have worked with him simply say that he wants to get things done immediately and that his passion becomes almost maniacal at times, resulting in his outbursts.

Regardless of the strengths and weakness of his leadership style, Wynn has built a successful empire. One reason may have been explained best by an expert on the gaming business who remarked, "I see Steve on the gaming business who remarked, "I see Steve Wynn as the prototypical charismatic leader, a kind of Henry Ford of the gambling industry. Yet he has these ticks, and he wants to make everything perfect. He many scream at you and humiliate you, but he's also the best person to work for, if you want to learn to do things the right way."

1. In terms of the various leadership styles described in the chapter, how would you describe Steve Wynn?
2. If you were making any suggestions to him regarding how he could improve his leadership style, what would you tell Wynn?
3. Which of the three major skills would be of most value to Wynn?

3. CASE STUDY

Rex Justice is a long-tem employee of the Carfax Corporation, and for the last several years he has been a supervisor in the financial section of the firm. He is very loyal to Carfax and works hard to follow the company policies and procedures and the orders of the managers above him. In fact, upper-level management think very highly of him; they can always count or Rex to meet any sort of demand that the company places on him. He is valued and well liked by all the top managers. His employees in the financial section have the opposite opinion of Rex. They feel that he is too concerned with pleasing the upper-level brass and not realy concerned enough with the needs and concerns of the employees in his department. For example, they feel that Rex never really pushes hard enough for a more substantial slice of the budget. Relative to other departments in the company, they feel they are underpaid and overworked. Also, whenever one of them goes to Rex with a new idea or suggestion for improvement, he always seems to have five reasons why it can't be done. There is considerable dissatisfaction in the department, and everyone thinks that Rex is just a puppet for management. Performance has begun to suffer because of his style and leadership. Upper-level management seem to be oblivious to the situation in the finance section.

1. How would you explain Rex's leadership style in terms of one or more of the approaches discussed in the chapter?
2. What advice would you give Rex to improve his approach to leadership?
3. Could a leadership training program be set up to help Rex? What would it consist of?

GE'S CONTROVERSIAL LEADER

In 1981, John W. Welch, Jr., became CEO of General Electric. His appointment ushered in an era of disdain for the elaborate planning and centralised control that had been the hallmark of his predecessor. Reginaid Jones, "Jones felt the others would be caretakers", says one former GE vice president, "Welch was the one who would take the company in radical directions if necessary."

Indeed, Welch has proved to be anything but a caretaker. He quickly articulated a plan to change GE from manufacturing company deriving more than half its revenues from heavy industry to one reaping a larger share of its earnings from technology and services. He also stated that GE would sell those of its businesses that weren't either first or second in their market.

Since becoming CEO, Welch has sold more than 250 businesses and used $20 billion to purchase more than 300 new ones. Among the acquisition are the RCA Corporation, the Employers Reinsurance Company, 80 per cent of Kidder, Peabody & Company, the medical equipment Business of Thomson SA, the appliance making Roper Corporation and the chemical business of the Borg Warner Corporation. In the process, he has eliminated more than 200,000 jobs through forced retirements, layoffs, resignations and outright divestitures.

His moves have caused revenues to increase by 50 per cent – up to about $70 billion. Admirers say that Welch has vision and is transforming GE from a stodgy bureaucracy to a nimble company much more fit for the challenges ahead. He was named "CEO of the Year" by the American Management Association in 1991. Detractors have dubbed Welch "Neutron Jack", after the bomb that destroys people but leaves buildings intact.

A notorious dislike of bureaucracy and red tape. Welch has cut layers of management, eliminating the group and sector levels that once fell between the heads of the various businesses and the CEO. Having fewer hierarchical levels fit in with his basic philosophy that managers should have the freedom to run their businesses as they see fit and to react to the fast changing environment.

"The early 80s were a hardware decade, getting the right stuff in the right place," Welch says. "The 90s and late 80s are what we call software. We're working desperately to get everyone participating in the process. To be a winner in the 90s, you have got to have the creativity of everybody in the organisation."

To that end, Welch has recently identified four types of leaders. Type One leaders deliver on commitments and share in the values of the company. Such leaders have a promising future at GE says Welch. Type Two leaders do not deliver on commitments and do not share company values. These leaders will not survive at GE. Type Three leaders miss commitments but share company values, so they will usually be given a second chance. Type Four leaders deliver on commitments, make all the numbers, but do not 'share in the values we must have,' says Welch. The type Four leader "is the individual who typically forces performance out of people rather than inspires it: the autocrat, the big shot, the tyrant. Too often, all of us have looked the other way," according to Welch. The tendency is to allow Type Four managers to continue to function "because they always deliver "– at least in the short run". Now says Welch, "in an environment where we must have every good idea from every man and woman in the organization, we cannot afford management styles that suppress and intimidate."

In order to further promote creativity and innovation, Welch has been advocating the development of a "boundaryless" company, in which workers at all levels are encouraged to communicate and share ideas with one another. He has also instituted the Best Practices Program, in which GE employees study the attitudes and management practices of other admirable companies and adapt the best for use at GE. Another means of fostering change is GE's Work-out Program, in which managers and their subordinates meet in a forum similar to New England town meeting and seek ways to eliminate unnecessary work and solve problems together.

According to Welch, "Leadership starts with absolute integrity. Leaders need to define and communicate their vision. They must have enormous energy and the ability to energise and excite others. Leaders embrace change, they know it creates opportunities. Leaders are accountable and decisive. They set and meet aggressive targets. They act sooner rather than later o issues." He noted recently, "I don't know what the world's going to be; all I know is it's going to be nothing like it is today. It's going to be faster; information is going to be everywhere." As a result, he says everyone at GE needs to come to work each day "on the razor's edge of a competitive battle."

Questions

1. Analyse the sources of power that are likely to be used by the four types of leaders identified by Welch.
2. Use path goal theory to analyze Welch's Leadership approach?

Multifactor Leadership

Questionnaire (MLQ) Form 6S

Instructions: This questionnaire provides a description of your leadership style. Twenty-one descriptive statements are listed below. Judge how frequently each statement fits you. The word others may mean your followers, clients, or group members.

Key: 01 = Not at all 1 = Once in a while 2 = Sometimes 3 = Fairly often 4 = Frequently, if not always.

1.	I make others feel good to be around me.	1	2	3	4
2.	I express with a few simple words what we could and should do.	1	2	3	4
3.	I enable others to think about old problems in new ways.	1	2	3	4
4.	I help others develop themselves.	1	2	3	4
5.	I tell others what to do if they want to be rewarded for their work.	1	2	3	4

6.	I am satisfied when others meet agreed-upon standards.	1	2	3	4
7.	I am content to let others continue working in the same way always.	1	2	3	4
8.	Others have complete faith in me.	1	2	3	4
9.	I provide appealing images about what we can do.	1	2	3	4
10.	I provide others with new ways of looking at puzzling things.	1	2	3	4
11.	I let others know how I think they are doing.	1	2	3	4
12.	I provide recognition/rewards when others reach their goals.	1	2	3	4
13.	As long as things are working, I do not try to change anything.	1	2	3	4
14.	Whatever others want to do is OK with me.	1	2	3	4
15.	Others are proud to be associated with me.	1	2	3	4
16.	I help others find meaning in their work.	1	2	3	4
17.	I get others to rethink ideas that they had never questioned before.	1	2	3	4
18.	I give personal attention to those who seem rejected.	1	2	3	4
19.	I call attention to what others can get for what they accomplish.	1	2	3	4
20.	I ask no more of others than what is absolutely essential.	1	2	3	4

Source: Copyright © 1992 B.M.Bass and B.J.Avolio. Adapted with permission. MLQ forms can be obtained from Mind Garden, Inc., 1690 Woodside Rd., Suite 202, Redwood City, CA 94061, USA: (650) 261 – 3500.

Scoring

The MLQ-6S measures your leadership on seven factors related to transformational leadership. Your score for each factor is determined by summing three specified items on the questionnaire. For example, to determine your score for factor 1, idealized influence, sum your responses for items 1,8, and 15. complete this procedure for all seven factors..

	Total
Idealised influence (items 1,8 and 15)	________Factor 1
Inspirational motivation (items 2, 9 and 16)	________Factor 2
Intellectual stimulation (items 3, 10 and 17)	________Factor 3
Individualized consideration (items 4, 11 and 18)	________Factor 4
Contingent reward (item 5, 12 and 19)	________Factor 5
Management-by-exception (item 6, 13and 20)	________Factor 6
Laissez-faire leadership (items 7, 14 and 21)	________Factor 7

Score range: high = 9-12, moderate = 5-8, low = 0-4

Scoring Interpretation

Factor 1. Idealized influence indicates whether you hold subordinates' trust, maintain their faith and respect, show dedication to them, appeal to their hopes and dreams, and act as their role model.

Factor 2. Inspirational motivation measures the degree to which you provide a vision, use appropriate symbols and images to help others focus on their work, and try to make others feel their work is significant.

Factor 3. Intellectual stimulation shows the degree to which you encourage others to be creative in looking at old problems in new ways, create an environment that is tolerant of seemingly extreme positions, and nurture people to question their own values and beliefs and those of the organizations.

Factor 4. individualized consideration indicates the degree to which you show interest in others' well-being, assign projects individually, and pay attention to those who seem less involved in the group.

Factor 5. Contingent reward shows the degree to which you tell others what to do in order to be rewarded, emphasize what you expect from them, and recognize their accomplishments.

Factor 6. Management-by-exception assesses whether you tell others the job requirements, are content with standard performance, and is a believer in "if it ain't broke, don't fix it."

Factor 7. *Laissez-faire* measures whether you require little of others, are content to let things ride, and let others do their own thing.

Scoring Interpretation

The PLIS measures subordinates' perceptions of their leaders' integrity in organizational settings. Your responses on the PLIS indicate the degree to which you see your supervisors behaviour as ethical.

Score the questionnaire by doing the following. Sum the responses on all 31 items. A low score on the questionnaire indicates that you perceive your supervisor to be highly ethical. A high score indicates that you see your supervisor to be very unethical. The interpretation of what the score represents in given below.

Total Score:____________

Interpretation: Your score is a measure of your perception of your supervisor's ethical integrity. Based on previous findings (Craig & Gustafson, 1998, the following interpretations can be made about your total score.

31-35	High Ethical	If you scored in this range, it means that you see your supervisor as highly ethical. Your impression is that your supervisor is very trustworthy and highly principled.

36-66 Moderate Scores in this range mean that your see your supervisor as moderately ethical. Your impression is that he or she sometimes engages in slightly unethical behaviour.

EXERCISE ON LEADERSHIP STYLE

Evaluating your Leadership Style

Working alone, complete and score the Leadership Style Survey.

In small groups, exchange scores, compute average score and develop responses to the discussion questions.

After the class reconvenes, group's spokepersons present group findings.

Discussion Questions

1. In what ways did your experience or lack of experience influence your responses to the survey?
2. In what ways did student scores and student responses to survey test items agree? In what ways did they disagree?
3. What do you think accounts for difference in student leadership attitudes?
4. How can students make constructive use of the survey results.

This survey describes various aspects of leadership behaviour. To measure your leadership style, respond to each statement according to the way you would act (or think you would act) if you were a work group leader.

EXERCISE ON *LAISSEZ-FAIRE*, DEMOCRATIC, AUTOCRATIC

Time : 1 hour

Procedure : Form two members in a group and discuss about each statement.

The following phrases focus on Characteristics/Qualites of Autocratic, Participative, and *Laissez-faire* leadership style to identify your style. It will help to apply your style based on situations. Please specify Leadership style and explain in your point of view.

1. Original work is encouraged.
2. Decisions are made by team members.
3. Decisions are made by leader.
4. Workers are encouraged to develop Creativity.
5. Everyone work is valued.
6. The leader gives praise and criticism.
7. Authority is not delegated.
8. Specific directions/suggestions are not allowed by team members.

9. Team members are Co-operative, Empathetic and Participative.
10. Leader prefers involve followers in decision making process.

For Answer Email: dracmohan_mannava@yahoo.com

EXERCISE ON IDENTIFYING INFLUENCE TACTICS

INSTRUCTIONS: After reading each tactic listed here, label it as being mostly an example of one of the following:

1 = ingratiation; E = exchange of favors; R = rationality; A = assertiveness; U = upward appeal

Tactic Code

1. I sympathized with the person about the added problems that my request caused.
2. I offered to help if the person would do what I wanted.
3. I set a time deadline for the person to do what I asked.
4. I obtained the informal support of higher-ups.
5. I used logic to convince him or her.
6. I made a formal appeal to higher levels to back up my request.
7. I had a showdown in which I confronted the person head-on.
8. I offered to make a personal sacrifice if the person would do what I wanted (for example, work late or harder).
9. I made him or her feel good about me before making my request.

For Answer Email: dracmohan_mannava@yahoo.com

EXERCISE ON HOW MUCH DO I CRAVE RECOGNITION?

Respond to the following statements on the following scale:

Disagree stongly (DS), disagree (D), neutral (N), and agree strongly (AS).

	DS	D	NA		AS
1. I keep (or would keep)almost every plaque, medal, Trophy I have ever received on display in my living quarters	1	2	3	4	5
2. I feel a nice warm glow each time somebody praises my efforts	1	2	3	4	5
3. When somebody tells me, "nice job," it makes my day.	1	2	3	4	5
4. When I compliment someone, I am really looking for a Compliment in return.	1	2	3	4	5
5. I would rather win an "employee-of-the-month"award than receive a $50 bonus for my good work.	1	2	3	4	5

	Always	Frequently	Occasionally	Seldom	Never
1. I would allow team members the freedom to do their jobs in their own way.	5	4	3	2	1
2. I would make important decisions on my own initiative without consulting the workers.	5	4	3	2	1
3. I would allow the team members to make their own decision.	5	4	3	2	1
4. I would not try to socialize with the workers.	5	4	3	2	1
5. I would allow team members to do their jobs as they see fit.	5	4	3	2	1
6. I would consider myself to be the group's spokesperson.	5	4	3	2	1
7. I would be warm, friendly and approachable.	5	4	3	2	1
8. I would be sure that the workers understand and follow all the rules and regulations.	5	4	3	2	1
9. I would demonstrate a real concern for the worker's welfare.	5	4	3	2	1
10. I would be the one to decide what is to be done and how it is to be done.	5	4	3	2	1
11. I would delegate authority to the workers.	5	4	3	2	1
12. I would urge the workers to meet production quotas.	5	4	3	2	1
13. I would trust the workers to use good judgement in decision making.	5	4	3	2	1
14. I would assign specific tasks to specific people.	5	4	3	2	1
15. I would let the workers establish their own work pace.	5	4	3	2	1
16. I would not feel that I have to explain my decisions to workers.	5	4	3	2	1
17. I would try to make each worker feel that his or her contribution is important.	5	4	3	2	1
18. I would establish the work schedules.	5	4	3	2	1
19. I would encourage workers to get involved in setting work goals.	5	4	3	2	1
20. I would be action oriented and result oriented.	5	4	3	2	1
21. I would get the workers involved in making decisions.	5	4	3	2	1
22. I would outline needed changes and monitor action closely.	5	4	3	2	1
23. I would help the group achieve consensus on important changes.	5	4	3	2	1
24. I would supervise closely to ensure that standards are met.	5	4	3	2	1
25. I would consistently reinforce good work.	5	4	3	2	1
26. I would nip problems in the bud.	5	4	3	2	1
27. I would consult the group before making decisions.	5	4	3	2	1

(***Source:*** Thomas S. Bateman and Scott A.Snell, *Management*, Irwin McGraw-Hill, 1999, pp 434 – 435).

6. If I had the resources to make a large donation to charity, I would never make the donation anonymously.	1	2	3	4	5
7. Thinking back to my childhood, I adored receiving a gold star Similar acknowledgement from my teacher for my good work.	1	2	3	4	5
8. I would be rather designated as *Time Magazine's* person of the Year than be one of the world's richest people.	1	2	3	4	5
9. I love to see my name in print.	1	2	3	4	5
10. I do not receive all the respect I deserve.	1	2	3	4	5

For Answer Email: dracmohan_mannava@yahoo.com

EXERCISE ON INNOVATION

	YES	NO
1. The reward system encourages innovation.	____	____
2. This organization publicly recognizes those who are innovative.	____	____
3. The reward system here benefits mainly those who do not rock the boat.	____	____
4. Our ability to function creatively is respected by the Leadership.	____	____
5. The main function of members of this organization is to follow orders that come down through channels.	____	____
6. Around here, a person can get into a lot of trouble by being different.	____	____
7. This organization can be described as flexible and continually adapting to change .	____	____
8. A person cannot do things that are too different around here without provoking anger.	____	____
9. The best way to get along in this organization is to think the way the rest of the group does.	____	____
10. People around here are expected to deal with problems in the same way.	____	____
11. This organization, is open and responsive to change.	____	____
12. The people in charge around here usually get credit for others' ideas.	____	____
13. In this organization, we tend to stick to tried and true ways.	____	____
14. This place seems to be more concerned with the status quo than with change.	____	____
15. Assistance in developing new ideas is readily available.	____	____
16. There are adequate resources devoted to innovation in this Organization.	____	____

17. There is adequate time available to pursue creative idea here. ____ ____
18. Lack of funding to pursue creative ideas is a problem in this Organization. ____ ____
19. Personnel shortages inhibit innovation in this organization. ____ ____
20. This organization gives me free time to pursue creative Ideas during the workday. ____ ____

For Answer Email: dracmohan_mannava@yahoo.com

REFERENCES

1. L.M.Prasad, "Principle and Practice of Management," Sultanchand and Sons, Educational Publishers 2001.
2. P.Subba Rao, "Personnel and Human Resource Management," Himalaya Publishing House, 2001.
3. L.M.Prasad, "Principles and Practice of Management," Sultanchand and Sons Educational Publishers 2001.
4. K.Aswathappa, "Organizational Behaviour," Himalaya Publishing House, 2000.
5. Robert J.House, A., 1976, "Theory of Charismatic Leadership", in J.G. Hunt and Larson Leadership, The Cutting Edge.
6. K.Aswathappa, "Organizational Behaviour," Himalaya Publishing House, 2001.
7. Robert Tannebaum and Warrant H.Schmidt, "How to Choose a Leadership Pattern", Harward Business Review, May – June 1973.
8. Robert Tannebaum and Warrant H.Schmidt, " How to Choose a Leadership Pattern", Harward Business Review, May – June 1973.
9. Robert Tannebaum and Warrant H.Schmidt, "How to Choose a Leadership Pattern" , Harvard Business Review, March April 1958.
10. Paul Hersey and Kennet H.Blanchard, "Management of Organizational Behaviour. Englewood Cliff, Prentice Hall, 1988.
11. R.R.Blake and J.S.Mouton, "The Managerial Grid," Houston: Gulf Publishing, 1964.
12. Likert, *op. cit.*
13. W.J.Reddin, "Managerial Effectiveness," New York McGraw Hill, 1970.
14. L.M.Prasad, "Principles and Practice of Management" Sultanchand and Sons Educational Publishers, 2001.
15. Stephen P.Robbins, "Organizational Behaviour," Prentice Hall of India, 1999.
16. Fred Luthans, "Organizational Behaviour," McGraw Hill International Edition, 1995.
17. A. Chandra Mohan, "The Leadership Styles of Indian Managers", "Andhra Pradesh Industrial Portal", September 1st, 2001.
18. Aruna Vaidyanadhan, "The Corporate India XI" , *The Economic Times*, June 4, 1999.

CHAPTER

4

Women and Leadership

Concept of Women Leadership – Women as Employees and Managers - Can Women be Leaders – Difference between Male and Female Leaders – Why few Female Leaders reach the Top – Exercise.

Learning Objectives of this Chapter are:

- To know the concept of women leadership.
- To understand the significance of women leadership.
- To study the women as employers and managers.
- To examine whether women can be leaders.
- To understand the difference between the male and female leaders.
- To identify the reason why few female leaders reach the top.

CONCEPT OF WOMEN LEADERSHIP

Women have been discriminated in our male dominated society. Mostly girls were married when they were in their teens, widow re-marriages were considered to be a social taboo, education beyond the primary or at the most, school level was rare; girls especially in rural and small towns, were deliberately under-nourished and denied access to outside world. Women were considered to be fit to cook food but not to work in business establishments. Even the constitution has not been free from bias against the fair sex. Daily newspapers publish reports about rape, bride burnings, dowry deaths and wives beaten to death. Women are afraid of going out alone after dark and cannot go for shopping without male escorts.

As we go into the future, discrimination against women will certainly go and they will sure occupy equal status along with male counterparts. Today girls are better educated, more assertive and bolder. Added to this is women's liberation movement, to protect and improve lot of women in business and other professionally talented women. The government is also keen on uplifting the status of women.

WOMEN AS MANAGERS AND EMPLOYEES

Participation of women in business as owners, managers and employees is less encouraging, considering the size of the population and the vast opportunities available. While women account for 48% of the population, the 1991 census the female workforce 20.85% occupying top positions are few and far between. Reasons are not difficult to seek. The main reasons are that women are known to have lower attachment to work and therefore content with lower positions. They do not consider themselves primary earners. They lack education and training. They are less preferred to men in recruitment and selection process because of legal and other problems.

SIGNIFICANCE OF WOMEN LEADERSHIP

The terms leader and manager will be used interchangeably in this chapter, the terms sex and gender will be used differently. Sex refers to biological differences including anatomy, physiology, and hormones, although some theorists argue that even sex is a continuum rather than a simple bipolar set of categories. The biological characteristics of males and females imply nothing, in and of themselves, about the cognitive, emotional , or interpersonal abilities relevant to the workplace and leadership. How, then, have men and women developed such different probabilities of becoming leaders in reputed business organizations of both Government and Non-Government. The answer lies in the meanings that most cultures have assigned to the categories of male and female. Gender refers to the way in which meaning and evaluations are associated with sex by members of a culture. In other words, masculinity and feminity have various set of characteristics associated with them, depending on the culture. The degree to which males and females are expected to behave are treated differently.

Some perception and sentiments and beliefs can be especially misleading when there are only two categories in a set (such as female/male or masculine/feminine) because several cognitive distortions arise (Gentile, 1996). First, people's thinking and observation become simplified because of the belief that everyone must fit into either one category or other. Second, the two categories also seem to imply that everyone within each category is identical. For example, the bipolar categories of sex and gender often seem to imply that only majority-group members are included when the terms are used. In other words, in the absence of further descriptors, the terms man and woman are often taken to mean white, heterosexual, healthy, and middle class or above (Bell, Denton, & Nkomo, 1993).

The third major distortion with a bipolar category set is the ease with which many people erroneously tend to value on category as superior to the other. In the case of sex and gender, hundreds of studies have documented the variety of ways in which male and masculine have been valued as superior to female and feminine. These prejudicial attitudes and discriminatory behaviours have damaged individuals, organizations, and society by limiting the ways in which people can contribute based on their unique, rather than their gender-role-bound, characteristics and talents.

The persuasiveness of the attitudes associated with sex and gender has resulted in workplaces becoming "gendered." This means that the allocation of responsibilities in organization and nearly all decisions about employees' career progress, resources, salaries, power and authority, and appropriate work behaviour are affected by the distinction between male and female, masculine and feminine. Although many executives and managers prefer to believe that organizations are objective about merit and are gender neutral, the data from many research studies indicate that most workplaces use gender, job-irrelevant as it should be, as a basis for many decisions that ultimately affect who becomes a leader. Just as workplace decision making is gendered, so is much of the distribution of responsibility at home, especially for working parents.

With these definitions as a foundation, the next section will provide a framework for the research trends to be explored in this chapter.

Brief Review of Literature

Over the past 20 years, researchers of women leaders and managers have build a large body of literature addressing three fundamental questions (Bell & Nkomo, 1992). The earliest question was, Can women be leaders? Once this was answered affirmatively, researchers asked, Do male and female leaders differ in their behaviour and effectiveness in organizations? Trends in the focus of these studies shifted emphasis; depending on the decade, the emphasis was sometimes on establishing differences sometimes on establishing similarities between men and women leaders (Maier, 1992). A third question has intrigued researchers: Why do so few women leaders reach the top? The purpose of this chapter is to review approaches and findings used to answer these three questions.

CAN WOMEN BE LEADERS

Based on the continuous evidence of sex discrimination in many arenas of life, the question in the heading for this section would no longer be posed and most people would agree that the answer is a resounding "yes!". This chapter presents comparative demographic data on female and male leaders, as well as an explanation of the benefit of this trend for employers. Of the approximately 135 million people employed in the United States in 2001, 46.6% were women (Women's Bureau, 2001). These women comprised about 585 of all U.S. women over age 20 (Bureau of Labor Statistics, 2002). Overall, women earned $0.76 for every dollar earned by men in 2001, although women managers earned only $0.66 for every dollar the bachelor's degrees in 2001 (Garofoli, 2002).

In 2002 women filled 15.7% of corporate officer (top management) positions, including 7.1% of chief financial officers and 16.1% of general counsels in the Fortune 500 composes of America's 500 largest companies (Catalyst, 2002a). While only 5.2% of the top-earning corporate officer slots were filled by women in 2002, they held 9.9% of the "clout titles" in the organization, including chairman, chief executive officer (CEO), and president (Catalyst, 2002a). Women held 12.4% of the sales on Fortune 500 corporate boards of directors in 2001, up from 10% in 1999; 66 of the 500 companies still had no women on their boards (Catalyst, 2002b).

At the very top of major corporation, there are six female CEOs in Fortune 500 companies and an additional five in Fortune 1000 companies (Sellers, 2002).

The 11 female CEOs of Fortune 500 and 1000 companies, with the rank of their companies in parentheses, are as follows: Carleton Fiorina of Hewlett-Packard (28), Marce Fufler of Mirant (52). Patricia Russo of Lucent (76), Anne Mulchay of Xerox (120), Andrea Jung of Avon Products (302), Marion Sandler of Golden West Financial Corporation (371), Patricia Forbes Liebernman of Truserv (513), Cinda Hallman of Spherion (539), Dorrit Bern of Charming Shoppes (699), Pamela Kirby of Quintiles Transnational (808), and Judy Odom of Software Spectrum (979).

However, an increasing number of women own and run their own companies. Over the past 1 decade women have started business at twice the rate of men and now own about 44% of the 20.4 million small business in the United States, despite the fact that only 5% of venture capital and 3% of government contracts are awarded to women-owned businesses (Pofeldt, 2002). In government, women serve in a growing number of leadership capacities, including 12% of state governorships (Women Governors, 2002), 13% of U.S. Senate positions, and 14% of U.S. House of Representatives positions (Ciabattari, 2002).

The growing trend of women filling leadership positions is reflected in the differences between two articles in *Fortune* magazine. In 1996, Fortune profiled the strategies of only 7 high-achieving women leaders with a proviso to watch the careers of an additional 15 (Sellers, 1996). By October 1998, however, *Fortune* concluded that a profile of 50 women leaders was warranted because women, at last, were achieving significant power in highly important industries (Sellers, 1998). The 2002 list of the 50 most powerful women in business was accompanied by an additional list of 5 women whose careers bear watching (Sellers, 2002).

The data presented above indicate that women's inclusion in leadership roles has increased over the past several decades and yet does not reflect their overall proportion of the labour force or population. Expanded leadership opportunities clearly benefit the individual women sought to fill such roles, but what explains organizational willingness to offer such opportunities (beyond the need to comply with legal requirements)? Enhanced productivity, competitive advantage, and financial performance are three reasons why developing and promoting women leaders are in the best interest of employers.

The resource-based theory of competitive advantage and strategy analysis (Barney, 1997) explains that an organization's primary source of competitive advantage is the capacity to optimize and use its internal resources in uncertain and dynamic contexts. Key among these internal resources are people's capabilities, including varying perspectives on problem solving. Underutilized women and people of colour are major sources of untapped value that can enhance an organization's creativity, change efforts, teamwork, and financial performance (Appold, Siengthai, & Kasarda, 1998; Flynn, 1994; Shrader, Blackburn, 1997; Thompson, 1999). Consequently, hiring, developing, and promoting women into leadership positions can be one of the most useful strategies an organization can adopt to succeed in an increasingly globalized and uncertain economy. In brief, recent demographic data on female and male leaders indicate both considerable progress and continued imbalance in the proportion of working women in leader roles. To the degree that women leaders are underutilized, organizations undermine an important source of competitive advantage. The next section will describe studies addressing the second major question posed by researchers.

DIFFERENCE BETWEEN MALE AND FEMALE LEADERS

Sometimes, the purpose of conducting research has simply been to understand the impact of gender on leadership behaviour and outcomes; other times, supporting belief systems about equality or one sex's superiority may have motivated researchers to collect data. In recent years, the large number of studies conducted to compare female and male leaders has allowed other researchers to conduct meta-analyses. A meta-analysis consists of a set of statistical procedures for analyzing all studies that include similar variables to determine what the overall trend in results is. This can be especially useful in leadership studies, since some studies have found sex differences whereas others have not. Female and male leaders did not differ overall in effectiveness, although more will be said later about this meta-analysis. Similarly, other reviews have demonstrated essential similarity in leader aptitude, in motivation to be a leader, in job satisfaction, in commitment, and in subordinate satisfaction (e.g., Dobbins & Platz, 1986; Donnell & Hall, 1980; Powell, 1993).

In what ways, then, might male and female leaders differ? Several authors have pointed to sex differences in worldwide, in socialization, and in life experience that may result in somewhat different mental models, or "implicit theories," of leadership (e.g., Belenky, Clinchy, Goldberger, & Tarule, 1986; Gilligan, 1982; Lowe & Gardner, 2000; Tannen, 1994). Other authors have illuminated sex differences in the organizational outcomes received by female and male leaders. This chapter has already described the relatively small percentage of women in leader roles relative to their proportion in the labour force and the salary inequities experienced even more sharply by women leaders than by women employees. Several studies have noted the relatively small number of corporate women leaders in line positions, seen as crucial for promotion to executive roles (e.g., Oakley, 2000).

Female and male leaders may also differ in the conditions that prove a good fit for their leadership style. In the meta-analysis on leader effectiveness already mentioned (Eagly *et. al.*, 1995), the researchers predicted that the social role theory of sex differences in social behaviour would explain the patterns in the literature. This theory proposes that people are generally expected to engage in activities and actions congruent with their culturally defined gender roles (Eagly, 1987). While overall effectiveness did not differ for male and female leaders, comparisons of leader effectiveness favoured men more and women less when three conditions were present: when the setting was male dominated (especially in the military); when a high percentage of subordinates were male; and when the role was seen as more congenial to men in terms of self-assessed competence, interest, and low requirements for co-operation with high requirements for control. Effectiveness comparisons favoured women leaders to the degree that these conditions were reversed. Additionally, effectiveness comparisons favoured women leaders for middle management in business, education, and government or social service, while they favoured male leaders in entry-level or supervisory positions, especially in the military.

Eagly and her associates (1992) concluded, "Leadership or managerial roles may be defined in a more masculine or feminine fashion, depending on the organizational context of management. It is the fit between leaders' gender and the specifics of the leadership role that influences leaders' effectiveness". In noting the conditions that seem to favour female or male leaders, the meta-analysis indicated that, across most sectors of the economy other than the military, women's effectiveness increased as they moved up the hierarchy and as co-operation rather than control was required. This pattern in the literature is consistent, not only with another meta-analysis indicating that women's social skills tend to be higher than men's (Eagly & Wood, 1991) but also with studies highlighting that many women leaders' preferred style of co-operative or "web leadership" (e.g., Helgesen, 1990; Lauterbach & Weiner, 1996; Rosener, 1990) provides a good fit with the evolving requirements for 21st century global leadership (e.g., Bartlett & Ghoshal, 1997; Fisher, 1998; Petrick, Scherer, Brodzinski, Quinn, & Ainina, 1999; Sharpe, 2000).

Finally, three recent studies underscore the pattern that, despite organizational obstacles, women leaders perform effectively. Advanced Teamware, Inc., conducted a study in which more than 6,000 bosses, peers, subordinates, and others were asked to complete comprehensive questionnaires about 915 middle- to senior-level managers and supervisors in large corporations. Of the 31 areas examined, women outperformed men in 28, including conflict resolution, work quality, adaptation to change, productivity, idea generation, and motivation of others. Men handled pressure and coped with their own frustration better than women did, while both groups scored equally on delegating authority (Micco, 1996).

Saville & Holdsworth, a consulting firm in New Zealand, conducted a study with 3,000 managers. While there were no differences between male and female managers on many of the 30 attributes measured, results indicated that women emphasized planning and organizing work and an empathic approach, while they placed less emphasis on the need to win at all costs ("Women", May,1997). Third, Lawrence A. Pfaff & Associates conducted a study in which 1,000 managers' bosses and employees evaluated their performance. Although some performance categories reflected no significant differences between women and men, in the 20 categories reflecting a statistically significant difference, women received higher scores from their bosses and employees. The largest gaps were in areas like planning and decisiveness (Gendron, 1995).

In brief, individual studies suggest several conclusions about differences between male and female leaders. Although quite similar to men in behaviour and effectiveness, women leaders tend to be more participative and less autocratic, a pattern that is well suited to 21st century global organizations. Since women leaders are evaluated more negatively by men when they behave in stereotypically masculine ways, the range of behaviour seen as appropriate for women leaders is more limited. Women leaders were seen as more effective in middle management positions in most sectors other than the military and in situations requiring co-operation, with a balance of men and women.

WHY FEW WOMEN LEADERS REACH THE TOP?

Several popularized explanations have been offered for the slow, albeit real, progress of women leaders over the past 30 years. One common explanation offered by theorists and male CEOs is the "pipeline theory," which argues that women's absence from executive positions is simply a function of not having been in managerial positions long enough for natural career progression to occur (Heilman, 1997; Ragins *et. al.*, 1998). A second explanation favoured by male CEOs in a recent study was women's lack of general management or line experience (Ragins *et. al*., 1998). A third explanation has proposed that women leaders are themselves the problem, whether because they are simply less suited to executive demands than men (Heilman, 1997), unavailable because so few are sufficiently qualified (Morrison, 1992), or lacking in self-confidence (Morris, 1998). How valid are these explanations?

Before coming to more data-based explanations for women's career advancement, evidence for each of the above popularized explanations will be reviewed. First, the pipeline theory has no data to support it. Heilman (1997) reviewed a number of studies indicating that if simple passage of time were the issue, women's representation at top levels would be many times what it was. McCorduck (1996) noted that since top corporate leaders were 99% male in 1970 and 95% male in 1995, it would take 300 years for U.S. women to achieve parity in business and 500 years to reach it in the U.S. Congress. A study of 70 executive women across the United States found that the average length of time they took to reach executive ranks in their companies was 11.5 years (Gallagher, 1996), a time period that should have easily allowed parity to be reached since, for example, the percentage of women in the Harvard MBA program has plateaued at about 26% since 1983 (Faircloth, 1998).

This chapter has already noted that corporate women leaders fill a small percentage of line positions (Catalyst, 1998a; Oakley, 2000), and some women leaders (47% of the sample) agreed with male CEOs (82% of the sample) that the absence of line experience was an advancement barrier (Ragins *et al*., 1998). In another study of 1,366 middle and top managers, however, researchers discovered that top executives were not distinguished from middle managers by their line experience but by the breadth of positions and departments in which they had worked. Thus, the extent to which extensive line experience is a primary determinant of women's career advancement remains an empirical question for future researchers.

The third popularized explanation of women's unsuitability for leadership has been refuted by the large number of published research findings and meta-analyses of studies detailed in the previous section of this chapter. Women leaders not only have demonstrated a strong achievement record but have also exhibited a number of personal qualities conducive to the executive ranks (e.g., Kelly & Dabul Marin, 1998). While women have reported lower self-confidence (Morris, 1998; Morrison, 1992; Watson & Hoffmann, 1996), it has not been found to affect career advancement directly but only indirectly through the career encouragement and training that women receive (Tharenou *et al*., 1994).

Data-based explanations for women's slow progress to the top have focused on the intangible, yet effective, barriers known collectively as the "glass ceiling" (Federal Glass Ceiling Commission, 1995). Many authors have listed and documented these barriers in detail (e.g., Eyring & Stead, 1998; Morrison, 1992; Ragins *et. al*., 1998), but this chapter will highlight only some of the major patterns found in recent research. Listed in Box 4.1, barriers to women's advancement may be broadly categorized as organizational, interpersonal, and personal.

Organizational barriers to women leaders' advancement include conditions and practices that put women at a disadvantage compared to equally educated and qualified male peers. *Higher* *standards of performance and effort for women* have been reported in many studies by both women leaders and male CEOs (Mainiero, 1994a; Morris, 1998; Morrison, 1992; Ragins *et. al*., 1998; Sutton & Moore, 1985). Women can expect this higher standard to continue, based on a recent survey of 1,200 professionals ages 25 to 35 (Catalyst, 200J). Men generally saw women enjoying equal pay for equal effort with highly expanded advancement opportunities, while women generally disagreed.

Box 4.1
Common Barriers to Women Leader's Advancement
Organizational barriers
Higher standards of performance and effort for women
Inhospitable corporate culture
Preference for homophily (gender similarity) as a basis for promotion decisions
Ignorance and inaction by male CEOs and "silent majority" male peers
Imbalance of inadequate recognition and support with excessive difficulties
Lack of definitive developmental opportunities
Interpersonal barriers
Male prejudice, stereotyping, preconceptions
Lack of emotional and interpersonal support
Exclusion from informal networks
Lack of white male mentors
Personal barriers
Lack of political savvy
Work-home conflict

Some of the recent studies conducted by Morrison, 1992; Chlott *et. al*., 1994), they found that an inhospitable culture makes a significant difference in the likelihood of women being promoted into lower and middle management positions and therefore being available for the pool of those who will be considered for upper management (Tharenou, 2001). Particularly, a males-only organizational hierarchy hindered women's promotions into lower and middle management, while having female leaders in the hierarchy fostered women's promotions at those levels. Another study, based on extensive interviews with 120 black and white women managers and executives and a survey of 825 black and white women managers, found that African American women "'worked from the understanding that they would never truly fit in" (Bell & Nkomo, 2001). While earlier research has discussed the debilitating effects of a bicultural life, this study uncovered that the African American women used their insider-outsider status as a means of galvanizing their energies and self-respect, regardless of disconfirming corporate messages.

Homophily refers to the tendency to prefer to work or interact with people who are similar demographically and attitudinally. While homophily can be useful for easing initial interaction in a group of people, it can also restrict creative thinking and balanced decision making (Cox, 1993). When top management in an organization is dominated by one demographic group (e.g., European American men) and when decisions about promotion are based, even in part, on their preference for working with people who are demographically similar, then a significant bias has entered the advancement process. The impact of a preference for homophily has been documented in major corporations (Appold *et. al.*, 1998; Cox, 1993; Morrison, 1992). Since women of colour differ in two demographic characteristics from European American men and in one demographic characteristic from European American women, they may be even more likely to experience marginalization at work (Bell *et. al.*, 1993). Related to this unspoken preference are the simple *lack of understanding* that male CEOs may have for the obstacles experienced by women leaders (Catalyst, 2001; Ragins *et. al.*, 1998) and the *avoidance of taking a stand* on women's advancement by the many men who do not consciously oppose gender equality (Hale, 1996).

The impact of *limiting the level of useful challenge* in assignments for women is to reduce the likelihood of promotion to executive ranks, and the nature of such decisions can be subtle. In a study of 507 managers (Ohlott *et al.*, 1994), both female and male leaders received opportunities to start new ventures and turn around businesses in trouble, but men were given higher levels of responsibility in these positions. This meant that the men's responsibilities entailed higher stakes (more crucial and visible), higher business diversity (managing multiple functions), and higher external pressure (more negotiation and/or international aspects). In contrast, women's responsibilities emphasized the need to influence employees despite having low leverage or formal authority, which suggested the women had been placed in situations known to involve difficult relationships. Thus, even though women leaders appeared to have been given equal opportunities, the features of the responsibilities they were given yielded lower development, thereby reducing their promotional potential.

Overall, women leaders developed via new responsibilities that were characterized by obstacles such as lack of support and resources, while male leaders developed via new responsibilities that were characterized by higher stakes, breadth, and external interface. Even with these differences, developmental opportunities that would decisively place high-potential individuals in the pool for promotion were found to be important, yet gender role had even more impact on women's income and level in the organization than did training, education, and work experience (Kirchmeyer, 1998). As would be expected, training, education, and work experience had far greater impact on men's career advancement than their gender role (Kirchmeyer, 1998; Tharenou *et. al.*, 1994).

The research reviewed in this section points to organizational practices that affect women's entry into leadership roles, but also to a variety of conversations and relationships within the workplace that help to explain sex differences in advancement (Heilman, 1997). **Interpersonal barriers** refer to those obstacles that occur primarily in the context of working relationships. Supportive relationships can be especially important in women's leadership advancement since women were often more likely to identify individuals rather than organizational practices when asked about what helped their career (Bell & Nkomo, 2001).

Gender *prejudice* can take many forms in organizational life and most often is not conscious. The most basic preconception is that a good manager is inherently masculine. In a comparison of samples drawn in 1999, 1984-1985, and 1976-1977, a recent study found this preconception still operates, although the preference for masculine characteristics decreased somewhat over the past 15 years (Powell, Butterfield, & Parent, 2002). Preconceptions of women leaders as less competent have meant that women must prove themselves repeatedly in each new situation (Ragins *et. al.*, 1998) and may not receive assignments with real risk and responsibility until they have excelled in trial situations (Ruderman & Ohlott, 1992). Preconceptions of women leaders as disinterested in challenge have meant that women must identify and explicitly ask for challenging assignments rather than simply having such assignments offered to them as equivalent high-potential men would (Ragins *et. al.*, 1998). Racial prejudice remains an additional advancement barrier for women of colour (Bell & Nkomo, 2001).

Men's discomfort with women leaders has taken many forms. Research has uncovered that women perceived a need to adapt their behavioural style so that men could avoid feeling intimidated (Ragins *et. al.*, 1998) and that a narrower range of acceptable behaviour existed for female than for male leaders (Eagly *et. al.*, 1992; Ragins *et. al.*, 1998). This means that male leaders were positively evaluated when they behaved either co-operatively or autocratically, but that female leaders were evaluated positively only when they behaved co-operatively (Eagly *et. al.*, 1992). Whether or not, most male employees viewed female employees as behaving inappropriately or as depleting workplace resources meant for men'(Hale, 1996), fear of reverse discrimination and backlash have increased (Burke & Black, 1997; Morrison, 1992; Ragins *et. al.*, 1998).

Prejudice about women leaders can have direct career ramifications. Women's evaluations of others' performance were not affected by the target's sex, but men tended to evaluate men more positively and women more negatively (Eagly *et. al.*, 1992). Women were more likely to be devalued when they composed a small proportion of the applicant pool considered for promotion, when performance standards and information were ambiguous (as often applies to managerial positions), when affirmative action was perceived as influencing selection decisions, and when organizational practices made demographic group membership (e.g., sex) pertinent (Heilman, 1997).

Several studies have documented that women leaders have experienced *lower support* throughout their careers than similarly employed men in terms of collegiality, acceptance, information, feedback, and flexibility (Morrison, 1992; Oakley, 2000; Ohlott *et. al.*, 1994; Ragins *et. al.*, 1998). Inclusion in *informal networks* provides important resources such as social contact with superiors, networking potential with peers within and beyond the organization, and the potential to influence management (Kelly & Dabul Marin, 1998). Again, several studies have found that women leaders have either tended to be excluded, have had to work harder to be included in informal networks (Morrison, 1992; Ohlott *et. al.*, 1994; Ragins *et. al.*, 1998), or have had to create formal opportunities for "informal" interaction (Bell & Nkomo, 2001).

One of the most critical types of relationship for career advancement is a *mentor relationship,* in which a senior individual provides task coaching, emotional encouragement, and sponsoring the protege with top-level decision makers. While a number of studies have documented the prevalence and impact of mentoring relationships for both male and female leaders (e.g., Dreher & Ash, 1990; Ragins *et. al*., 1998), a recent study found that European American male mentors had a dramatic impact on salary and that other European American men were most likely to be their proteges (Dreher & Cox, 1996).

In another sample of 160 executives, women and men were equally likely to be mentors, but women were more likely to have same-sex proteges while men were more likely to have proteges of both sexes (Ragins & Scandura, 1994). While a mentor of any sex, race, or ethnicity can be highly important (Dreher & Cox, 1996; Gallagher, 1996), recent research has demonstrated that bad mentoring may be worse than none at all and that formal mentoring programs may be less effective for women than for men (Ragins, Cotton, & Miller, 2000). Having a supportive boss who can sponsor career advancement has remained a perennial issue for women of colour as well (Bell & Nkomo, 2001; Catalyst 1998b, 2002b).

Personal barriers to women leaders' advancement refer to elements of their personal lives or a lack of knowledge that may be an obstacle. Women leaders themselves have reported naivete and lower *political savvy* as a barrier, particularly in earlier career stages (Bell & Nkomo, 2001; Bierema, 1999; Morrison, 1992; Ragins *et. al*., 1998). The need to build alliances, navigate competing priorities, and develop to a point of functioning as a change agent has been described in several studies (Bell & Nkomo, 2001; Bierema, 1999; Mainiero, 1994b). To mature organizationally, black women leaders have adopted perseverance, a willingness to change employers or functions to gain upward mobility, and self-generated developmental opportunities (Bell & Nkomo, 2001; Catalyst, 2002c).

Perhaps as serious for many women leaders are the *non-work obligations* for which they remain primarily responsible in a household, although one recent study found that a configuration of multiple work and non-work roles with positive affect actually enhanced women managers' psychological resources, social support, and management skills (Ruderman, Ohlott, Penzer, & King, 2002). Nonetheless, the need for better balance and the impossibility of "having it all" have been frequent themes in women leaders' descriptions of their lives (Catalyst, 1998a; Faircloth, 1998; Gallagher, 1996; Morris, 1998; Sellers, 1996, 1998), and finding peace with one's life configuration has emerged as a major theme in two recent studies of white and black women executives and managers (Bell & Nkomo, 2001; Ruderman & Ohlott, 2002).

While some women have coped by purchasing domestic services, having a supportive or non-employed husband, or scaling back their families (Catalyst, 1996; Gallagher, 1996; Kirchmeyer, 1998; Morris, 2002), using organizational supports such as flex-time or parental leave was generally not seen as a genuine option (Catalyst, 1996; Hochschild, 1997). Others have acknowledged that work-home conflict has been an obstacle (Kelly & Dabul Marin, 1998; Morrison, 1992; Tharenou *et. al*., 1994). While a non-employed spouse was favourable to advancement for both men and women (Kirchmeyer, 1998), homes with families overall proved to be a source of support for male leaders' advancement but a source of demand for female leaders (Tharenou *et. al*., 1994).

In summary, women's career advancement in leadership roles has been hampered by organizational, interpersonal, and personal barriers. Although these barriers may be subtle and have often been enacted unconsciously, they have nonetheless functioned to keep the number of women in leadership positions disproportionately low for both white women and women of colour. While one author has concluded that the problem is too systemic to be solved with changes in organizational practice and actually requires changes in federal law (Tharenou, 2001), the studies described above provide the seeds of solutions in both the inner and outer worlds of women leaders. Many of the organizational practices that would increase the flexibility, authority, and recognition available to women leaders have also been suggested as ways that organizations could retain more of the women who might otherwise leave corporate life to start their own businesses (Gordon & Whelan, 1998; Morris, 1995; Royal, 1998; Sellers, 1998).

Exercise on Gender Consciousness Questionnaire

Instruction: Indicate the degree to which each statement reflects your personal beliefs or expectations. Use the following scale:

Key: 1 – False 2 = More false than true 3 = More true than false 4 = True

1. If my child were to become ill during workday hours, I would expect my working spouse to take care of the situation.
2. I prefer to work with a boss who has the same sex as mine.
3. If it had a son and a daughter who were equally educated and qualified for a position, it makes sense that my son would earn more money than my daughter for doing the same work.
4. Organisations should focus on controlling costs and maximizing profits, not an accommodating non-work responsibilities.
5. If my spouse were offered a career opportunity that exceeded my current job, I would not expect to relocate in order to foster my spouse's career.
6. People of the other sex are generally less suited or qualified to be leaders than members of my own sex.
7. I expect my working spouse to take primary responsibility for household chores.
8. Individuals should be expected to adapt themselves to organizational policies and practices, rather than the other way around.
9. I expect to earn more than my spouse, and I would not be comfortable if my spouse earned more than 1 did.
10. Members of my sex are easier to work with than members of the other sex.
11. If members of the other sex want to be promoted, they should pay attention to making their work behaviour non-threatening for members of my sex.
12. Being in control of any situation should be the top priority for a leader.
13. It seems natural for people at work to listen without interrupting me and to include my ideas in most decisions that are made.

14. When members of the other sex are promoted into leadership positions, I usually think that some form of favouritism was part of the decision.
15. I expect to work in an organization where members of my sex make most of the decisions.
16. When people or groups have competing goals, my priority as a leader is to make sure the outcome reflects my priorities.
17. Members of the other sex who seek leader position should be careful not to reduce opportunities for members of my sex. Members of the other sex are too sensitive and tend to misinterpret interpersonal situations at work.
18. Finding an influential mentor to help me with my career should be easy.
19. Leaders should not expect to live balanced lives; work must come first.

Scoring

The Gender Consciousness Questionnaire is designed to measure your beliefs in three areas: expectation of privilege, preference for similarity, and preference for control. Score the questionnaire by doing the following:

- Expectation of Privilege: Sum your responses on all the odd-numbered items.
- Preference for similarity: Sum your responses on items 2,6,10,14, and 18.
- Preference for control: Sum your responses on items 4,8,12,16 and 20.

Scoring Interpretation

Several basic beliefs underlie many of the statements in this questionnaire. There are no correct answers to any question. Your responses simply indicate the degree to which you hold a particular belief.

- **Expectation of Privilege**

High Score	30 – 40
Moderate Score	16 – 29
Low Score	1 – 15

A high score on this group of items indicates that you tend to expect that your perspective or your needs will take precedence in your work and home life. The alternative would be a recognition that others' concerns and perspectives have as much validity as one's own.

- **Preference for Similarity**

High score	15 – 20
Moderate Score	6 – 14
Low Score	1 – 5

A high score on this group of items indicates that you tend to more positively evaluate people whose sex is the same as yours. A preference for similarity need not be limited to sex but can also apply to other demographic characteristics such as race, age, or social class. The alternative would be a recognition that individuals can make valuable contribution whether they are demographically similar or different from oneself.

➢ **Preference for Control**

High score	15 – 20
Moderate score	6 – 14
Low Score	1 – 5

A high score on this group of items indicates that you tend to subscribe to an organizational value set with an emphasis on monetary outcomes, control of individuals, and more autocratic decision-making processes. The alternative would be a balance of individual and organizational priorities, a balance between profit and human or planetary needs, and a more collaborative approach to problem solving and decision making.

Case Study on Women Leadership

Others Seek Her Opinions, But the CEO Never Knows

Lisa Weber never doubted that she would be a partner in her Wall Street firm. A graduate of a prestigious business school, with a doctorate in economics, she taught briefly at a major university. She was the first woman hired as a market analyst in her well–regarded firm. Within two years, she had become one of four senior portfolio managers reporting directly to a senior partner. Her clients give her the highest commendations for her outstanding performance, and over the past two years, she has brought in the largest number of new accounts to the firm.

Despite the admiration of her colleagues and their seeming acceptance of her, there is a disturbing, if flattering, aspect to her job. Most of her peers and some of the partners visit her office during the day to discuss in private her opinions on market performance and financial projections. She enjoys these private sessions but is dismayed that at the weekly staff meetings the CEO, Michael Breyer, usually says something like, "Okay, let's get started and bring Lisa up-to-date on some of the trouble spots." None of her peers or the partners mention that Lisa knows as much as they do about what's going on in the firm. She never protests this slight to her competence and knowledge of firm business, nor does she mention the almost daily private meetings where her advice is sought. As the only woman on the executive level, she prefers to be considered a team player and "one of the boys."

During the past year, one of her peers was promoted to partner, although Lisa's performance clearly surpassed his, as measured by the success of her accounts and the amount of new business she brought to the firm. Having heard no mention of partnership for herself, she approached her boss, one of the partners, and asked about the path to a partnership. He replied, "You're doing great, Lisa, but what happens if you are a partner and you make a huge mistake? How would you take it? And what about our clients? There's never been a female partner in the 103 years of our firm."

Shortly therafter, another woman, Pamela Tobias, was hired as a marketing analyst. Once, when the CEO saw Lisa and Pamela together, he called out to the men, "Hey, guys, two women in one room. That's scary."

During the next six months, Lisa meets several times with the CEO to make her case for a partnership on the basis of her performance. She finally realizes that there is no possibility of change in the foreseeable future and makes a decision to leave and form her own investment firm.

Questions

1. Which advancement barriers and patterns apply to Lisa's situation?
2. What could Michael Breyer do differently to retain and support Lisa more effectively?
3. What could Lisa do differently to foster her own advancement?
4. What could the organization provide to support and develop Lisa's and Pamela's effectiveness?
5. What could the organization provide to raise the gender consciousness of Michael Breyer and Lisa's male colleagues?

Source : Peter G. Northouse " Leadership Theory and Practice" Response Books, New Delhi, 2003.

REFERENCES

1. Robert Tannebaum and Fred Massarik, "Leadership " A frame of Reference," in Leadership and Organisation – A Behavioural Science Approach, New York, McGraw-Hill, 1961,
2. R.D.Mann, "A Review of the Relationship between Personality and Performance in Small Group", Psychological Bulletin, 56(1959).
3. John R. Schermerhorn, Jr., *et. al.*, " Managing Organisational Behaviour", New York, John Wiley and Sons, 1985,
4. Joe Kelly, "Organisational Behaviour – Its Data, First Principles, and Applications", New Delhi, Surjeet Publications, 1987.
5. E.H Schein, "Organisational Psychology", New Delhi, Prentice Hall of India, 1983.
6. Andrew J.H.Dubrin, "The Practice of Supervision", New Delhi, Universal Books Stall, 1988.
7. Acker, J., (1992). "Gendering Organizational Theory." In A. Mills & P. Tancred (Eds.), Gendering Organizational Analysis, Newbury Park, CA:Sage.
8. Bell, E., (1990). "The Bicultural Life Experience of Career-Oriented Black Women", *Journal of Organisational Behaviour.*
9. Bierema, L., (1999) "A Model of Executive Women's Learning and Development", *Adult Education Quarterly*,
10. Catalyst, (1996). "Women in Corporate Leadership: Progress and Prospects." Retrieved June 4, 1999, from http://www.catalystwomen.org.

11. Daniels, C., (2002, July 22). "The Most Powerful Black Executive in America." *Fortune*.

12. Dobbins, G., & Platz, S., (1986). "Sex Differences in Leadership." *Academy of Management Review*.

13. Eagly, A., Karau, S., & Makhijani, M., (1995). "Gender and the Effectiveness of Leader: A Meta-analysis." *Psychological Bulletin*.

14. Federal Glass Ceiling Commission, (1995). Good for Business: Making Full Use of the Nation's Human Capital. Washinton, DC: U.S.Department of Labour.

15. Raginsm B., & Scandura, T., (1994). "Gender Differences in Expected Outcomes of Mentoring Relationships." *Academy of Management Journal*.

16. Women's Bureau, U.S.Department of Labour, (2001). 20 Leading Occupations of Employed Women: 2001 Annual Averages. Retrieved December 8, 2002, from http://www.dol.gov/wb.

CHAPTER 5

Leadership Ethics

Meaning and Significance – Definition of Ethics – Ethical theories – Central Points to Leadership Ethics – Some Research Trends on Leadership Ethics – Principles of Ethical Leadership – Exercise – Case Study.

Learning Objectives of this Chapter are:

- To understand the meaning and significance of leadership ethics.
- To study the definitions of leadership ethics.
- To examine the ethical theories.
- To identify the central points to leadership ethics.
- To know some research trends on leadership ethics.
- To explain the principles of ethical leadership.

MEANING AND SIGNIFICANCE

This chapter is different from other chapters in this book. Generally, the other chapters focus on Leadership Characteristic, Theories and Styles. Whereas, this chapter presents a broad set of ethical view points. Human beings have been concerned with the ethics of our leaders. Later, our history books are replete with descriptions of good kings and bad kings, great empires and evil empires, and strong presidents and weak presidents. But in spite of a wealth of biographical accounts of great leaders and their morals, very little research has been published on the theoretical foundations of leadership ethics. While there have been many studies on business ethics in general since the early 1970s, these studies have been only tangentially related to leadership ethics.

This chapter presents leadership ethics by defining ethics, giving an overview of ethical theories, discussing why ethics is central to leadership, and describing the unique perspectives of Heifetz, Burns, and Greenleaf. The chapter continues with a discussion of five principles of ethical leadership: respect, service, justice, honesty, and community. Finally, some strengths and weaknesses of present-day leadership ethics are mentioned.

DEFINITIONS OF ETHICS

The word *ethics* has its roots in the Greek word *ethos,* which means "customs," "conduct," or "character." Ethics is concerned with the kinds of values and morals an individual or society finds desirable or appropriate. Furthermore, ethics is concerned with the virtuousness of individuals and their motives. Ethical theory provides a system of rules or principles that guide us in making decisions about what is "right or wrong" and "good or bad" in a particular situation. It provides a basis for understanding what it means to be a morally decent human being. Thus, it is a set of principles of values and morals relating to the behaviour of the individuals.

ETHICAL THEORIES

For the purposes of studying ethics and leadership, ethical theories can be thought of as falling within two broad domains: theories about leaders' *conduct* and theories about leaders' *character*. Stated another way, ethical theories are about the actions of leaders, on the one hand, and who they are as people, on the other. Throughout the chapter, our discussions about ethics and leadership will always fall within one of these two domains.

Ethical theories are concerned with the conduct of leaders. They are divided into two kinds: theories that stress the *consequences* of leaders' actions, and those that emphasize the *duty* or *rules* governing leaders' actions. Teleological theories, from the Greek word *telos,* meaning "ends" or "purposes," try to answer questions about right and wrong by focusing on whether an individual's conduct will produce desirable consequences. The question, "What is right?" from the teleological perspective is answered by looking at results — at the outcomes. In effect, the consequences of an individual's actions determine the goodness or badness of a particular behaviour.

In assessing consequences, there are three different approaches to making decisions regarding moral conduct. One *is ethical egoism,* which states that an individual should act so as to create the greatest good for herself or himself. A leader with this orientation would take a job or career that he or she selfishly enjoys (Avolio & Locke, 2002). Self-interest is an ethical stance closely related to transactional leadership theories (Bass & Steidlmeier, 1999). Ethical egoism is common in some business contexts in which a company and its employees make decisions in ways that will achieve its goal of maximizing profits.

Ethical Theories Based on Self-interest Versus Interest for Others

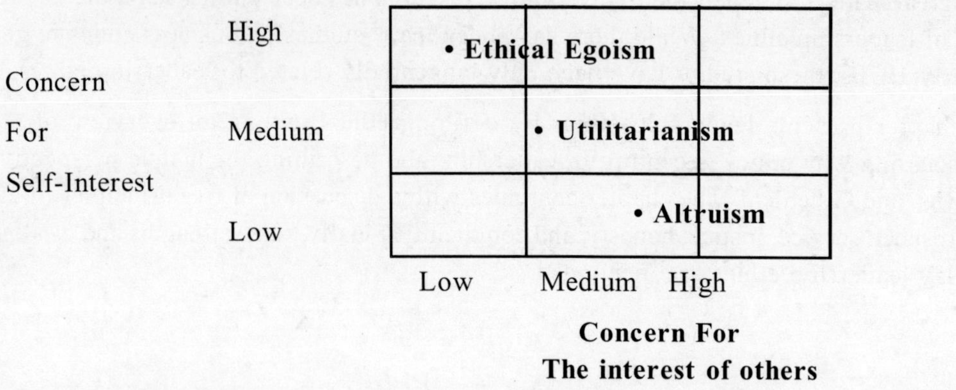

A second teleological approach is *utilitarianism,* which states that we should behave so as to create the greatest good for the greatest number. From this viewpoint, the morally correct action is the action that maximizes social benefits while minimizing social costs (Schumann, 2001). When the U.S. government allocates a large part of the federal budget for preventive health care rather than for catastrophic illnesses, it is acting from a utilitarian perspective—putting money where it will have the best result for the largest number of citizens. Closely related to utilitarianism, and opposite of ethical egoism, is *altruism,* an approach that suggests that actions are moral if their primary purpose is to show concern for the best interests of others. From this perspective, a leader may be called on to act in the interests of others, even when it runs contrary to his or her own self-interests (Bowie, 1991). Authentic transformational leadership is based on altruistic principles (Bass & Steidlmeier, 1999; Kanungo & Mendonca, 1996). The strongest simple of altruist ethics can be found in the work of Mother Teresa, who gave her entire life to help poor people.

While teleological and deontological theories approach ethics by looking at the behaviour or conduct of a leader, a second set of theories approaches ethics from the viewpoint of a leader's character. These theories are called virtue-based theories, and they focus on who leaders are as people. In this perspective, virtues are rooted in the heart of the individual and in his or her disposition (Pojman, 1995). Furthermore, it is believed that virtues and moral abilities are not innate but can be acquired and learned through practice. People can be taught by their families and communities to be morally appropriate human beings.

Although virtue theories have only recently regained their popularity, their origin can be traced back in the Western tradition to the Greek period and the works of Plato and Aristotle. The Greek term associated with these theories is *aretaic,* which means "excellence" or "virtue." Consistent with Aristotle, current advocates of virtue-based theory stress that more attention should be given to the development and training of moral values (Velasquez, 1992). Rather than tell people what to *do,* attention should be directed toward telling people what to *be*—by helping them to become more virtuous.

What, then, are the virtues of an ethical person? There are many, all of which seem to be important. Based on the writings of Aristotle, a moral person demonstrates the following virtues: courage, temperance, generosity, self-control, honesty, sociability, modesty, fairness, and justice (Velasquez, 1992). For Aristotle, virtues allowed individuals to live well in communities. Applying ethics to leadership and management, Velasquez has suggested that managers should develop virtues such as perseverance, public-spiritedness, integrity, truthfulness, fidelity, benevolence, and humility.

In essence, virtue-based ethics is about being and becoming a good, worthy human being. While people can learn and develop good values, this theory maintains that virtues are present within the individual's disposition. When practiced over time, from youth to adulthood, good values become habitual and part of the persons themselves. From telling the truth, people become truthful; from giving to the poor, people become benevolent; and from being fair to others, people become just. Our virtues are derived from our actions and our actions manifest our virtues (Frankena, 1973; Pojman, 1995).

CENTRAL POINTS TO LEADERSHIP ETHICS

Leadership Ethics are more important, the are related to principles and values. Every leader has a distinct philosophy and point of view. All leaders "have an agenda, a series of beliefs, proposals, values, ideas, and issues that they wish to 'put on the table'" (Gini, 1998). The values promoted by the leader have a significant impact on the values exhibited by the organization (cf. Carlson & Perrewe, 1995; Schminke, Ambrose, & Noel, 1997; Trevino, 1986). Again, because of their influence, leaders play a major role in establishing the ethical climate of their organizations. They will help the leader to achieve individual and organizational goals.

In brief, ethics is central to leadership because of the nature of the process of influence, the need to engage followers to accomplish mutual goals, and the impact leaders have on establishing the organization's values.

SOME RESEARCH TRENDS ON LEADERSHIP ETHICS

Some of the research have been conducted by prominent leadership scholars who have addressed issues related to ethics and leadership. Although many additional viewpoints exist, those presented are representative of what is currently the predominant thinking in the area of ethics and leadership.

Heifetz's Perspective on Ethical Leadership

Based on his observations and analysis of many world leaders like President Lyndon Johnson, Mohandas Gandhi, and Margaret Sanger, (Ronald Heifetz (1994) has formulated a unique approach to ethical leadership; it concludes that leaders help followers to confront conflict and to effect changes from conflict. Heifetz's perspective is related to ethical leadership because it deals with values—values of workers, and the values of the organizations and communities in which they work. According to Heifetz, leadership involves the use of authority to help followers deal with the conflicting values that emerge in rapidly changing work environments and social cultures.

Leaders must use authority to mobilize people to face tough issues. The leader provides a "holding environment" in which there is trust, nurturance, and empathy. Within a supportive context, followers can feel safe to confront and deal with hard problems. Specifically, leaders use authority to get people to pay attention to the issues, to act as a reality test regarding information, to manage and frame issues, to orchestrate conflicting perspectives, and to facilitate the decision-making process (Heifetz, 1994,). The leader's duties are to assist the followers in struggling with change and personal growth.

Burns's Perspective on Ethical Leadership

This study has been conducted by Burns. It is similar to Heifetz's Perspective Theory. It is important for leaders to engage themselves with followers and help them in their personal struggles regarding conflicting values. In the process, the connection between the leader and the follower raises the level of morality in both the leader and the follower.

The origins of Burns's position on leadership ethics are rooted in the works of such writers as Abraham Maslow, Milton Rokeach, and Lawrence Kohlberg (Ciulla, 1998). The influence of these writers can be seen in how Burns emphasizes the leader's role to attend to the personal motivations and moral development of the follower. For Burns, it is the responsibility of the leader to help followers assess their own values and needs in order to raise them to a higher level of functioning, to a level that will stress values such as liberty, justice, and equality (Ciulla, 1998).

Greenleaf's Perspective on Ethical Leadership

In the early 1970s, Robert Greenleaf developed a somewhat paradoxical approach to leadership called *servant leadership.* It is an approach that has gained increased popularity in recent years (cf. Block, 1993; De Free, 1989, 1992). With its strong altruistic ethical overtones, servant leadership emphasizes that leaders should be attentive to the concerns of their followers and empathize with them; they should take care of them and nurture them.

Greenleaf (1970, 1977) argued that leadership was bestowed on a person who was by nature a servant. In fact, the way an individual emerges as a leader is by first becoming a servant. A servant leader focuses on the needs of followers and helps them to become more knowledgeable, more free, more autonomous, and more like servants themselves. They enrich others by their presence.

In addition to serving, the servant leader has a social responsibility to be concerned with the "have-nots" and to recognize them as equal stakeholders in the life of the organization. Where inequalities and social injustices exist, a servant leader tries to remove them (Graham, 1991). In becoming a servant leader, a leader uses less institutional power and less control, while shifting authority to those who are being led. Servant leadership values everyone's involvement in community life because it is within a community that one fully experiences respect, tract, and individual strength. Greenleaf places a great deal of emphasis on listening, empathy, and unconditional acceptance of others.

In the novel *The Journey to the East,* by Herman Hesse (1956), there is an example of leadership that was the inspiration behind Greenleaf's formulation of servant leadership. The story is about a group of travellers on a mythical journey who are accompanied by a servant who does menial chores for the travellers but also sustains them with his spirits and song. The servant's presence has an extraordinary impact on the group, but when the servant becomes lost and disappears, the group of travellers falls into disarray and abandons their journey. Without the servant, they are unable to carry on. It was the servant who was leading the group. He emerged as a leader by caring for the travellers.

A common theme running through all three of the perspectives (i.e., Heifetz, Burns, and Greenleaf) is that the leader-follower relationship is central to ethical leadership. In addition, they all emphasize that it is critically important for leaders to pay close attention to the unique needs of their followers.

In many ways, the ideas presented by these leadership scholars are parallel to and consonant with the *ethic of caring* set forth by Gilligan (1982), who contended that personal relationships should be the beginning point of ethics. In the past 20 years, the "caring principle" has become recognized by scholars as one of the predominant moral principles. From a caring perspective, a leader's actions are morally correct if they express care in protecting the people with whom the leader has special relationships (Schumann, 2001). An ethic of caring is extremely important in organizations because it is the main ingredient in building trust and co-operative relationships (Brady, 1999).

PRINCIPLES OF ETHICAL LEADERSHIP

These principles are broadly divided into five types. The importance of these principles has been discussed in a variety of disciplines including biomedical ethics (Beauchamp & Childress, 1994), business ethics, counselling psychology, and leadership education. These principles provide a foundation for the development of sound ethical leadership: *respect, service, justice, honesty,* and *community* (see figure 5.1).

Principles of Respect

Philosopher Immanuel Kant (1724-1804) argued that it is our duty to treat others with respect. Leaders who respect others also allow them to be themselves, with creative wants and desires. They approach other persons with a sense of unconditional worth and valuable individual differences (Kitchener, 1984). Respect includes giving credence to others' ideas and confirming them as human beings. At times, it may require that leaders have to refer to others. As Burns (1978) suggested, leaders should nurture followers in becoming aware of their own needs, values, and purposes and assist them in integrating these with the leader's.

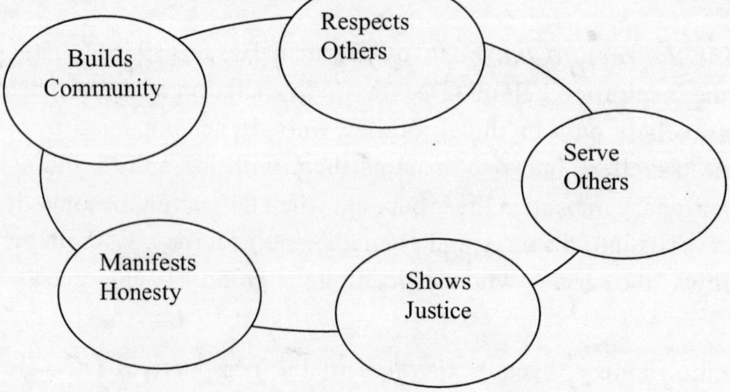

Fig. 5.1: Principles of Ethical Leadership

Respect for others is a complex ethic that is similar to but goes deeper than the kind of respect that parents teach children when they are little. Respect means that a leader listens closely to his or her subordinates, is empathic, and is tolerant of opposing points of view. It means treating subordinates in ways that confirm their beliefs, attitudes, and values. When a leader exhibits respect to subordinates, subordinates can feel competent about their work. In short, leaders who show respect in fact treat others as worthy human beings.

Principle of Service

Earlier we have discussed, two ethical theories—one is concerned for self and another based on the interests of others. They are related to ethical egoism and ethical altruism. The service principle is clearly an example of altruism. Leaders who serve are altruistic; they place their followers welfare foremost in their plans. In the workplace, altruistic service behaviour can be observed in activities such as mentoring, empowerment behaviours, team building, and citizenship behaviours etc. The leader's ethical responsibility to serve others is very similar to the ethical principle in health care of beneficence. Beneficence is derived from the Hippocratic tradition, which implies that health professionals ought to make choices that benefit patients. In a general way, beneficence asserts that providers have a duty to help others pursue their own legitimate interests and goals (Beauchamp & Childress, 1994). Similar to health professionals, ethical leaders have a responsibility to attend to others, be of service to them, and make decisions pertaining to them that are beneficial and not harmful to their welfare.

In brief, whether it be Greenleaf's notion of waiting on the have-nots or Senge's notion of giving oneself to a larger purpose, the idea behind service is contributing to the greater good of others. In practicing the principle of service, ethical leaders must be willing to be follower centred, must place others' interests foremost in their work, and must act in ways which will be benefited to others.

Principles of Justice

Ethical leaders are concerned about issues of fairness and justice. They make it a top priority to treat all of their subordinates in an equal manner. Justice demands that leaders place issues of fairness at the centre of their decision making. As a rule, no one should receive special treatment or special consideration except when their particular situation demands it. In instances where individuals are treated differently, the grounds for differential treatment need to be clear, reasonable, and based on sound moral values.

These principles of justice can be shown in the Table 5.1, consider the following hypothetical example. Imagine you are the owner of a small tracking company, which employs 50 drivers. You have just opened a new route, and it promises to be one that pays well and has an ideal schedule. Only one driver can be assigned to the route, but seven drivers have applied for it. Each feels he or she should have an *equal opportunity* to get the route. One of the drivers recently lost his wife to

Table 5.1 Principles of Distributive Justice

These principles are applied in different situations

To each person

- an equal
- according to individual need
- according to that person's rights
- according to individual effort
- according to societal contribution
- according to merit

breast cancer and is struggling to care for three young children *(individual need).* Two of the drivers are minorities and one of them feels strongly that he has a *right* to the job. One of the drivers has logged more driving hours for 3 consecutive years and she feels her *effort* makes her the logical candidate for the new route. One of the drivers serves on the National Safety Board and has a 20-year accident-free driving record *(societal contribution).* Two drivers have been with the company since its inception and their *performance* has been meritorious year after year.

Principle of Honesty

Leaders are always advised to maintain honesty in achieving leadership success. To be a good leader, leaders need to be honest. The importance of being honest can be understood more clearly when we consider the opposite of honesty: dishonesty (cf. Jaksa & Pritchard, 1988). Dishonesty is a form of lying, a way of misrepresenting reality. Dishonesty may bring with it many objectionable outcomes, and foremost is the distrust it creates. When leaders are not honest, others come to see them as undependable and unreliable. People lose faith in what leaders say and stand for; their respect for leaders is diminished. As a result, the leader's impact is compromised because others no longer trust and believe in the leader.

When we relate to others, dishonesty also has a negative impact. It puts a strain on how people are connected to each other. When we lie to others, we are in essence saying that we are willing to manipulate the relationship on our own terms. We are saying that we do not trust the other person in the relationship to be able to deal with information we have. In reality, we are putting ourselves ahead of the relationship by saying that we know what is best for the relationship. The long-term effect of this type of behaviour is that it weakens relationships. Dishonesty, even when used with good intentions, contributes to the breakdown of relationships.

But being honest is not just about telling the truth. It has to do with being open with others and representing reality as fully and completely as possible. However, this is not an easy task because there are times when telling the complete truth can be destructive or counter-productive. The challenge for leaders is to strike a balance between being open and candid while at the same time monitoring what is appropriate to disclose in a particular situation. It is important for leaders to be authentic but at the same time it is essential that they be sensitive to the attitudes and feelings of others. Honest leadership involves a wide set of behaviours.

Principles of Community

In Chapter 1, we defined leadership as the process of influencing others to reach a common or communal goal. This definition has a clear ethical dimension because it refers to a *common* goal. A common goal requires that the leader and followers agree on the direction to be taken by the group. Leaders need to take into account their own and followers' purposes, while working toward goals that are suitable for both of them. This factor, concern for others, is the distinctive feature that delineates *authentic* transformational leaders from transformational leaders (Bass & Steidlmeier, 1999). Concern for the common good means that leaders cannot impose their will on others. They need to search for goals that are compatible with everyone.

A transformational leader tries to move the group toward a common good that is beneficial for both, the leader and the followers. In moving toward mutual goals, both the leader and followers are changed. It is this feature that makes Burns's theory unique. For Burns, leadership has to be grounded in the leader-follower relationship. It cannot be controlled by the leader, such as Hitler's influence in Germany when Hitler coerced people to meet his own agenda—and followed goals that did not advance the goodness of humankind. An ethical leader takes into account the purposes of everyone involved in the group and is attentive to the interests of the community and the culture. Such a leader demonstrates an ethic of caring toward others and does not force others or ignore the intentions of others.

Exercise on Perceived Leader Intergrity Scale (PLIS)

Instructions: The following items concern your immediate supervisor. You should consider your immediate supervisor to be the person who you feel has the most control over your daily work activities. Circle responses to indicate how well each item describes your immediate supervisor.

Key: 1 = Not at all 2 = Somewhat 3 = Very Much 4 = Exactly

1.	Would use my mistakes to attack me personally.	1 2 3 4
2.	Always get even.	1 2 3 4
3.	Gives special favours to certain "pet" employees, but not to me.	1 2 3 4
4.	Would lie to me.	1 2 3 4
5.	Would risk me to protect himself/herself in work matters.	1 2 3 4
6.	Deliberately fuels conflict among employees.	1 2 3 4
7.	Is evil.	1 2 3 4
8.	Would use my performance appraisal to criticize me as a person.	1 2 3 4
9.	Has it in for me.	1 2 3 4
10.	Would allow me to be blamed for his/her mistakes.	1 2 3 4

11. Would falsify records if it would help his/her work situation. 1 2 3 4
12. Lacks high morals. 1 2 3 4
13. Makes fun of my mistakes instead of coaching me as to how to do my job better. 1 2 3 4
14. Would deliberately exaggerate my mistakes to make me look bad when describing my performance to his/her superiors. 1 2 3 4
15. Is vindictive. 1 2 3 4
16. Would blame me for his/her own mistake. 1 2 3 4
17. Avoids coaching me becauses (s)he wants me to fail. 1 2 3 4
18. Would treat me better if I belonged to a different ethnic group. 1 2 3 4
19. Would deliberately distort what I say. 1 2 3 4
20. Deliberately makes employees angry at each other. 1 2 3 4
21. Is a hypocrite. 1 2 3 4
22. Would limit my training opportunities to prevent me from advancing 1 2 3 4
23. Would blackmail an employee if (s)he thought (s)he could get away with it. 1 2 3 4
24. Enjoys turning down my requests. 1 2 3 4
25. Would make trouble for me if I got on his/her bad side. 1 2 3 4
26. Would take credit for my ideas. 1 2 3 4
27. Would steal from the organisation. 1 2 3 4
28. Would risk me to get back at someone else. 1 2 3 4
29. Would engage in sabotage against the organisation. 1 2 3 4
30. Would fire people just because (s)he doesn't like them if (s)he could get away with it. 1 2 3 4
31. Would do things which violate organizational policy and then expect his/her subordinates to cover for him/her. 1 2 3 4

Source: Based on a version of the PLIS that appeared in Leadership Quarterly, 9 (2), S.B.Craig and S.B.Gustafson, "Perchieved Leader Integrity Scale: An Instrument for Assessing Employee Perceptions of Leader Integrity, "Used with permission of the authors.

Case Study A Struggling Company with Not Enough Cash

Joe Woodman bought a small struggling computer company. After several difficult years, revenues started to grow and it seemed, according to the financial statements, that profits were growing as well. But in reality, the business did not have enough cash.

The company's key stakeholders, such as the bank, vendors and investors, were applying pressure on Joe to improve earnings and cash flow. They threatened to take over the business if major changes were not made. About the same time and making matters worse, Joe was notified that several contracts, constituting about 25% of his top-line revenues would be lost to the competition.

Joe responded by laying off employees, freezing wages, and closing several marginal operations, but these efforts were not enough. Joe was still badly in need of more cash and professional management. To remain viable, he had three options.

1. He could negotiate a "capital for control" type exchange with the investor and the banks. If he did this, the banks could help recruit new talent and also offer interim financing to support the company while restructuring occurred. On the downside, with this option his status within the organization would significantly change; instead of being the owner, Joe would become more of a senior manager.
2. Joe could maintain control and pursue hiring turn-around management, explaining to them that the company was in a critical turn-around phase and that the organization's future depended on the new manager's ability to generate credibility and positive performance in 1 year's time. He would have to disclose the wage freezes of the past 2 years and explain that he could not initially offer competitive salaries or certain traditional benefits. If he took this option, Joe would have difficulty recruiting skilled managers because they would not want to come into a situation with failing operations, no operating cash, and the prospects of a dramatically dwindling revenue base. If it succeeds, this option would allow Joe to keep control and save his reputation.
3. Joe could remain in control and pursue hiring turn-around management but he would not fully explain the serious situation. He might say that the company is one of the fastest-growing companies in the industry, that it just completed an operational turn-around, had regained profitability, and was now upgrading staff to take the company to the next level. He could support this positive picture by representing proforma financial information as though it were actual. This approach would probably be successful initially in gaining new qualified staff, but the new managers might join only to leave soon afterward. They would probably not develop into loyal, long-term employees because of Joe's breach of trust. This option would give Joe the opportunity to maintain control and keep all his workers employed.

Questions

1. Of the three options available to Joe, which is the most ethical?
2. How does egoism come into play in this case? In which of the three options is altruism most apparent?
3. Which option would provide the greatest good for the greatest number? From an ethical perspective, what is Joe's duty in this situation?
4. What pressures does Joe face regarding honesty and telling the truth about his situation?

REFERENCES

1. Avolio, B.J., & Locke, E.E., (2002), Contrasting Different Philosophies of Leader Motivation: Altruism Versus Egoism. *Leadership Quarterly*, 13, pp.169–191.
2. Beauchamp, T.L., & Bowie, N.E., (1988), Ethical Theory and Business (3rd ed.) Englewood Cliffs, NJ: Prentice Hall.
3. Brady, F.N., (1999), A Systematic Approach to Teaching Ethics in Business. *Journal of Business Ethics,*
4. Convey, S.R., (1990), Principle – Centered Leadership. New York:
5. Fr Pree, M.(1992), Leadership Jazz. New York: Dell.
6. Greenleaf, R.K., (1970), The servant as leader. Newton Centre, MA: Robert K. Greenleaf Centre.
7. Greenleaf R.K., (1977), Servant Leadership: A Journey into the Nature of Legitimate Power and Greatness. New York:
8. Johnson, C.R., (2001), Meeting the Ethical Challenges of Leadership. Thousand Oaks, CA:Sage.
9. Kanungo, R.N., &Mendonca, M., (1996), Ethical Dimensions of Leadership Thousand Oaks, CA: Sage.
10. Pojman, L.P., (1995), Ethical Theory: Classical and Contemporary Readings (2nd ed.). Belmont, CA:Wadsworth.
11. Schumann, P.L., (2001), A Moral Principles Framework for Human Resource Management Ethics. *Human Resource Management Reveiew*, 11.
12. Trevino, L.K., (1986), Ethical Decision Making in Organizations: A Person–Situation Interactionist Model. *Academy of Management Review*,
13. Velasquez, M.G., (1992), Business Ethics: Concepts and Cases (3rd ed.). Englewood Cliffs, NJ: Prentice Hall.

CHAPTER 6

Nature and Significance of Management

Meaning of Management - Definition of Management – Nature of Management – Concept of Management – Roles of a Manager – Management Skills – Effective vs. Successful Managerial Activities – Management is a Science or Art – Management is a Profession – Professional Management vs. Family Management – Functions of Management – Evolution of Management Thought – Case Study

Learning Objectives of this Chapter are:

- To know the meaning of management.
- To understand the definition of management.
- To study the nature of management.
- To analyze the concept and significance of management.
- To examine the roles of managers.
- To understand the skills of the managers.
- To identify the levels of management.
- To clarify the qualities of effective manager and successful managers.
- To study the management as science or art.
- To understand management as a profession.
- To know the difference between professional management and family management.
- To study the functions of management.
- To examine the management thoughts.

MEANING OF MANAGEMENT

Management is a wider term. It carries different meanings depending on the context it is used. It is variously described as a "discipline", a "process" and a "group of people" vested with the authority to make decisions. Thus, the term management is used in three alternative ways: Management is the process which consist various activities. It is an organized activity to assign the duties to different people working in various departments and divisions. Thus, management means managing the things and managing the people.

Management is the art of getting things done through other people. Management is the process of doing various activities in order to achieve individual as well as organizational goals or objectives. It is a process which includes planning, organizing, directing and controlling of various activities in an effective manner to achieve desired goals. Management is a discipline, it is a dynamic life giving a limit. It is a science. It is an art. It is a profession. It is a multi-dimensional activity.

DEFINITION OF MANAGEMENT

It is difficult to define the management, in fact no clear cut definitions has been accepted universally. One of the popular definition is given by Mary Farker Follett, she defines thus, **"it is the art of getting things done through people."** Management has been defined by different authors in different aspects. Some of the important definitions of management are as follows:

> *Management can be defined according to Koontz "Management is the art of getting things done through and with the people in formally organized groups."*
>
> *It can be defined by George R. Terry "Consisting of planning, organizing, actuating and controlling, performed to determining and accomplish the objectives by the use of people and resources."*
>
> *According to Peter Drucker "Management is a multi purpose organ which manages the business, which manages managers, which manages worker and the work."*

NATURE OF MANAGEMENT

Management is a group of activity. No individual can satisfy all his desires by himself. Hence, he unites with his fellow-beings and works in an organized group to achieve what he cannot achieve individually. Wherever there is an organized group of people working towards a common goal or objective, some type of management becomes essential. Management makes the people to realize the objectives of the group. It directs their efforts towards the achievement of these objectives. Management aims at achieving economic and social objectives. It exists to achieve some definite goals or objectives. It is a means towards the accomplishment of pre-determined goals. All activities of management are goal-oriented. Effective management is always management by objectives. Management is not an end itself. It is a means to achieve the group objectives. Land, labour and capital are the important factors of production. They are essential for the production of goods and services. Management is also a factor of production. It is required to co-ordinate the other factors of production for the accomplishment of pre-determined goals. The four other factors may prove ineffective in the absence of management. Management occupies a central place among productive factors.

Management is a distinct process performed. It is different from the activities, techniques and procedures. The process of management consists of such functions as planning, organizing, staffing, directing, co-ordinating, motivating and controlling. Management is done by people, through people and for people. It is a social process because it is concerned with inter-personal relations. Human factor is the important element in management. Management is concerned with performance in pursuit of organizational objectives. The performance of the organization as a whole will determine its survival in society. Management is a dynamic function. It has to be performed continuously.

Management is intangible activity. It is an unseen or invisible force. It cannot be seen or touched but its presence can be felt everywhere in the form of results. Management is a science because it has developed certain principles which are of universal application. But the results of management depend upon the personal skill of managers. Management is required in all types of organizations. Wherever there is some human activity, there is management. In the present days, management is recognized as a profession. It has a systematic and specialized body of knowledge consisting of principles, techniques and laws. According to the nature of work and the scope of authority, management is needed at all levels of the organization. It is needed at the top level, middle level and supervisory level of the organization. Management has to deal with human behaviour under dynamic conditions. Therefore, it depends upon wide knowledge derived from several disciplines like engineering, sociology, psychology, economics, mathematics and anthropology.

CONCEPT OF MANAGEMENT

The concept of management is used in four alternative ways, they are:

1. *Management as a discipline.*
2. *Management as a process.*
3. *Management as a group of people.*
4. *Management as a multi purpose organ.*

1. Management as a discipline: Management is a separate discipline. It is a separate branch of knowledge or subject just like engineering, law, physics, chemistry, economics and so on. It has well- defined concepts and principles. Management is now recognized as a distinct discipline or body of knowledge. It is being regarded as one of the important branches of social sciences. As a body of knowledge or science, management deals with the techniques, principles and skills required to manage business enterprise. These principles deal with human behaviour. They have been formulated on the basis of observation, research and analysis and experience of management executives.

2. Management as a process: A process of systematic organized activities. Management is described as a process. Used as a process, management refers to all that a manager does. It includes various functions which are performed by managers to make the efficient use of the available material and human resources to achieve the desired objectives. Thus, management is a distinct process consisting of planning, organizing, staffing, directing, co-ordinating and controlling. It is a never-ending and dynamic process. It is a result-oriented process. A majority of authors believe that it is a process of getting things done by others.

3. Management as a group of people: Management refers a group of people working together to achieve common goals. People are placed from top level to bottom level in various departments and sections of the organization. It includes the chief executive and all those persons in the organization who have supervisory responsibility over others. Managers occupy positions at different levels of authority but perform the same basic functions.

4. Management as a multi-purpose organ: It is a process of organizing various activities and people of various departments. It refers to the process of organizing business, process of organizing managers and process of organizing worker and work. Thus, it means management of business, management of managers, management of workers and work.

ROLES OF A MANAGER

Manager has to play an important role in any organization in introducing the new techniques and ideas to achieve the individual as well as organizational goals. Thus, the manager occupies different positions in different situations and plays different roles because people in each situation have different expectations of him concerning his functions. In the late 1960s, a graduate student at MIT, Henry Mintzberg, undertook a careful study of five executives to determine what these managers did on their jobs. On the basis of his observations of these managers, Mintzberg concluded that managers perform 10 different, highly interrelated roles, or sets of behaviours attributable to their jobs. It can be shown in Exhibit 6.1. According, to Mintzberg, a manager should be regarded as playing the following three major roles which can be sub-divided into ten different roles. They are as follows:

1. Interpersonal Roles
2. Informational Roles
3. Decisional Roles

1. Interpersonal Roles

In this role, every manager has to perform some duties of a ceremonial nature, such as greeting the touring dignitaries, attending the wedding of an employee, taking an important customer to lunch and so on. As a leader every manager must motivate and encourage his employees. He must also try to reconcile their individual needs with the goals of the organization. In his role of liaison, every manager must cultivate contacts outside his vertical chain of command to collect information useful for his organization.

2. Information Roles

All managers, to some degree, collect information from organizations and institutions outside their own. Typically, they get information by reading magazines and talking with other people to learn of changes in the public's tastes, what competitors may be planning, and the like. Mintzberg called this the monitor role. Managers also act as a conduit to transmit information to organizational members.

This is the disseminator role. Managers additionally perform a spokesperson role when they represent the organization to outsiders.

3. Decisional Roles

Finally, Mintzberg identified four roles that revolve around the making of choices. In the entrepreneur role, managers initiate and oversee new projects that will improve their organisation's performance. As disturbance handlers, managers take corrective action in response to unforeseen problems. As resource allocators, managers are responsible for allocating human, physical and monetary resources. Last, managers perform a negotiator role, in which they discuss issues and bargain with other units to gain advantages for their own unit.

MANAGEMENT SKILLS

Robert Katz has identified three essential management skills; Technical Skills, Human Skills, and Conceptual Skills. These three important management skills possessed by the managers help to understand various problems and analyse difference complex situations. They are as follows:

Technical Skills: The ability to apply specialized knowledge or expertise.

Human Skills: The ability to work with, understand, and motivate other people, both individually and in groups.

Conceptual Skills: The mental ability to analyze and diagnose complex situations.

EFFECTIVE vs. SUCCESSFUL MANAGERIAL ACTIVITIES

Fred Luthans and his associates looked at the issue of what managers do from a somewhat different perspective. They asked the question: Do managers who move up most quickly in an organization do the same activities and with the same emphasis as managers who do the best job? You would tend to think that the managers who were the most effective in their jobs would also be the ones who were promoted fastest. But that's not what appears to happen. Luthans and his associates studied more than 450 managers. What they found was that these managers all engaged in four managerial activities:

1. *Traditional Management.* Decision making, planning, and controlling.
2. *Communication.* Exchanging routine information and processing paperwork.
3. *Human Resource Management.* Motivating, disciplining, managing conflict, staffing and training.
4. *Networking.* Socializing, politicking, and interacting with outsiders.

Exhibit 6.1: Managerial Roles

Mintzberg's Managerial Roles

Role	*Description*	*Example*
Interpersonal		
Figurehead	Is symbolic head; required to perform a number of routine duties of a legal or social nature	Handles ceremonies, status request, solicitations.
Leader	Is responsible for the motivation and directive of subordinates	Performs virtually all managerial activities involving subordinates
Liaison	Maintain a network of outside contacts who provide favours and information	Acknowledges mail, external board work.
Informational		
Monitor	Receives wide variety of information, serves as nerve centre of internal and external information of the organization	Handles all mail and contacts categorised as concerned primarily with receiving information.
Disseminator	Transmits information received from outsiders or from other subordinates to members of the organization	Forwards mail into organization for information purposes; makes verbal contacts involving information flow to subordinates such as review sessions.
Spokesperson	Transmits information to outsiders on organisation's plans, policies, actions, and serves as expert on organization's industry	Attends board meetings; handles contacts involving transmission of information to outsiders.
Decisional		
Entrepreneur	Searches organization and its environment for opportunities and initiates projects to bring about change	Holds strategy and review sessions involving initiation or design of improvement projects.
Disturbance Handler	Is responsible for corrective action when organization faces important, unexpected disturbances	Holds strategy and review sessions involving disturbances and crises.
Resource Allocator	Makes or approves significant	Handles scheduling requests for authorization; budgeting; the programming of subordinate's work.
Negotiator	Is responsible for representing the organization at major negotiations	Handles contract negotiation.

(***Source:*** Adapted from *The Nature of Management Work,* by M.Mintzberg).

The "average" manager in the study spend 32 percent of his or her time in traditional management activities, 29 percent communicating, 20 percent in human resource management activities, and 19 percent networking. However, the amount of time and effort that different managers spent on those four activities varied a great deal. Specifically, as shown in the Exhibit, managers who were successful (defined in terms of the speed of promotion within their organization) had a very different emphasis than managers who were effective (Defined in terms of the quantity and quality of their performance and the satisfaction and commitment of their employees). Among successful managers, networking made the largest relative contribution to success, and human resource management activities made the least relative contribution. Among effective managers, communication made the largest relative contribution and networking the least.

This study adds important insights to our knowledge of what managers do. On average, managers spend approximately 20 to 30 percent of their time on each of the four activities: traditional management, communication, human resource management, and networking. However, successful managers don't give the same emphasis to each of those activities as do effective managers. In fact, their emphases are almost the opposite. This finding challenges the historical assumption that promotions are based on performance, vividly illustrating the importance that social and political skills play in getting ahead in organizations.

MANAGEMENT IS A SCIENCE OR ART

Management is both science and art. Science refers practical application of knowledge, on the other hand art refers the understanding of how a particular work can be accomplished. Thus, management is also called as psydeo science which means partly an art and partly a science. The concept of management is universal and very old. Different views have been expressed about its nature by different authorities. Some call it an "art", and some others call it as a "science", this controversy has created a great deal of confusion. Following discussion will make it clear.

Management as an Art : Art involves the practical application of skills and knowledge to achieve concrete results. It is the practical way of doing specific things. The function of the art is to effect change and to achieve desired results. In the words of Terry "Art is bringing about of a desired result through application of skill". Art is essentially creative and the success of an artist is measured by the results he achieves. Art is a personalized process and every artist has his own style. Art is practice-based and perfection in it requires continuous practice over a long period of time. The following are thus the essential features of art.

1. Personal Skill & Experience
2. Practical Knowledge
3. Result-Orientation
4. Regular practice aimed at perfection
5. Creativity and Innovation

Management as a Science: The word "Science" literally means "knowledge". It is a systematized body of knowledge acquired by mankind through observation and experimentation. In the words of Keynes "Science is a systematized body of knowledge which establishes relationship between cause and effect". The essential features of science are as follows:

1. Science is a systematized body of knowledge that uses scientific methods for observation.
2. The principles are evolved on the basis of continued observation.
3. The principles are exact and have universal applicability without any limitation.
4. The principles establish a cause and effect relationship between various factors.
5. The validity of scientific principles can be verified, and they provide a reliable basis for predicting future events, and
6. The organized body of knowledge can be taught and learnt in the classroom and outside.

MANAGEMENT IS A PROFESSION

When we have concluded that management is partly an art and partly a science. It has been proved that it is a profession particularly in practicing various principles and theories. Professional managers are working in both government and non-government organization. The following features are essential for the professional managers:

Essential Features of Professional Managers

1. Existence of an organized and systematic knowledge.
2. Formalized methods of acquiring training and experience.
3. Existence of an association with professionalisation as its goal.
4. Existence of an ethical code to regulate the behaviour of the members of the profession.
5. Changing of fees based on service, but with due regard for the priority of service over the desire for monetary reward.

Management, as we all know, does not possess all the above characteristics of a profession. Unlike medicine or law, management does not have any fixed norms of managerial behaviour. There is no uniform code of conduct or licensing of managers. Further, the entry to managerial jobs is not restricted to individuals with a special academic degree only. Managing a business is no longer just a matter or intuition or a family ability. It has now come to be studied and taught as a subject by itself. In India, we have at present six national institutes of management at Ahmedabad, Bangalore, Kolkata, Lucknow, Indore and Kozhikode; besides there are a number of university departments which offer M.B.A. programmes to young graduates to enable them to take up the profession of management. Peter F. Drucker is, however, of the view that holding of an academic degree should not be a condition to get an entry into the management profession. He says that " no greater damage could be done to our economy or to our society than to attempt to professionalise management by licensing managers, for instance, or by limiting access to management to people with a special academic degree."

PROFESSIONAL MANAGEMENT vs. FAMILY MANAGEMENT

The phrase "professional management" is also sometimes used as an antithesis to "family management". It is said that all family managements must be replaced by professional management – managers by birth should yield place to managers by profession. This view is not totally correct because there is nothing basically wrong in perpetuating a family dynasty so long it also continues to be dynamic. A study covering 30 nations around the world points out that 75% of all firms in the world are family firms. In some of these firms family inheritance has been continuing for centuries. For instance, in Kikkoman Corporation of Japan – the world's leading supplier of soya sauce, descendants of the founders still control and run the firm after 17 generations since its birth more than 300 years ago. The phenomenal progress of Ford Motors, Exxon, IBM, Du Pont, etc. bears testimony to the quality of leadership, dynamism, versatility and vision of the respective families of Ford, Rockefeller, Watson and Du Pont. The growth of the corporate sector in India is our inspiring saga of dynamism and toil of some business families, at a time when professionalism was quite unknown. In the words of K.K.Birla, "If people like Sir Jamshetji Tata or Rai Bahadur Gujarmal Modi were to start their business career again, I would any day put my rupee on them than on the best of the professionals.

Levels of Management

Every business organization, irrespective of its size, has many managerial positions in its structure. These positions are created through the process of delegation of authority from top to lower levels. Each position is marked by authority, responsibility function, roles and relationships. The contents and nature vary depending on the level at which the position lies. These managerial position lying in the chain of command may be classified into various groups or levels of management. Levels of management refers to a line of separation between different positions held by different persons in an organization. The number of levels of management in an organization depends upon its size, technology and the range of production. Broadly speaking, there are two levels of management, namely, administrative management is concerned with "thinking function" such as policy determination, planning and fixation of standards. Operative management, on the other hand, is concerned with the "doing function" which include use of money, materials, machinery and men, implementation of policies laid down by administrative management and directing operations to achieve the objectives of the organization. Although all managers perform the same function of planning, organizing, directly and controlling, there are levels among them. The number of management levels may differ from a company to company. On the basis of authority and responsibility, in a Joint-stock company, the management levels may be classified as follows:

I. Top level management

II. Middle level management, and

III. Lower level or supervisory level management.

In a very large enterprise, the middle management may be sub-divided into upper middle management and lower middle management.

I. Top level management: In a Joint-stock company, equity shareholders are the real owners of the company. They are in a large number, widely scattered and not interested in the management. So, they select their representatives as directors. Top level management consists of owners, Board of Directors and the chief executives, like the managing director, general manager and the secretary. Board of Directors is accountable to the shareholders in the annual general meeting of the company. It is basically an organ of overall review and control. Chief executive may be an individual or a group consisting of chairman and functional directors. Chief executive is concerned with the overall management of the company's operations. He maintains co-ordination among different departments of the company. He also keeps the organization in harmony with its external environment. Louis Allen states that " the top management is the policy making group responsible for the overall direction and success of all activities of the company". The major function of the top level management are as under:

1. To analyze and interpret changes in the external environment of the company.
2. To establish long-term corporate plans for the entire organization covering all areas of operations.
3. To formulate and approve the master budgets and department's budgets.
4. To design broad organization structure.
5. To select key officials and executives for the company.
6. To co-ordinate and integrate the activities of different departments and divisions of the company.
7. To provide overall direction and leadership to the company.
8. To exercise overall review and control of the financial and operating results of the company.
9. To maintain liaison with outside parties having a stake in business such as government, trade unions and trade associations.

II. Middle level management: Middle level management is the second level of managerial hierarcy. It consists of departmental managers, deputy managers, foreman and administrative officers etc. These executives are mainly concerned with the overall functioning of their respective departments. They act as a link between top and lower level management. Middle level management is also known as "departmental management" or "functional management". The main functions of middle level managers are as under:

1. To interpret and explain the plans and policies formulated by top level management to lower level managers.
2. To prepare departmental plan covering all the activities of the department within the basic framework of the corporate plan.
3. To establish departmental goals and decide upon various ways and means for achieving these goals.

4. To perform all other managerial functions with regard to departmental activities for securing smooth running of the entire department.
5. To issue detailed order and instruction to lower level managers and co-ordinate the activities of various work units at lower level.
6. To train, motivate and develop supervisory personnel.
7. To make recommendations to top management for the better implementation of plans and policies.

III. Lower level of supervisory level management: This is the lower or first level of management in an organization. This level consists of first line supervisors, inspectors, section officers etc., they are in direct touch with "core group" of workers, such as operators, assemblers, mechanics, salesmen and clerks, etc. They directly supervise the work performed by core group workers. They issue orders and instruction to them, educate them about the method of doing the work and regularly supervise their activities. They serve as a channel of communication between management and workforce.

The lower level managers generally have to perform the following functions:

1. To get the things done by "core group" workers.
2. To prepare plan for their activities, known as "scheduling". Scheduling lays down what is to be done, by whom it will be done, and, how and when it will be done.
3. To issue necessary orders and instructions to the workers regarding the work being performed by them.
4. To assign the work to the workers and seek its completion within the given period of time and quality specifications.
5. To guide, assist and help the workers by explaining work procedures to them and solving their problems.
6. To motivate the workers and to maintain a team spirit among them.
7. To put up the case of workers to higher level managers for various welfare schemes, incentives and for improving physical working conditions.
8. To arrange materials, machines and tools for the workers and provide training to them.

Thus, management at all levels perform the same function of management i.e., planning, organizing, co-ordinating, staffing and controlling, but in a varied degree. The relative importance of these functions varies at different levels.

FUNCTIONS OF MANAGEMENT

There is enough disagreement among management writers on the classification of managerial functions. Some classify these functions into four types, some into five and some into six or seven. The terminology is also not always alike, different authors offering different names for the same functions of management. Newman and Summer recognise only four functions, namely, organising, planning, leading and controlling. Henri Fayol identifies five functions of management, *viz*., planning, organising, commanding, co-ordinating and controlling. Luther Gulick states seven such functions under the catch word "POSDCORB" which stands for planning, organising, staffing, directing, co-ordinating, reporting and budgeting.

Warren Haynes and Joseph Massie classify management functions into decision-making, organising, staffing, planning, controlling, communicating and directing. Koontz and O'Donnell divide these functions into planning organising, staffing, directing and controlling.

For our purpose, we shall designate the following four as the functions of a manager: planning, organising, directing, and controlling. We will examine these functions in greater detail in the following chapters. We will also briefly refer to "innovation" and "representation" as two additional managerial functions considered important by Ernest Dale.

Planning

Planning is the function that determines in advance *what* should be done. It is looking ahead and preparing for the future. It is a process of deciding the business objectives and charting out the methods of attaining those objectives. In other words, it is the determination of what is to be done, how and where it is to be done, who is to do it and how results are to be evaluated. This is done not only for the organisation as a whole but for every division, department or sub-unit of the organisation. Thus, planning is a function which is performed by managers at all levels—top, middle and supervisory. Plans made by top management for the organisation as a whole may cover periods as long as five or ten years. Plans made by middle or first line managers, cover much shorter periods. Such plans may be for the next day work, for example, or for a two-hour meeting to take place in a week.

Organising

To organise a business is to provide it with everything useful to its functioning: personnel, raw materials tools, capital. All this may be divided into two main sections, the human organisation and the material organisation. Once managers have established objectives and developed plans to achieve them, they must design and develop a human organisation that will be able to carry out those plans successfully According to Allen, this organisation refers to "the structure which results from identifying and grouping work, defining and delegating responsibility and authority, and establishing relationships."

Staffing may also be considered an important function involved in building the human resources.

In staffing, the manager attempts to find the right person for each job. Staffing fixes a manager's responsibility to recruit and to make certain that there is enough manpower available to fill the various positions needed in the organisation. Staffing involves the selection and training of future managers and suitable system of compensation. Staffing obviously cannot be done once and for all, since people are continually leaving, getting fired, retiring and dying. Often too, the changes in the organisation create new positions, and these must be filled.

It should be noted that different objectives require different kinds of organisation to achieve them. For example, an organisation for scientific research will have to be very different from one for manufacturing bicycles. Producing bicycles requires assembly-line techniques, whereas scientific research requires teams of scientists and experts in various disciplines. Such people cannot be organised on an assembly-line basis.

Directing

After plans have been made and the organisation has been established and staffed, the next step is to move towards its defined objectives. This function can be called by various names: "leading", "directing", "motivating", "actuating", and so on. But whatever the name used to identify it, in carrying out this function the manager explains to his people what they have to do and helps them do it to the best of their ability. Directing, thus involves three sub-functions—communication, leadership and motivation. Communication is the process of passing information and understanding from one person to another Leadership is the process by which a manager guides and influences the work of his subordinates. Motivation means arousing desire in the minds of workers to give their best to the enterprise. It is the act of stimulating or inspiring workers. If the workers of an enterprise are properly motivated they will pull their weight effectively, give their loyalty to the enterprise, and carry out their task effectively. The broad categories of motivation are: financial and non-financial. Financial motivation takes the form of salary, bonus, profit-sharing, etc., while non-financial motivation takes the form of job security, opportunity of advancement, recognition, praise, etc.

Controlling

The manager must ensure that everything occurs in conformity with the plans adopted, the instructions issued and the principles established. This is the controlling function of management, and involves three elements.

1. Establishing standards of performance.
2. Measuring current performance and comparing it against the established standards.
3. Taking action to correct any performance that does not meet those standards.

In the absence of sound control, there is no guarantee that the objectives which have been set will be realised. The management may go on committing mistakes without knowing them. Control compels events to conform to plans.

Innovation

These days, it is not necessary for an organisation to grow bigger. But it is necessary that it constantly grows better. This makes innovation an important function of a manager. Innovation means creating new ideas which may either result in the development of new products or finding new uses for the old ones. Thus, a salesman who can persuade Eskimos to purchase refrigerators to prevent food from freezing is as much an innovator as the one who invents a new product. One may, however, consider innovation not a separate function but only a part of planning.

Representation

A manager is also required now-a-days to spend a part of his time in representing his organisation before various outside groups which have some stake in the organisation. These stake-holders can be government officials, labour unions, financial institutions, suppliers, customers, etc. They wield influence over theorganisation. A manager must win their support by effectively managing the social impact of his organisation.

Management Process

What we have presented here is a model of the *management process.* A model is a simplification of the real world, used to convey complex relationships in more understandable terms. The relationships described above are by no means as straightforward as our model implies. For example, the four functions do not necessarily occur in the sequence presented in our model (except, perhaps when a new organisation is being formed). In fact, various combinations of these activities usually go on simultaneously in an organisation. Thus, for example, when a manager controls employees' actions, he establishes standards of performance which is also a part of the planning function.

Professor Haimann has rightly observed that it is helpful to **think of these** managerial functions as a circular, continuous movement. They blend into each other like **the flowing** water of a river and at times there is no clear line of demarcation when one **ends** and the other **begins (Fig. 1.1).** In fact, they have no separate entities.

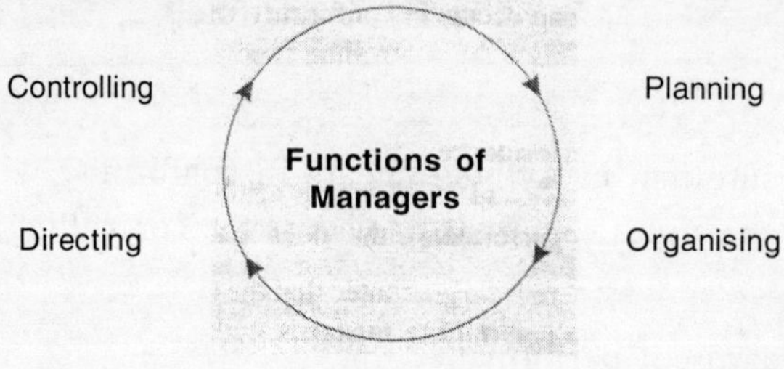

EVOLUTION OF MANAGEMENT THOUGHT

During the past five decades, management has become a more scientific discipline with certain standardized principles and practices. Many researchers have conducted studies to identify the various principles on scientific management as well as administrative management. Upon the studies conducted by eminent scholars, the evolution of management thought has been divided into three parts. They are as follows:

1. **Early classical approaches:** These are broadly divided into two types such as, scientific management and administrative management.

2. **Neo-classical approaches:** These are also broadly divided into two types such as human relations' movements and behavioural approaches.

3. **Modern approaches:** Modern approaches are divided into three approaches. They are, Quantitative approach, System approach & Contingency approach.

EARLY CLASSICAL APPROACHES

Scientific Management

Frederick Winslow Taylor (1856-1915) has been recognized as the Father of Scientific Management. He exerted a great influence on the development of management thought through his experiments and writings. During his career spanning a period of 26 years, he conducted a series of experiments in three companies: Midvale Steel, Simonds Rolling Machine and Bethlehem Steel.

While serving as the Chief Engineer of Midvale Steel Company, Taylor made several important contributions which are classified under scientific management.

1. Time and Motion Study: F.W. Taylor had been considered a machinist himself; he knew how piece-work employees used to hold back production to its one-third level because they feared that their employers would cut their piece rate as soon as there was a rise in production. The real trouble, Taylor thought was that no one knew how much work was reasonable to expect a man to do. He, therefore, started time and motion study, under which each motion of a job was to be timed with the help of a stop watch and shorter and fewer motions were to be developed.

2. Differential Payment: Taylor has introduced differential piece work. It is also called as new payment plan and incentives which is linked with production. Under this plan a worker received low piece rate if he produced the standard number of pieces and high rate if he surpassed the standard.

3. Drastic Reorganization: Taylor suggested two new concepts such as separation of planning and doing and functional foremanship. In those days, it used to be customary for each worker to plan his own work. The worker himself used to select his tools and decide the order in which the operations were to be performed. The foreman simply told the worker what jobs to perform, not how to do them.

4. Scientific Recruitment and Training: Taylor also suggested that there should be scientific selection and development of the worker. He said that the management should develop and train every worker to bring out his best faculties and to enable him to do a higher and more interesting work.

5. Intimate Friendly Co-operation between the Management and Workers: Taylor said that for the above suggestions to succeed, 'a complete mental revolution' on the part of management and labour was required. Rather than quarrel over whatever profits there were, they should both try to increase production. By doing so, profits would be increased to such an extent that labour and management would no longer have to compete for them.

Administrative Management

While Taylor is considered the Father of Scientific Management, Henri Fayol (1841-1925) is considered the Father of Administrative Management theory with focus on the development of broad administrative principles applicable to general and higher managerial levels. He was a French mining engineer turned a leading industrialist and successful manager. He wrote a monograph in

French in 1916, entitled 'General and Industrial Administration'. Until this book was translated into English in 1929, little was known about him by the western world. Fayol provided a broad analytical framework of the process of administration.

Fayol wrote that all activities of business enterprises could be divided into six groups: technical, commercial, financial, accounting, security and administrative or managerial. Fayol's primary focus, of course, was on this last managerial activity because he felt managerial skills had been the most neglected aspect of business operations. He defined management in terms of five functions: planning, organizing commanding, co-ordinating and controlling. Fayol's five management functions are similar to the functions of planning, organizing, directing and controlling that we have described in an earlier chapter. Many management theorists and even practitioners have found this classification very useful and realistic.

FAYOL'S 14 PRINCIPLES OF MANAGEMENT

Fayol also presented 14 principles of management as general guidelines to the management process and management practice. These are as follows:

1. Division of Work: Division of work in the management process produces more and better work with the same effort. They must be entrusted to specialists in related fields.

2. Authority and Responsibility: A manager may exercise formal authority and also personal power. Formal authority is derived from his official position, while personal power is the result of intelligence, experience, moral worth, ability to lead, past service, etc. Responsibility is closely related to authority and it arises wherever authority is exercised.

3. Discipline: Discipline is more important and it is essential for smooth running of business. Discipline refers to obedience to the authority and observation of rules and regulations in an effective manner. Thus, discipline provides better results.

4. Unity of Command: This principle refers each employee should receive instructions about a particular work from one superior only.

5. Unity of Direction: It refers people should follow the direction of one's superior or managers.

6. Subordination of Individual Interest to General Interest: In a business concern, an individual is always interested in maximizing his own satisfaction through more money, recognition, status, etc. This is very often against the general interest which lies in maximizing production. Hence, the need to subordinate the individual interest to general interest.

7. Remuneration: The remuneration paid to the personnel of the firm should be fair. It should be based on general business conditions, cost of living, and productivity of the concerned employees and the capacity of the firm to pay. Fair remuneration increases workers' efficiency and morale and fosters good relations between them and the management.

8. Centralization: The management must decide the degree of centralisation or decentralisation of authority on the basis of the nature of the circumstances, size of the undertaking, the type of activities and the nature of organizational structure. Thus, centralization plays an important role to achieve the organizational goals.

9. Scalar Chain: Scalar chain means the hierarchy of authority from the highest executive to the lowest one for the purpose of communication. It states superior-subordinate relationship and the authority of superiors in relation to subordinates at various levels. It is also called as Gang Plank.

In the following figure, we find two ladders of authority—one from *E* to *A* and the other from *P* to *A*. In a strict observance of the scalar chain, any communication from *D* to *O* would go all the way up to *A* and down the other side of the triangle to *O*. This is a time consuming procedure. Fayol suggested that if there is need for swift action *D* and *O* may be authorised by their respective superiors (C and N) to have direct contact with each other. A gang plank can be thrown across between *D* and *O*. By this method, the scalar principle is safeguarded and at the same time the subordinate officers are enabled to take swift action.

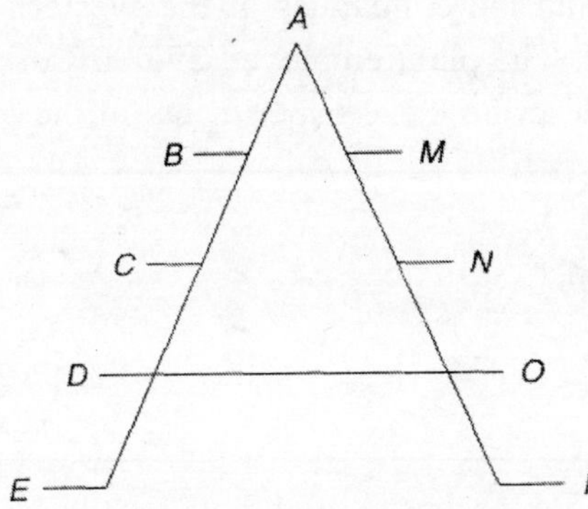

Fig. 6.1: Gang Plank

10. Order: This principles explains right man for the right job, right time and right place. This principles provides efficiency and effectiveness in doing the employees jobs.

11. Equity: This principles refers equal and fair treatment of employees. Thus, employees expect the management to be equally just to everybody. Thus, this principle ensures healthy human relations and industrial relations between management and employees.

12. Stability of Tenure of Personnel: It is essential for every employees in order to motivate the employees to do the work effectively and with efficiency. Thus, they can develop morale and job satisfaction for better work.

13. Initiative: Initiative refers freedom to think out and execute a plan. According to Fayol, initiative is one of the keenest satisfactions for an intelligent man to experience, and hence, he advises managers to give their employees sufficient scope to show their initiative. Employees should be encouraged to make all kinds of suggestions to conceive and carry out their plans, even when some mistakes result.

14. Esprit de Corps: This principle says that union is strength. The management should create team spirit among the employees. Only when all the personnel pull together as a team, there is scope for realizing the objectives of the concern. Harmony and unity among the staff are a great source of strength to the undertaking. Thus, this principle provides better results.

NEO-CLASSICAL APPROACHES

The Human Relations Movement

The human relations movement emerged in part because managers found that Taylor's scientific management and Fayol's administrative management did not quite achieve complete production efficiency and work place harmony. Managers still faced difficulties because employees did not always follow predicted or rational patterns of behaviour. Thus, there was an increased interest in helping managers deal more effectively with the "people side" of their organizations. The real inspiration for the movement, however, came from the Hawthorne experiments which were done by Prof. Elton Mayo and his colleagues at the Western Electric Company's plant in Cicero, Illinois from 1927 to 1932. The plant employed 29,000 workers to manufacture telephone parts and equipment. We briefly describe these experiments in the following four parts:

1. Illumination Experiments.
2. Relay Assembly Test Room.
3. Interviewing Programme.
4. Bank Wiring Test Room.

We will briefly examine these experiments and their results.

Illumination Experiments: This was the first phase of this study. In this phase, the popular belief that productivity is positively correlated with illumination was tested. Experiments were done on a group of workers. Their productivity was measured at various levels of illumination. But the results were erratic. Puzzled with this phenomenon, researchers, improved their methodology.

Relay Assembly Test Room: In this phase, the object of the study was broadened. It now aimed at knowing not only the impact of illumination on production but also of such other factors as length of the working day, rest pauses, their frequency and duration and other physical conditions. A group of six women workers, who were friendly to each other, were selected for this experiment. These women workers were told about the experiment and were made to work in a very informal atmosphere with a supervisor-researcher in a separate room. The supervisor-researcher acted as their friend, philosopher and guide. During the study, several variations were made in the working conditions to find which combination of conditions was most ideal for production. Surprisingly, the researchers found that the production of the group had no relation with working conditions. It went on increasing and stabilized at a high level even when all the improvements were taken away and the poor pre-test conditions were reintroduced. How this phenomenon came about, nobody knew.

Interviewing Programme: In this phase, they wanted to know as to what were the basic factors responsible for human behaviour at work. For this purpose they interviewed more than 20,000 workers. At first, direct questions were asked relating to the type of supervision, working conditions, living conditions and so on. But since the replies were guarded, the technique was changed to non-directive type of interviewing, in which workers were free to talk about their favourite topics related to their work environment. This study revealed that the workers' social relations inside the organization had an unmistakable influence on their attitudes and behaviours.

Bank Wiring Observation Room: This phase involved an in-depth observation of 14 men making terminal banks of telephone wiring assemblies, to determine the effect of informal group norms and formal economic incentives on productivity. It was found that the group evolved its own production norms for each individual worker, which was much lower than those set by the management. Workers would produce that much and no more, thereby defeating the incentive system. This artificial restriction of production saved workers from a possible cut in their piece rates or an upward revision of their standards by the management and protected weaker and slower workers from being reprimanded or thrown out of the job—these being the days of the Great Depression.

Behavioural Approach

This approach is an improved and a more mature version of the human relations approach to management. Douglas McGregor, Abraham Maslow, Kurt Lewin, Chester Barnard, Mary Parker Follett, George Homans, Rensis Likert, Chris Argyris, and Warren Bennis are some of the foremost behavioural scientists who made signal contributions to the development of the behavioural approach to management. These scientists were more rigorously trained in various social sciences (such as psychology, sociology, and anthropology) and used more sophisticated research methods. Thus, these people came to be regarded as "behavioural scientists" rather than members of the "human relations" school. The findings of these people have enormously helped us in understanding organizational behaviour.

Behavioural scientists are highly critical of the classical organisation structures which are built around the traditional concepts of hierarchical authority, unity of command, line and staff relationships and narrow spans of control. They argue that in these organisations there is lot of domination of the work place by managers which causes subordinates to become passive and dependent on them. Behaviourists prefer more flexible organisation structures and jobs built around the capabilities and aptitudes of average employees.

The behavioural approach recognizes the practical and situational constraints on human rationality for making optimal decisions. It says that in actual practice, the decision-making is done in a sub-optimal manner. Also, behavioural scientists attach great weightage to participative and group decision-making because it is felt that business problems are so complex that it is neither fair nor feasible to make individuals responsible for solving them.

Behaviourists underline the desirability of humanising the administration of the control process and encouraging the process of self-direction and control instead of imposed control. They also favour participation in the establishment, measurement and evaluation of standards of performance, prompt information feedback to those whose performance is off the mark and the need for positive and reformative measures instead of punitive measures.

Behavioural scientists consider organisations as groups of individuals with certain goals. They have, therefore, made wide-ranging studies of human groups—big and small. They have studied such issues as why individuals join groups, group size, structure and process, group cohesiveness, and so on.

Behavioural scientists have made extensive studies on leadership. Their view is that while in general, the democratic-participative style is desirable, the autocratic, task-oriented style may also be appropriate in certain situations.

To behavioural scientists, the realistic model of human motivation is *complex man*. This model suggests that different people react differently to the same situation or react the same way to different situations. No two people are exactly alike, and the manager should tailor his attempts to influence people according to their individual needs.

The behavioural approach to organisational conflict and change is quite pragmatic. It recognises that conflict is inevitable and sometimes is even desirable and should be faced with understanding and determination, that every organisational change involves technological and social aspects and that it is generally the social aspect of a change which people resist.

MODERN APPROACHES

Quantitative Approach

This approach is also called the management science approach. It gained momentum during the Second World War when UK and USA were desperately trying to seek solutions to a number of new, complex problems in warfare. The interdisciplinary groups of scientists who were engaged for this purpose were known as Operations Research (OR) teams because their work consisted of analysing operations and carrying out applied scientific research.

It is clear from the above description that the focus of the quantitative approach is on decision-making—to provide quantitative tools and techniques for making objectively rational decisions. This approach facilitates disciplined thinking, while defining management problems and establishing relationships among the variables involved. The keynote of this approach is precision and perfection which is achieved by expressing relationships and facts in quantitative terms. The approach has been widely used in planning and control activities where problems can be precisely identified and defined in quantitative terms. But its use is still uncommon in such areas as organising, staffing and leading the organisation where the problems are more human than technical in nature.

Systems Approach

A common pitfall of the classical, behavioural, and quantitative schools is that they stress one aspect of the organization at the expense of others. Whereas, the classical approach emphasises the "task" and "structure", the behavioural approach emphasises "people" and the quantitative approach emphasises "mathematical decision-making". However, it is difficult to know which aspect is most useful and appropriate in a given situation. What is needed is one broad, detailed, conceptual framework that can help a manager diagnose a problem and decide which tool or combination of tools will best do the job. The systems approach provides him "this integrated approach to management problems.

Contingency Approach

The contingency approach is the second approach (the first being the systems approach) that attempts to integrate the various schools of management thought. According to this approach, management principles and concepts of various schools have no general and universal applicability under all conditions. In other words, there is no one best way of doing things under all conditions. Methods and techniques which are highly effective in one situation may not work in other situations. What is good for the goose may not be good for the gander. Results differ because situations differ. Accordingly, the contingency approach suggests that the task of managers is to try to identify which technique will, in a particular situation best contribute to the attainment of management goals. Managers have, therefore, to develop a sort of situational sensitivity and practical selectivity.

Contingency views are applicable in designing organizational structure, in deciding the degree of decentralization, in planning information decision systems, in motivational and leadership approaches, in establishing communication and control systems, in resolving conflicts and managing change, in employee development and training programmes and in several other areas of organization and management. A detail of these views is given at relevant places in the chapters ahead.

Case Study on Management Profession

Ashok, a senior sales executive had been working with XYZ and Sons, a reputed publishing firm for the last 15 years. The firm has wide-ranging publications of textbooks for school and college students. The firms is owned by a family having four brothers and eldest one who is about 55 years old, still a bachelor, looks after all activities of production and distribution. The role of other brothers is to 'follow up' in nature and to be supportive. About 100 employees are working in the firm including 15 employees in the sales department having no line of authority and all of them are accountable to the owner. Most of the employees working in the organization are not satisfied with the behavioural pattern of the owner barring a few, being considered faithful to him. Mr. Ashok, working for a longer period of time with same clientele has developed good interpersonal relations and rapport with various librarians and professors. He supplies specimen copies of books to the teachers in time and follow them up in getting the books recommended to the students. He is very popular among teachers because of his good behaviour, professional knowledge and other qualities of salesmanship. He is 35 years old, not very ambitious but equally concerned about his future. He has also a feeling that he has not been given any recognition by the owner for his sincerity and hard work. Recently, he had some argument with the owner over the distribution of specimen copies to the teachers, because the owner has been suspecting some wastage and leakage on the part of Ashok. Though he had clarified his position in this regard. But the owner kept on suspecting his integrity without sufficient grounds. Finally, when Ashok knew it through some other employees in the office, he decided to leave the firm. Within a couple of months he left the firm and joined another one, owner of which is young and dynamic and seriously interested for broadening product line with new publications specially in the field of management. It is reliably learnt that within a short span of about one year sales volume of XYZ and sons has declined considerably. The owner is greatly worried about it and he has appointed Shyam Verma in place of Ashok who is also having some experience in this field. But he is finding it very difficult to cope with the situation and to check the decline.

Read the above case and answer the following questions.

(a) What is wrong with XYZ and Sons?

(b) Enumerate all possible reasons due to which Ashok left the firm.

(c) Give your suggestions for controlling decline in the sales volume of XYZ & Sons.

(***Source:*** M.Sakthivel Murugan, "Management Principles and Practices" New Age International Publishers, New Delhi, 2004.)

Case Study on The New Manager

Mr. Avinash was appointed as general manager, administration in Phoenix Industries Limited. He joined the company only about two years back. Prior to joining this company, he served another company for two years. He did his M.B.A from a reputed institution. He considered himself as a high flier. After getting promotion as general manager, administration, he felt quite excited and was quite enthusiastic about his new job. The post of general manager was sufficiently at high level. However, because of young age and lack of adequate experience, Mr. Avinash was considered as junior executive by most of his subordinates.

The administration department of the company had four major sub-units: purchasing, record maintenance, printing and secretarial services. Each sub-unit was headed by a manager. These four managers were directly reporting of Mr. Avinash. They had combined experience of over 80 years with an average age of 45 years. Most of them had been with the company for a fairly long period of time and that too with their present units. Since Mr. Avinash was quite less experienced and young, these four managers viewed his appointment with hesitancy and suspicion. Also, they had liking for the previous general manager and were sorry to see him leave the company.

The new general manager, Avinash, started holding weekly meetings of the department. However, he noticed that managers were hesitant to speak in the meetings; he was the only one to speak. He made some changes in the operating procedures that he felt would increase efficiency and announced them in weekly departmental meeting. There were no reactions to the changes. But later he noticed that the managers continued to follow the old procedures. He talked to them individually but felt that they were not opening up to him. The problem continued.

After about two months, Avinash started receiving complaints from other departments about the services they received from the administration department. These complaints mostly related to printing and purchasing. Avinash believed that his department should provide the best possible services and, therefore, admonished his managers in a weekly departmental meeting. He still received little response from them. He contined to receive complaints and was becoming increasingly frustrated. One day, he became very upset at the third complaint that week, over jobs done in the printing unit. He stormed out of his office down to the printing unit. The manager of the printing unit was out. Avinash called over the chief print operator, chewed him out, and told him to re-do the job on the same day. When printing unit manager returned and learned what happened, he immediately called a meeting with the three other managers and described the events to them. On this, commented the manager of the purchasing unit, "We have to do something. Avinash is too young, incompetent, and is a tyrant." "I agree, he dictates to us in departmental meetings, and how he goes behind our back to our employees. He shows no confidence in us. I am fed up with this situation," said manager-secretarial services. Finally the manager-maintenance chimed in, "I don't think we have much choice. Avinash is regarded high by top level management. We can't talk to him and higher ups, and if we continue doing things this way, our careers will be ruined. Therefore, I think that we should look for some other job opportunities." They all reluctantly agreed with this statement and the meeting ended.

Questions

1. Describe the nature of the problems in this case.
2. Explain what could have been done to prevent the problems.
3. Outline the means you would propose to solve the problems.

(***Source:*** M. Sakthivel Murugan, "Management Principles and Practices" New Age International Publishers, New Delhi, 2004.)

REFERENCES

1. P. C. Tripathi , P. N. Reddy, "Principles of Management", Tata McGraw Hill, New Delhi,2006.
2. M.Sakthivel, Murugan, "Management Principles and Practices, New Age International Publishers, New Delhi, 2005.
3. James E.Post, Anne T. Lawrence and James Weber, "Business and Society", Ninth Edition, McGraw-Hill, 1999.
4. Cutis W.Cook and Phillip L.Hunsaker, "Management and Organisational Behaviour", Third Edition, McGraw-Hill, Irwin, 2001.
5. Stephen P.Robbins, "Organisational Behaviour – Concepts, Controversies and Applications" PHI, 1989.

6. Beach, Dale, S., Personnel "The Management of People at Work", New York, MacMillan, 1980.
7. Drucker, Peter F., "The Practice of Management", New York, Harper & Row, 1954.
8. Flippo, Edwin B., "Principles of Personnel Management", Tokyo, McGraw-Hill Kogakusha, Ltd., 1989.
9. Kinard, Jerry, "Management", Laxington, D.C., Health & Co., 1988.
10. Koontz, Harold and O'Donnell, Cyril, (ed.) "Management: A Book of Readings", New York, McGraw-Hill Inc., 1972.
11. Koontz, Harold, O'Donnell, Cyril, and Weihrich, Heinz, "Management", Tokyo, McGraw-Hill, Kogakusha Ltd., 1994.
12. Mayo, Elton, "The Human Problems of an Industrial Civilizations", New York, Macmillan Publishing Company, Inc., 1969.
13. Newman, William H., "Administrative Action", New York, Prentice Hall Inc., 1956.
14. Stogdill, R.N., "Handbook of Leadership", New York, Free Press, 1974.
15. Taylor, F.W., "Scientific Management", New York, Harper and Borther, 1947.
16. Terry, George R., "Principles of Management", Homewood, Illinois, Richard D. Irwin Inc., 1974.

CHAPTER

7

Communication

Communication – Meaning and Definitions of Communication – Attributes of Communication – Objectives of Communication – Grapevine Communication – Methods of Communication – Listening – Steps Involved in the Process of Listening – Importance of Listening – Improving Listening Skills – Tips for Good Listening – Exercises – Case Studies

Learning Objectives of this Chapter are:

- To know the meaning and definition of communication.
- To understand the attributes of communication.
- To study the objectives of communication.
- To study the grapevine communication.
- To explain the methods of communication.
- To know the meaning of listening.
- To study the step involved in the process of listening.
- To identify tips for good listening.

MEANING OF COMMUNICATION

The word communication is used in common talk, usually to mean speaking or writing or sending message to another person. Communication is an important aspect of behaviour. Human communication is complicated by all factors that influence human behaviour. Communication is a transfer of information, ideas, views and opinions from one person to another person. Communication plays an important role in achieving organizational goals/objectives. Communication refers to is a process by which meanings are perceived and understood among human beings. Thus, communication is a process of exchange of facts and ideas from one person to another.

DEFINITIONS OF COMMUNICATION

Communication is a process of passing information and understanding from one person to another.

– Keith Davis

Communication is any behaviour that results is an exchange of meaning.

– The American Mgt. Association

Communication is a process of passing information from sender to receiver, the information being understood by both sender and receiver.

QUALITIES/ATTRIBUTES OF COMMUNICATION

- Communication is unintentional as well as intentional
- Communication is a dynamic process
- Communication is a systematic process
- Communication is both, transaction and interaction.

10 Major Objectives of Communication

- Information
- Orders and Directions
- Education and Training
- Persuasion and propaganda
- Raising Morale
- Advice/Suggestions
- Operations
- Instructions
- Warning
- Motivation

Primary Objectives

- To get an understanding response and to change attitude
- To maximize production sales and profit

Secondary Objectives

- To assist in attainment of operating objectives of business
- To help improve performance and job satisfaction of employees
- To enhance the corporate image with the employees
- To understand economic, social and political issues
- To keep management informed of trends, and reasons among employers and public.

GRAPEVINE COMMUNICATION

There are two important channels of communication in the organisation. Formal and Informal Communication. Formal communication is called as official communication on the other hand informal communication is also called Grapevine. Every organisation has one informal communication network. Grapevine has its own origin in the social relationships within the organisations and outside the organisations. People talk naturally about various activities which are going on in the industries, at the same time people also will create messages without having evidence. Thus, Grapevine circulates information from one individual to many people in various departments of the organisation. There are four basic forms of informal communication network. They are as follows:

1. **Single Stand** – It involves the passing of information through a long line of persons to the ultimate recipient.
2. **Gossip** – In a gossip chain, A actively seeks and tells everyone. Single individual spreads the news.
3. **Probability** – Probability chain is a random process in which A transmits the information to others non selectively, in accordance with the laws of probability and then these others tell still others in a similar manner.
4. **Cluster** – A selectively tells persons in whom he has trust and confidence. Others also relay the information selectively.

METHODS OF COMMUNICATION

Communication methods are broadly divided into two types such as verbal communication and non-verbal communication. Communication through words are called verbal communication. Communication through other symbols are called non-verbal communication. It can be presented in the following chart.

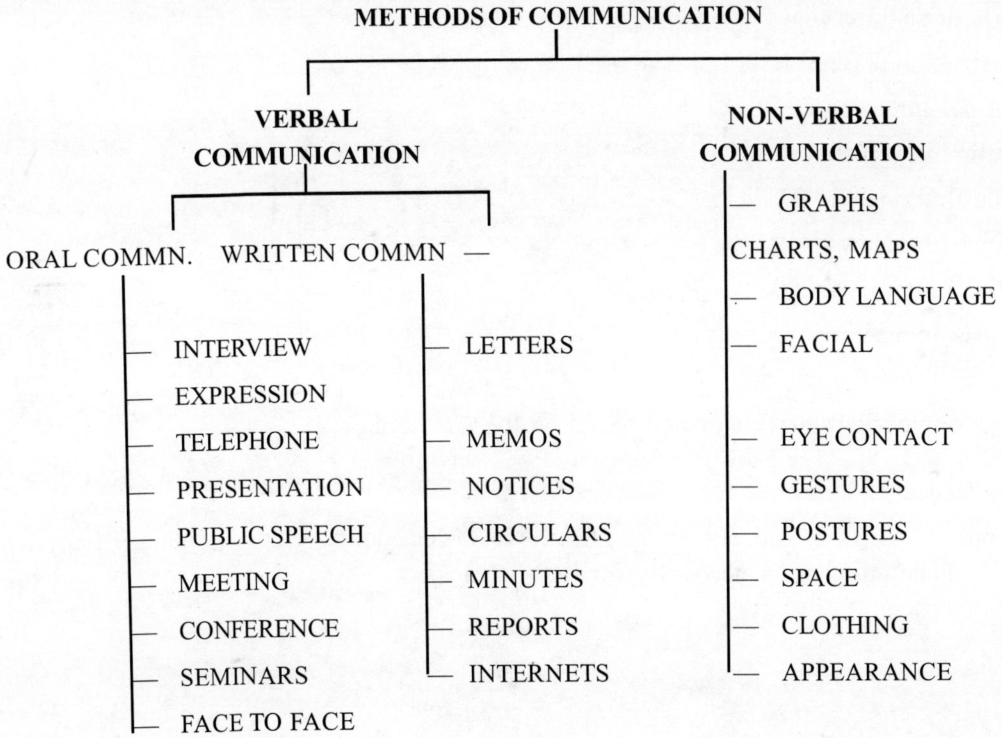

Verbal Communication

Verbal communication is divided into two types i.e., oral communication and written communication and communication is more natural and immediate. In natural situations we speak to communicate about activities which are going on in an industry.

ORAL COMMUNICATION

Oral communication is the face to face situations between two or more persons or among group of persons. There are various methods of oral communication.

- Interview
- Telephone Talk
- Presentation
- Public Speech
- Meeting, Conferences
- Seminars
- Face to Face conversation

Interview

It is face to face conversation among two or more persons for a definite future purpose. Different types of interview are conducted in the organization. They are as follows:

- Structured Interviews
- Unstructured Interviews
- Formal Interviews
- Preliminary Interview
- Final Interview
- Panel Interview
- Group Interviews
- Stress Interviews
- In-depth interviews, etc.

The above interviews are conducted based on the situation.

Telephone Talks

Telephone talk depends entirely upon on the voice. It does not have the advantage of physical presence. Telephone etiquette is necessary for both parties.

Meeting

Mccting involves number of persons coming together to discuss about agenda, chairman, or leader, or president, and other members present in the meeting. Different type of meetings are conducted in Business organisations.

Public Speech

Public speech is a face to face setting. It is an open public meeting. There is a distance between speaker and audience. The purpose of public speech is to evaluate and improve. Public speaking is organized to discuss mostly problems of people. Audience are attracted in public speaking if it organized in a systematic way. Public speaking skills are necessary for managers to analyse the problems which are happening in a group or in any industry.

Face to Face conversation

Oral communication is best when it is face to face. A face to face setting is possible between two individuals among small group of persons, at an interview or meeting in a seminar hall.

Internet

An international computer network connecting other networks and computers from companies and university, etc. Internet is different from interanet. Internet is networks of world.

Intranet

Computer networks of particular company of university or institution. It is connected to use the same software as the net. Simply, it is a connection of an intranet system.

Written Communication

Written communication is used for many purposes. Many types of documents are used for official works. Various forms are used to send the message.

They are as following:

- Letters
- Notice
- Circulars
- Minutes
- Memos

Letters

Letters are most widely used form of written communication. A letter has complex layout which has to be carefully followed. Different types of letters are used in sending message. They are as follows : Letter of congratulations, letter of intimation about the various programmers, call letter for written tests, call letter for interview, leave letter, etc.

Memos

Memorandum is also called as memo in a short form. It is an informed or formal message between the members of an organisation and easily related to day-to-day working instruction.

Notice

A notice is used when many people are working in the organisation. Notices are sent to all departments of organisation to pass the information. Notice should be understood by all employees. Some notices are put on the notice board.

Circular

A circular is a detailed document giving information, instruction, guidelines, or orders on specific matters of college, university, Government of India and professional bodies.

Minutes

Minutes are written record of decision taken at a meeting. Organisations have their own conventions for record of decisions and discussion. Minutes are generally written or typed or pasted in a minutes book. Agenda for the meeting given in advance of the meeting. Points will be discussed as per agenda in advance.

Report

A report is a document prepared by an individual or committee entrusted with the tasks of collecting information an a given subject. It requires careful research, collecting and presentation of findings, conclusion and recommendations. Reports are varying length and may be anything from two pages to a full book divided into chapters. Reports are classified into various types such as research reports, project reports, first information survey reports and other reports, etc.

NON-VERBAL COMMUNICATION

The verbal means of communication includes the use of language whether spoken or written. Non-verbal methods can be used consciously to enhance what we speak. A trained speaker can use gestures, facial expression and postures to pronounce meaning of words. Non-verbal communication is very ancient and are of the earliest type of communication. It developed much before an communication.

For traffic signals non-verbal communication is absolutely essential, visual non-verbal communication methods are extremely useful for conveying ideas related to geography, location data etc. Human beings more responded to picture colour than to languages. News on TV is more interesting and effective than the radio.

Methods of Non-Verbal Communication

Colour: Colour is a very important and powerful means of communication. Colours are associated with different feelings like black with death and sorrow, white for peace and purify, red with danger, green with signal for clearance. Pictorial representation, sophisticated photograph and coloured pictures are used for advertisements.

Graphs and charts: Represents the statistical informatics, charts and graphs must be property titled and labelled for information.

Maps: Maps represents tertiary geographical information and climate condition and transport points, etc.

Body Language

It is also called as Kinesics Body Language in a comprehensive term for communication by the use of part of the body other than tongue. It includes whole range of gestures, facial expressions postures, mini, touch, the physical space between the communicators, dress and all kinds of body movements.

Facial Expressions

Facial expression is an obvious communication factor. A cheerful face and gloomy face. A happy or appreciated smile, looks of surprise and sorrow. This communicates mostly emotions and attitudes.

E.g.: Face is the index of mind.

The thoughts and feelings of the mind express on the face.

Eye contact

Eyes are most effective/expressed part of the human face. A person who is lying usually blinks his eyes many times.

Gestures

Gestures are movements of hands, head and body. These are closely related to personality. No two persons make exactly the same gestures.

Postures

The way we hold our body, the way we stand, set in later something about an feelings, though attitudes and health. Sitting shifting may show tensure. Sitting very comfortable shows relaxed mood, graceful posture is a great asset in any profession.

Space

A manager can use space to create an impression of status. The way we use space plays an important role in body language.

Clothing and Appearance

What we are wearing conveys something about us. It requires good taste and judgement to create some impression. A persons general appearance depends upon several things. Besides clothing, other factors like accessories, footwear, jewellery, handbag, briefcase, etc.

Silence

Silence is also called a method of communication. Silence may be in the form of punishment.

"Speech is Silver

Silence is Golden"

It is a well-known proverb given by Thomas Carlyle.

Silence can be a very effective way of communication. Silence is not a negative absence of speech but a positive withdrawal of speech. In face to face situation silence may indicate several things.

Silence has been classified into four types: warm silence, cold silence, natural silence and demanding silence.

Warm Silence

When old friends meet after a long time. They are so choked by affection.

Cold Silence

When enemies are coming face-to-face with each other.

Demanding Silence

When employee has not finished his work which was assigned to him by his superior. Boss makes enquires about it.

Natural Silence

When two persons are meeting and who have nothing to start the conversation.

LISTENING

Listening is the receiver's activity of communication. Listener is to be a responsible person to pay attention to understand the message of the speaker. A successful manager generally pays higher attention on listening. An effective manager's communication time is spending roughly in the following proportion:

Listening	45%
Speaking	30%
Reading	16%
Writing	9%

Though listening is very critical in our daily activities, it is necessary to improve the listening skill.

Most of the people are not good listeners. Listening capacity can be improved by understanding steps involved in the process of listening.

4 Steps of Listening

— Hearing is the first step of listening.

Listener has to pay attention to hear the message of the speaker, then you can repeat the same message.

— Interpretation is the second step.

Listener has to understand words, vocabulary, experience, attitudes, cultural and background etc. objectwise listen and may be misunderstood.

— Evaluation is the third step.

At this stage the listener decides what is to be done. Evaluation is crucial to give correct judgement in the listening process.

— Response is the final step.

In this stage listener has to give response to speaker when you have got the message and your reaction for the message.

IMPORTANCE OF LISTENING

Listening is making effort to get the speaker's full meaning. Listening is not only understanding the content of the message but also understanding the feeling of the speaker. Listening is an intellectual activity.

Any working encouragement in an organisation depends for success on your ability to listen. Unless someone listens carefully there is no use to make any effort to communicate. Employee has to listen carefully to the instruction given by his superior to complete the work. An employee cannot carry out the work unless instructions are carefully listened. If you listen to employee carefully you can find out employees have enthusiasm and when effective listening presides, there are better results to solve any problem. Effective listening is selected to various future like motivation make of employee.

Benefits of Listening

- Finding out more information
- Learning about people and how their minds are working
- Improving relations with different kinds of people
- Raising morale of the employees
- Obtaining suggestions and new ideas
- Discover why employees are performing well or poorly
- To help in solving various problems.

Blocks to Effective Listening

Unfortunately most of the people are not good listeners and they are not able to listen with full concentration for more than two or three minutes at a time, people cannot pay attention continuously to listen speaker's day a message. In general people do not receive any training in listening. There are many reasons why people are not able to listen. Some persons have self control and they like keep us talking continuously allow then sharing concentration risk other. They want others to listen items. They are not willing to listen what others are

Barriers to Listening

Distraction in your own mind.

When you mind may be allowed to given thinking but your daily action. The next location what last weekend party end semester exam, there will be no listening. Semester working about your personal problem engagements.

Wandering Attention

Average speaking speed is about 150 words a minute.

Listening capacity is 500 words a minute.

This is use of the most difficult barrier between speaking and listening Listener's mind goes on various departments

Planning to present a good argument

Trying to plan a good answer to your question is a nice distraction while you are listening. If speakers makes of a conversational statement which ultimately resulted to subjects. Audience way get confirm in preparing argument a question to ASIS may be missed rest of the speech.

Lack of Interest

Topic is not interesting to audience it may be caused faculty listening audience may be regretted the subject of speaker. A responsible person has to make efforts to create interest in communicating efficiency.

Avoiding the efforts to understand what is difficult

Some audience switch off their attention it creates mind more and more lazy. They can not pay attention in understanding the message of speaker. Radios and TV are useful.

Tendency to criticize

Criticising the speaker's appearance, manner and voice is another cause of poor listening. It may be caused to poor listening.

Emotional blocks

Some people have dead spots this is a tendency not to catch ideas and opinion of the speaker. People may have the message wrongly, some people find it difficult to listen to stories of incidents.

Importance

Lack of patience is the common barrier in listening activity, some people do have patience to wait until the completing his speak. They want to answer and add their own points in the discussion. When someone is continuously talking about his own experiences and expectation it may also cause impatience in listening activity.

Poor Health

Poor state of health reduces listening capacity of the audience. No doubt, any physical pains or ill health may be the cause to reduce the listening efficiency. People cannot pay attention without having good health.

Notice

If there is noice in the environment it makes very difficult to pay attention and to understand the speaker's message. When you are sitting in the class room/seminar.

IMPROVING LISTENING SKILLS

- Each individual has to pay attention. Training for good listening is largely a personal responsibility.
- You must create interest to improve the listening capacity, your listening capacity depends upon your attitude. You must feel respect for people and you must create interest to share ideas and views.
- You should accept speaker's message though it is non-judgmental a non moralizing
- Concentrate your mind on the speaker's message.
- Use you eyes as well as you ears to listen.

TIPS FOR GOOD LISTENING

- Stop talking.
- Try to be in the speaker's position. This is called empathy.
- Write down main points and get them checked for correctness. This creates good impression of the speaker.
- Don't create distractions and should not irritate the speaker.
- Be patient to listen to speaker's message.
- Ask questions at suitable moment to get clear understanding.
- Keep an open mind.

Ten Commandments of Effective Communication

(Given by American Management Association)

(1) Seek to clarify your ideas before communicating.

(2) Examine the true purpose of each communication.

(3) Consider the total physical and human setting whenever you communicate (for example sense of timing, privacy or otherwise, social climate pervading work relationships, custom and past practice)

(4) Consult with others, where appropriate, in planning communications.

(5) Be mindful, while you communicate, of the overtones as well as the basic content of your message.

(6) Take the opportunity, when it arises, to convey something of help or value to the receiver.

(7) Follow up your communication.

(8) Communicate for tomorrow as well as today.

(9) Be sure your actions support your communication.

(10) Last, but by no means the least : seek not only to be understood but to understand — be a good listener.

EXERCISES AND CASE STUDIES

EXERCISE 1

Exercise on Attentive Listening Skills

The objective of this exercise is to show the importance of listening skills to interpersonal success.

Form groups, there should be a minimum of three students to a group and a maximum of seven per group.

Each group has 30 minutes to address the following four questions. The groups should begin by brain storming answers and then narrowing their selection to the three most significant answers. Appoint one member of the group to transcribe answers on the board and another to tell the class why the group selected these answers.

1. How do you know when a person is listening to you?
2. Describe a situation in which you exhibited outstanding listening behaviour. How did it influence the speaker's subsequent communication behaviorus?
3. How do you know when a person is ignoring you?

Describe a situation in which you ignored someone. What impact did it have on that person's subsequent communication behaviours?

(***Source:*** Adapted from T.Clark, "Sharing the Importance of Attentive Listening Skills", *Journal of Management Education,* April 1999.)

EXERCISE 2

Exercise on Effective Communication

Step 1: Below are some statements that were made by employees to their manager —- select the response that best represents active listening.

1. Each day brings new problems. You solve one and here comes another.... What's the use?

________ a. I'm surprised to hear you say that.

________ b. That's the way it is. There's no use getting upset over it.

________ c. I know it's frustrating and sometimes discouraging to run into problem after problem.

________ d. Give me an example, so I know what you're referring to.

2. At your meeting yesterday, I was counting on you for some support. All you did was sit there and you never said anything!

________ a. I was expecting you to ask for my opinion.

________ b. You're evidently upset with the way I handled things at the meeting.

________ c. Hey, I said some things on your behalf. You must have not heard me.

________ d. I had my reasons for being quiet.

3. I don't know when I'm going to get that report done. I'm already swamped with work.

________ a. See if you can get someone to help you.

________ b. All of us have been in that situation, believe me.

________ c. What do you mean swamped?

________ d. You sound concerned about your workload.

4. I've been scheduled to be out of town again on Friday. This is the third week end that's been messed up!

________ a. Why don't you talk with someone higher up and get it changed?

________ b. Going on the road must be a burden to you.

________ c. Everyone has to be on the road - it's part of the job.

________ d. I'm sure this is the last trip you'll have to make for a while.

5. It seems like other people are always getting the easy jobs. How come I always get the hard ones?

________ a. You feel I'm picking on you and that I'm being unfair in assigning.

________ b. What evidence do you have for saying that?

________ c. If you'd look at the work schedule, you'd see that everyone has had easy jobs.

________ d. What about that job I gave you yesterday?

6. When I first joined this company, I thought there would be plenty of chances to move up. Here I am, four years later, still doing the same thing.

________ a. Let's talk about some of the things you could do to be promoted.

________ b. May be you just haven't worked hard enough.

________ c. Don't worry, I 'm sure your chance will come soon.

________ d. Getting ahead must be important to you. You sound disappointed.

7. Performance evaluations are here again. I wish I could just give all my people good ratings – it sure would be easier.

________ a. I know, but that's not possible.

________ b. We all feel that way. Don't get upset over it.

________ c. Performance evaluations seem to bother you.

________ d. Just do the best you can.

8. It's the same old thing day in and day out. Any child could do this job!

________ a. Your work is evidently getting you down and making you feel useless.

________ b. I always thought you liked your job.

________ c. What good is complaining going to do?

________ d. If you've got some idea on improving your job, I'll be happy to listen.

9. I really appreciate getting the promotion. I just hope I can do the job.

________ a. Don't worry. I'm sure you'll get better as you get more experience.

________ b. What makes you think you can't do the job.

________ c. Don't worry. Most people have those same feelings.

________ d. I'm sure you can do it, or you wouldn't have been promoted.

10. I' m tired. That last sale really wore me out. I don't think I can handle another customer.

________ a. Sure, you can. Just rest a few minutes and you'll be fine.

________ b. What have you been doing that's gotten you so tried?

________ c. You look like you're exhausted.

________ d. We all get to feeling that way; don't worry about it.

Step 2: Your instructor has information about the appropriate response. You can verify your answers with this data.

EXERCISE 3

Exercise on Listening

Objective: This exercise has been designed to understand the importance of listening in communication process. This exercise will help the students or trainees to improve communication skills, particularly listening abilities.

Procedure: The class can be divided into groups of three students each. He or she will assign, in each group, the role of speaker to one, of listener to second, and of judge to the third. The speaker, then, shall talk, on any topic, for about five minutes. The listener shall listen and after the talk, will report to the judge about what he or she has heard. The judge (only this person has been allowed to take notes while the speaker talks), shall point out the points missed by the listener and wrong interpretations, if any, made. The roles of the three are reversed and the process repeated so that the group members will have the feel of all the sides.

In the reassembled class, each group shall make its presentation about the roles played, experiences felt, points missed and points wrongly and rightly interpreted.

The lecturer shall moderate the presentations stressing the importance of listening in effective communication.

EXERCISE 4

Exercise on Attentive Listening

Objective

To illustrate the difficulty of attentive listening even in simple exercises.

Procedure

Ask the group to take a sheet of blank paper and number from 1-15. They are to listen carefully to each question and do all calculations mentally, writing only the answers down on the paper. Read the questions found on the following page at a normal rate of speech.

Discussion Questions

1. How many of us just "quit listening" when we get confused or "Lost" with a question?
2. Have you seen times when people seem to "quit listening" when you're giving instructions?
3. What can we do to prevent this loss of attention or to encourage active listening?

Material Required

Questions found on the following page

Worksheet: Following Oral Directions

1. Start with 8; double it; add 4; divide by 5; the answer is ____________
2. Start with 11; substract 3; add 4; add 3; divide by 3; the answer is ____________
3. Start with 15; add 10; divide by 5; multiply by 6; add 6; divide by 4; the answer is ____________

4. From a number that is 4 larger than 13, add 5; divide by 2; substract 3; the answer is ____________
5. From a number that is 2 smaller than 9, add 6; add 5; multiply by 2; divide by 4; the answer is ____________
6. Add 6 to 12; substract 9; add 10; substract 13; double it; the answer is ____________
7. Add 4 to 5; add 6 ; add 7 ; add 9 ; add 9; divide by 4 ; the answer is ____________
8. Substract 6 from 11 ; add 5 ; multiply by 5 ; substract 15 ; substract 10 ; add 1; the answer is ____________
9. From a number that is 6 larger that 6, add 3 ; divide by 5; multiply by 4; add 1 ; the answer is ____________
10. Take the square root of 36; add 5; add 14; divide by 5; add 3; divide by 4; the answer is ____________
11. From a number that is 5 larger than 6, substract 3 ; add 2 ; add 3 ; add 9 ; divide by 2 ; the answer is ____________
12. In the series of numbers, 4-7-8-6-9-12, the first three numbers were ____________
13. In the series of numbers, 4-6-9-9-7-6-3, the sum of the first three number is ____________
14. In the series of number, 7- 9-6-8-4-9-6-10 the lowest odd number is ____________
15. In the series of numbers, 4-5-7-8-6-2-1-9, the sum of these numbers is ____________

Answer:

(1) 4; (2) 5; (3) 9; (4) 8; (5) 9; (6) 12; (7) 10; (8) 26; (9) 13; (10) 2; (11) 11; (12) 4-7-8; (13) 19; (14) 7; (15) 42.

CASE STUDY ON COMMUNICATION

1. Case: Doing My Own Thing

Rita Lowe has worked for the same boss for 11 years. Over coffee one day, her friend Sara asked her, "What is it like to work for old Charlie?" Rita replied, "Oh, I guess it's okay. He pretty much leaves me alone. I more or less do my own thing." Then Sara said, "Well, you've been at that same job for 11 years. How are you doing in it? Does it look like you will ever be promoted? If you don't mind me saying so, I can't for the life of me see that what you do has anything to do with the operation." Rita replied, "Well, first of all, I really don't have any idea of how I am doing. Charlie never tells me, but I've always taken the attitude that no news is good news. As for what I do and how it contributes to the operation around here, Charlie mumbled something when I started the job about being important to the operation, but that was it. We really don't communicate very well."

1. Analyze Rita's last statement: "We really don't communicate very well." What is the status of manager-subordinate communication in this work relationship? Katz and Kahn identified five purposes of the manager-subordinate communication process. Which ones are being badly neglected in this case?
2. It was said in this chapter that communication is a dynamic, personal process. Does the situation described verify this contention? Be specific in your answer.
3. Are there any implications in this situation for upward communication and for interactive communication? How could feedback be used more effectively?

2. Case

Michelle Adams is the maintenance supervisor of a large taxi-cab company. She had been very concerned because the cab-drivers were not reporting potential mechanical problems. Several months ago she implemented a preventive maintenance program. This program depended on the drivers' filling out a detailed report in writing or into the office computer system when they suspected any problem. But this was not happening. On a number of occasions a cab left the garage with major problems that the previous driver was aware of but had not reported. Calling out the field repair teams to fix the breakdowns not only was costing the company much time and trouble but also was very unsafe in some cases and created a high degree of customer ill will. The drivers themselves suffered from a loss of fares and trips, and in some cases their lives were endangered by these mechanical failures. After many oral and written threats and admonishments, Michelle decided to try a new approach. She would respond directly to each report of a potential mechanical problem sent in by a driver with a return memo indicating what the maintenance crew had found wrong with the cab and what had been done to take care of the problem. In addition, the personal memo thanked the driver for reporting the problem and encouraged reporting any further problems with the cabs. In less than a month the number of field repair calls had decreased by half, and the number of turned-in potential problem reports had tripled.

1. In communication terms, how do you explain the success of Michelle's follow-up memos to the drivers?
2. Explain and give examples of the three communication processes in this company (that is, downward, upward, and interactive).

"ANALYZE THE GRAPEVINE PATTERN"

Case Discussion

In Secunderabad a maintenance employee of the A to Z Constructions Co., asked for three months leave of absence for personal reasons. The request was granted because it was in accord with the company and Union policy. A few weeks later, Mr. N. Subbaya the Industrial Relations manager of 'A to Z heard by grape vine that Mr. Ranga Reddy actually had taken this leave to work on a construction project in another part of the state. The report was that Ranga needed some extra money and he had taken this job in order to earn contract construction wages as an electrician because these wages were nearly twice those carned on his regular maintenance job.

The act of taking leave for personal reasons, with the hidden purpose of working for another employer during the leave period was contrary to the labour contract; and the penalty for this could be dismissal. After investigation to determine that the grapevine probably was correct, Mr. N. Subbaya prepared a "Notice of hearing concerning dismissal action" to be mailed to Ranga at his local address where his wife and children remained. The letter of notice was dictated by Subbaya on Monday morning.

The same night Ranga called Subbaya at his home, saying that he had heard that the notice was being prepared and that he felt there was a misunderstanding. He said that he thought his action was acceptable under the contract but if it was not acceptable, he wanted to return immediately, because he did not want to give up his permanent job.

When Subbaya pressed him to learn how he knew about his pending dismissal notice, Ranga said that his wife had called him that evening telling him that at the local supermarket the mother of their son's friend had told her about the pending dismissal order.

(1) Is there any evidence in this case that both management and employees use the grape vine for their benefit? Discuss.

(2) Assume grape vine facts are as follows:
"Subbaya's secretary told a fringe benefit clerk about the dismissal notice; the clerk not realizing the information might be confidential told someone else". If you were Subbaya would you try to suppress grape vine leaks of this type? How?

(3) After Ranga's telephone call, what action should Subbaya take? Discuss.

CASE STUDY MESSAGE EXPANSION

On Tuesday morning Mr. Dixit, the Divisional Manager, told Prashant : "Find out how many people do we have working in our Nasik branch. I know the president is going to ask for this information during our meeting on Friday, and I want to be prepared".

Prashant promptlty passed on the message to Raghav, the Secretary. Immediately, Raghav called the Nasik branch and told Meenal. The Secretary there, "Our presient has asked for a complete list of everyone who works in Nasik branch. We need it all within two days".

Meenal then expanded the message further by telling Mr. Nagesh, the Branch Manager, that the president wants personnel records of all the branch employees to be sent to the head office at the earliest.

Within half an hour, a team of seven members started working on the assigned task. The team worked over-time and the very next day that is Wednesday afternoon the data arrived at the head office in two large boxes sent through special courier.

Mr. Dixit was astonished to see this message expansion when a simple order was distorted as it came down the line, Actually speaking, Mr. Dixit merely wanted Prashant to come up with the number of employees that is two hundered and fifty three people, that's all, instead, the order was turned into major project involving so many people, thus the message in his order was expanded in terms of interpretation and impact.

"LACK OF EFFECTIVE COMMUNICATION"

A massive fire took place in a paper mill on the outskirts of a big industrial town. This mill belonged to an Industrialist in the neighbourhood of the Factory "National Engineering Co.", who has a fully equipped Fire Tender available, round the clock, for any eventuality.

Both companies had a non-hostile relationship and the management of the mill was aware of the Fire Tender readily available next door.

An official of the mill, therefore, rang up the safety officer of the National Engineering Co., to help urgently by sending their fire tender.

The safety officer was aware that Fire Tender could not be sent outside the premise without prior permission of his superiors. However, as the Officer on telephone was in a hurry, the safety Officer plainly replied that the tender was not in proper mechanical condition and hence cound not be sent outside. The officer of the mill discontinued the conversion in frustration.

Thereafter, the safety officer informed the personnel manager about the above call. Meanwhile, the annoyed officer of the mill, frantically looking for help, rang up the residence of the Chief Executive of National Engineering Co., once again requesting for help where he was assured all the help.

Next day when interrogated by the chief Executive, the personnel manager had to explain that the safety officer had given a reply without consulting anyone which created an unwanted annoyance and misunderstanding.

This incident would not have become so severe had the safety officer told the officer of the mill that he would check the position/status of the Fire Tender, availability of the Driver etc. and call him back. The safety officer then could have checked with personnel manager and could have again spoken to the official of the mill. He could have politely expressed his inability for not sending the fire tender, as it was under breakdown, and would have taken 5-6 hours to reach the spot. Safety officer also could have concluded while regretting the request for tender by offering any other help to the official of the mill.

Analyse the case in the light of barriers to effective communication, and managerial leadership.

CHAPTER 8

Motivation

Meaning and Definitions of Motivation –Motivational Framework - Nature of Motivation –Important of Motivation - Process of Motivation - Theories of Motivation - Content Theories – Process Theories – Case Studies – Exercises.

Learning Objectives of this Chapter are:

- To know the meaning and definitions of motivation.
- To understand the objectives of motivation.
- To understand the nature of motivation.
- To analyze the importance of motivation.
- To examine the theories of motivation.
- To identify the difference between content theories and process theories.

INTRODUCTION

Motivation is derived from the word motive which means to move towards a desired goal. In psychology, motivation is the driving force (desire) behind all actions of all organisms. Motivation is the set of forces that cause people to behave in certain ways. Performance of an individual depends on his ability backed by motivation. Most motivation theorists assume that motivation is involved in the performance of all learned responses; that is, a learned behaviour will not occur unless it is energized. The major question among psychologists, in general, is whether motivation is a primary or secondary influence on behaviour. That is, are changes in behaviour better explained by principles of environmental/ ecological influences, perception, memory, cognitive development, emotion, explanatory style, or personality or are concepts unique to motivation more pertinent.

DEFINITION OF MOTIVATION

According to S.P. Robbins: "The process that account for an individual intensity, direction and persistence of effort towards attaining a goal.

According to McFarland: "Motivation refers to the way in which urges, drives, desires; aspirations; striving; or needs direct, control or explain the behaviour of human beings".

According to Scott: "Motivation means a process of stimulating people to action to accomplish desired goals".

MOTIVATIONAL FRAMEWORK

Motivation is the set of factors which leads people to behave in different situations. It is important in every organization to achieve the individual as well as organization goals. Motivation determines the performance of employees. This framework provides a useful way to see how motivational processes occur. When people experience a need deficiency, they seek ways to satisfy it, which results in a choice of goal-directed behaviours. After performing the behaviour, the individual experiences rewards or punishments that affect the original need deficiency. The following figure can be explained for the motivational framework.

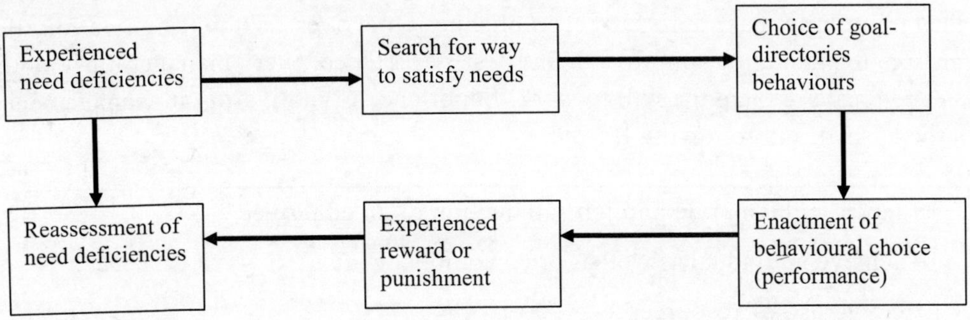

Fig. 8.1: Motivational Frame Work

NATURE OF MOTIVATION

Based on the definitions of motivation, we can derive its nature relevant for human behaviour in an organization. Motivation is not an easily observed phenomenon. We observe an individual's actions and then interpret his observed behaviour in terms of underlying motivation. This sometimes leaves a wide margin of error. Our interpretation does not necessarily reveal the individual's true motivation. The following points reveal the complexities involved in understanding true motivation:

1. Motivation is a continuous process
2. Individuals differ in their motivation
3. Sometimes the individual himself is unaware of his motivation
4. Motivations change
5. Motivations are expressed differently
6. Motivation is complex
7. Motivation may be positive or negative
8. Motivation is a physiological concept
9. Motivation is a goal oriental behaviour
10. Motivation is related to job satisfaction

IMPORTANCE OF MOTIVATION

Motivation is an important part of managing process. Lip Kert has called motivation as "the core of the management". It is one of the most crucial factors that determine the efficiency and effectiveness of an organization. All organizational facilities will go waste in the lack of motivated people to utilize these facilities effectively. A team of highly qualified and motivated employees is, therefore, necessary for achieving objectives of an organization. It is only through motivation process, they contribute maximum for accomplishing objectives. Without motivation, they may not have an urge to maintain or improve their efficiency. Hence, every manager must motivate his subordinates to create in them the will to work. Importance of motivation in management may be judged on the basis of the following factors:

1. To increase the morale and job satisfaction of an employee
2. To achieve individual as well as organizational goals
3. Effective use of resources
4. Higher efficiency
5. Accomplishment of organizational goals
6. Reduction in labour turnover and absenteeism
7. Healthy industrial relations
8. Facilitates change
9. Improved corporate image

The concepts of Motivation is interrelated to the following terms:

- Motives
- Needs
- Wants
- Drives
- Wishes
- Incentives

PROCESS OF MOTIVATION

Motivation is a six phased process beginning from the inner state or need deficiency and ending with need fulfillment. Let us assume that an employee desires to have a promotion. This desire for promotion represents need deficiency also called inner state of disequilibrium, tension or urge, which is the starting point in the motivation model. The employee is expected to search for strategies to get promotion and make a choice among them. There are two ways of getting promotion — putting in better performance, pleasing the boss, the employee puts in regular attendance, completes allotted work on schedule and work hard. The fourth stage in motivation model represents assessment of employee performance by his boss. In the light of evaluation of performance, the employee is either promoted (reward) or promotion is denied to him (punishment). Awarding or denying promotion represents the fifth phase in motivation model. If sincere and hard work has benefited the employee through promotin, he feels encouraged to repeat better performance. If promotion is denied to the employee, his better performance not withstanding, the employee feels discouraged. He may not repeat better performance. He will probably wonder whether it was worth working hard. He may give up the idea of striving for promotion.

Motivation Model
1. **Need Deficiency**
2. **Search and Choice of Strategy**
3. **Goal Directed Behaviour**
4. **Revaluation of Needs**
5. **Reward or Punishment**
6. **Evaluation of performance**

THEORIES OF MOTIVATION

There are several theories and approaches to study the motivation. All these theories will help us to understand the basic nature of motivation exactly. All the theories of motivation can be broadly divided into two categories. They are as follows 1. Content Theories 2. Process Theories. Content theories are classified as follows: Maslow's Need Hierarchy Theory, Herzberg's Two Factor Theory, Alderfer's ERG Theory, McClelland's Achievement Motivation Theory. On the other hand Process theories are classified as follows: Vroom's Expectancy Model, Adam's Equity Theory, Porter and Lawler's Performance Satisfaction Theory. They are presented in the following figure:

Theories of Motivation

Content Theories	Process Theories
Maslow's Need Hierarchy Theory,	Vroom's Expectancy Model
Herzberg's Two-Factor Theory,	Adam's Equity Theory
Alderfer's ERG Theory	Porter and Lawler's Performance Satisfaction Theory
McClelland's Achievement Motivation Theory	Theory X and Theory Y

CONTENT THEORIES

Maslow's Need Hierarchy Theory

Maslow's theory of motivation identified by Abraham Harold Maslow. This theory has been applied by Abraham Maslow in the industry to study the motivation of the employee. This is the simplest and most widely applied theory of motivation. Maslow proposed that motivation is based on a number of human needs. These are arranged in a hierarchy that requires the 'lower', more basic needs to be satisfied before the increasingly less basic ones above. Maslow identified five motivational factors. They are presented in the following figure:

1. Basic physiological need
2. Safety needs or security needs
3. Social needs or love needs
4. Esteemed needs
5. Self actualization

Basic Physiological Needs

The Basic Physiological Needs are relating to the minimum needs of the employees to live in the society. They are food, drink, air, sleep, sex, protection from extreme temperature and sensory stimulation. These physiological needs are directly connected with the biological maintenance of the organism and must be gratified at some minimum level, before the individual is motivated by higher-order needs. These needs are crucial to the understanding of human behaviour.

Safety Needs

Once basic physiological needs are satisfied, another set of motivational needs become a dominant. They are also called as security needs . The primary motivating force here is to ensure a reasonable degree of continuity, order, structure and predictability in one's environment. These needs relate to the security of the employment and working environment. These needs will help the employee to get the job security in the organisation. Some of the safety needs of employees include pension schemes, group insurance, provident fund, gratuity, safe working conditions, grievance procedure, system of seniority to govern lay-off and others.

Social Needs

These needs are also called love needs. Love needs are third level needs in the hierarchy. Once basic physiological needs and Safety needs are satisfied and next level will become a dominant. Social needs are relating to love and affection, affiliation, association and relationship with other employees working in the organisation. In the organizational context, social needs represent the need for a compatible work group, peer acceptance, professional friendship, and friendly supervision. Managers do well to encourage informal groups. Besides, supervision requires to be effective, and friendly behaviour with employees.

Esteemed Needs

According to the Maslow's Hierarchy Theory, these needs are also called as egoistic needs. These needs are sub-classified into two types. Such as self-respect and self-esteem. The self respect includes such things as desire for competence, confidence, personal strength, adequacy, achievement, independence, and freedom. An individual needs to know that he or she is competent and capable of mastering tasks and challenges in life. On the other hand, self-esteem includes prestige, recognition, acceptance, attention, status, reputation, and appreciation. In the organizational context, self-esteem needs correspond to job title, merit pay, peer/supervisory recognition, challenging work, responsibility and publicity in company publications.

Self Actualisation Needs

These are the secondary level needs of an employee. These needs provide full job satisfaction of an employee. Maslow characterized self-actualisation as the desire to become everything that one is capable of becoming. The person who has achieved this highest level presses towards the full use and exploitation of his or her talents, capacities, and potentialities. Thus, this need is the highest level of need which provides maximum satisfaction of an employee.

Hygiene Theory of Motivation

Hygiene theory is based on the premise that things leading to job satisfaction are distinct from those leading to job dissatisfaction. Things people find satisfying in their jobs are therefore not always the opposite of things they find dissatisfying. Maslow's theory has been modified by Herzberg, it is called as two-factor theory of motivation. According to Herzberg the first group of needs are such things as company policy and administration, supervision, working conditions, interpersonal relations, salary, status, job security and personal life. Herzberg called these factors as 'dissatisfiers' and not motivators. By this he means that their presence or existence does not motivate in the sense of yielding satisfaction, but their absence would result in dissatisfaction. These factors are presented in the following figure:

Motivational Factors or Dissatisfiers or Hygiene Factors	**Motivational Factors or Satisfiers**
Job Content	Job Content
Extrinstic Factor	Intrinsic Factors
Compency Policy and Administration	Achievement
Quality of Supervision	Recognition
Relations with supervisors	Advancement
Peer Relations	Work Itself
Relations with Subordinates	Possibility of Growth
Pay	Responsibility
Job Security	
Work conditions	
Status	

Alderfer's ERG Theory of Motivation

This theory was identified by Alderfer. He identified three core needs. ERG stands for Existence, Relatedness and Growth. Existence – Needs relating to basic survival, such as food. Relatedness – Needs relating to relationship with others. Growth – Needs relating to personal development. The ERG theory differs from the need hierarchy theory in three respects. First, instead of five hierarchy of needs, the ERG theory hypothesizes only three. Second, the need hierarchy theory postulates a rigid step – like progression. The ERG theory, instead, hypothesizes that more than one need may be operative at the same time. In other words, Alderfer suggests that there does not exist a rigid hierarchy where a lower-level need must be substantially gratified before one can move on. A person can be working on growth even though existence or relatedness needs are unsatisfied. Third, Maslow had stated that a person will stay at certain level until that need is satisfied.

Comparison of Maslow's, Herzberg's and Alderfer's ERG Theories

We can compare Maslow's hierarchy theory, Herzberg's two factors theory and Alderfer's ERG three factors theories. Most of the maintenance factors of Herzberg come under low level needs of Maslow. Maslow says when the lower level needs are satisfied, they stop being motivatiors and what Herzberg says is the same in the sense that they are maintenance factors. But one particular difference that can be talked of here is that Maslow emphasizes that any unsatisfied need, whether of lower or higher level, will motivate people and Herzberg clearly identifies certain needs and call them as maintenance factors which can never be motivators. They can be presented in the following figure.

Herzberg's Model

Herzberg's Model	**Maslow's Model**	**Alderfer's Model**
Motivating	5. Need for Self Actualisation	Growth
	4 Esteem Needs or egoistic needs	
Maintenance	3. Social Needs or Love needs	Relatedness
Factors	2. Security or Safety Needs	Existence
	1. Physiological Needs	

McClelland's Needs Theory of Motivation

McClelland has identified three types of basic motivating needs. He classified these as need for power, need for affiliation and need for achievement. Considerable research work was done by McClelland and his associates in this respect, particularly on achievement motive. The ability to induce or influence behaviour is called power. It is the ability to manipulate or control the activities of others to suit one's own objectives. People with a high need for power seek positions of leadership. They develop interpersonal relations. They are forceful, outspoken, hard headed and demanding. Thus, according to these theory, David C. McClelland identified three needs. They are as follows:

Achievement need : The drive to excel, to achieve in relation to a set of standards, to strive to succeed. McClelland has identified four basic characteristics of people with a high need for achievement. They are 1. Moderate risks 2. Immediate feedback 3. Indifference to reward 4. Task-orientation.

Affiliation need: The desire for friendly and close interpersonal relationships. Man is a social animal. He seeks interactive and wants to be with people towards whom he feels a sense of belonging and who accept him in their company. Affiliation is a common social need, but some feel it more intensively than others. It is concerned with maintaining pleasant social relationship, enjoying a sense of intimacy and understanding, and enjoy consoling and helping others in trouble.

Power need: The need to make others behave in a way that they would not have behaved otherwise. It is the ability to manipulate or control the activities of others to suit one's own objectives. People with a high need for power seek positions of leadership. They develop interpersonal relations.

PROCESS THEORIES

Vroom's Theory of Motivation

Victor H. Vroom has identified the theory based on the motivational process. It is called expectancy theory of motivation. This theory is based on traditional expression that "everything done in the world is done in Hope". According to Vroom, people will be motivated to do things to achieve some goals to the extent that they expect that certain actions on their part will help them to achieve the goal. Vroom's expectancy model of motivation is built around the concepts of valence and expectancy Therefore, this model is referred to as "VE theory" Various terms used in Vroom's model are explained below: Thus, this theory explains that the strength of tendency depends on the strength of an expectation that the act will be followed by a given outcome and on the attractiveness of that outcome to the individual. Vroom explains that motivation is a product of how much one wants something and one's estimate of the probability that a certain action will lead to it. This relationship is stated in the following formula: V X E = M.

Valence (Strength of one's desire for Something)	X	Expectancy (Probability of getting it with a certain action)	=	Motivation (Strength of drive towards an action)

Valence: It is strength of a person's It is the relative strength of the employee. Valence is an expression of amount of employee's desired goal. If employee strongly wants promotion, it is said that promotion has high valence for that employee. Salaries, security, benefits, reorganization, responsibility and work itself, etc., are the outcomes with different value for different people. The above factors differ from one individual to another individual.

Expectancy

Expectancy is the strength of an employee. It is also related to the belief of a particular outcome. Expectancy represents employee judgement of probability that achieving one result will lead to another result. Expectancy implies the extent to which a person believe that his effort will lead to high performance. It is the possibility that a particular action will lead to the first level outcome. Managers can improve expectancy by matching jobs to people.

Adam's Equity Theory of Motivation

James Stacy Adams proposed the equity theory of motivation in 1965. It was based on the belief that an individual's motivation is influenced by his perception. Adams believed that an individual compares the ratio of his inputs and outcomes. Adams has identified the following formula to express his idea: Equity exist when –

$$\frac{\text{Person's Outcomes}}{\text{Person's Inputs}} = \frac{\text{Other's Outcomes}}{\text{Other's Inputs}}$$

Inequity exists under two conditions:

1. When the person feels that in comparison, he suffers a negative inequity, that is he has been rewarded less for his efforts than another.

$$\frac{\text{Person's Outcomes}}{\text{Person's Inputs}} < \frac{\text{Other's Outcomes}}{\text{Other's Inputs}}$$

2. When the person experiences a positive inequity, that is, through comparison he finds himself rewarded more than the other person for a similar degree of effort.

$$\frac{\text{Person's Outcomes}}{\text{Person's Inputs}} > \frac{\text{Other's Outcomes}}{\text{Other's Inputs}}$$

Thus, this theory explains that individuals consider their job inputs such as effort, experience, education, seniority, skill and competence and compare outcomes such as salary level, status, pay raises, recognition, promotion and other factors and then they compare this ratio with those of other comparable persons and then respond so as to eliminate any inequities. In order to restore equity, individuals can make one of the six alternative choices. They are as follows:

(i) Change their inputs
(ii) Change their outcomes
(iii) Distort perception of self
(iv) Distort perception of others
(v) Choose a different referent
(vi) Leave the field

The Porter and Lawler Theory of Motivation

This theory has developed by Lyman W. Porter and Edward E. Lawler. The most important and surprising contribution of Porter and Lawler is that according to them performance leads to satisfaction, rather than satisfaction leading to performance. It is a severe blow to the long-held assumptions that satisfaction leads to performance. Another equally important contribute of Porter and Lawler is that they consider motivation, performance and satisfaction as separate variables. Traditionally people believe that motivation leads to performance which in turn leads to satisfaction. Porter and Lawler start with the premise that motivation does not equal satisfaction and/or performance. They point out that effort does not directly lead to performance. It is mediated by abilities/traits and role perception. More important in the Porter Lawler model is what happens after the performance. The rewards that follow and how these are perceived will determine satisfaction. This can be presented in the following figure:

Theory X and Theory Y

McGregor has developed the Theory X and Theory Y. Basically, he was a US behavioural scientist. He has identified certain assumptions regarding human behaviour in his survey of motivation

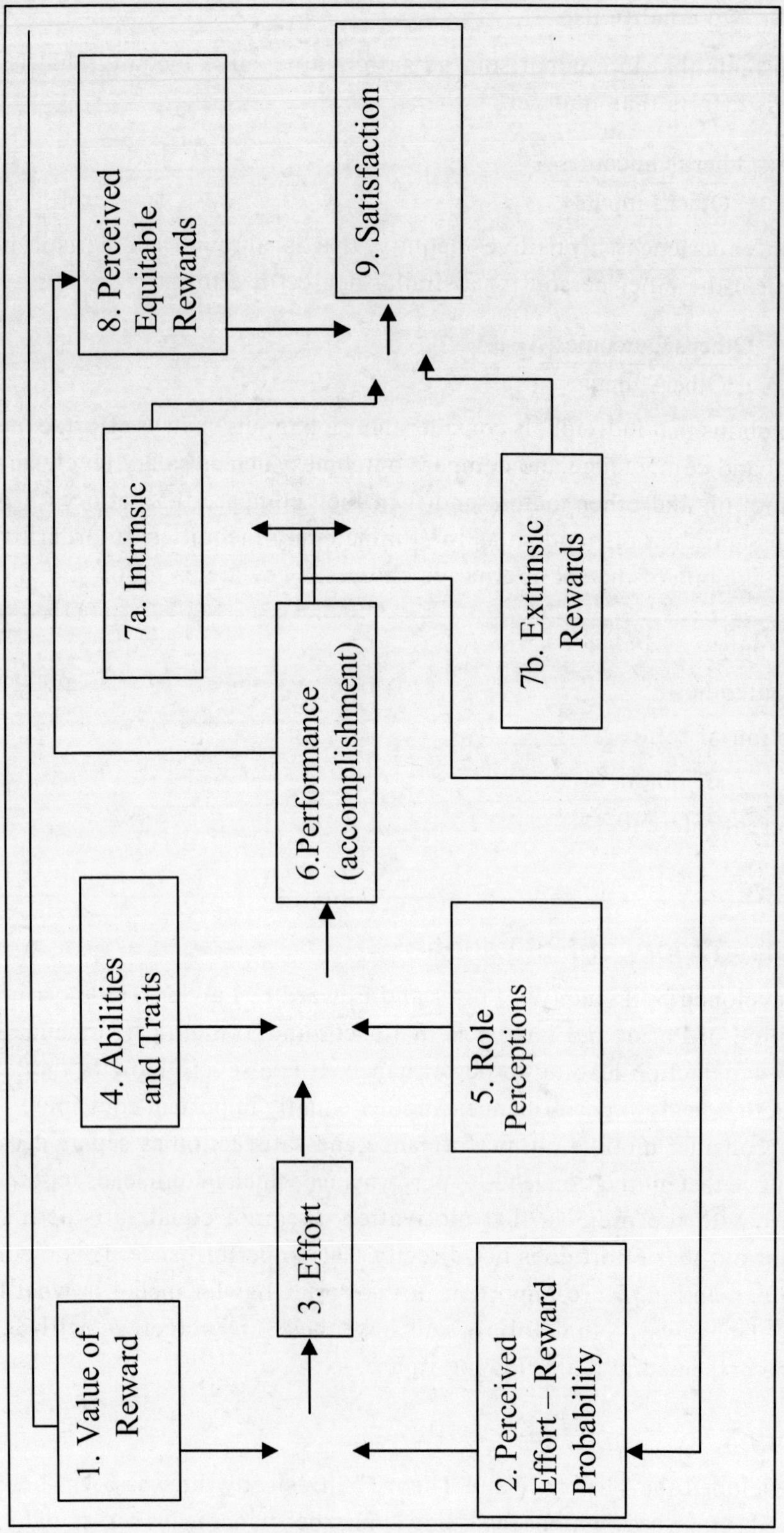

(***Source:*** Layman W. Porter and Edward E. Lawler III, *Managerial Attitudes and Performance*, Irwin, Homewood, III. 1968, P.165.)

Theory X	Theory Y
1. Management is responsible for organizing the elements of productive enterprises such as money, materials, equipment and people, in the interest of economic ends. 2. With respect to people, there is a process of directing their efforts, motivating them, controlling their actions, modifying their behaviour to fit the needs of the organisation. 3. Without active intervention by management, people would be passive to organizational needs. They must be persuaded, rewarded, punished, controlled, and their activities must be directed. Thus, management consists of getting things done by others. 4. The average man is by nature indolent. He works as little as possible. 5. He lacks ambition, dislikes responsibility, prefers to be led. 6. He is inherently self-centred, indifferent to organizational needs. 7. He is, by nature, resistant to change. 8. He is gullible, not very bright, the ready victim of the schemer.	1. The expenditure of physical and mental effort is as natural as play and rest. The average human being has no inherent dislike for work. Work, if meaningful, should be a source of satisfaction and it can be voluntarily performed. 2. External control and the threat of punishment are not the only means of motivating people to work and achieve organizational goals. Man will exercise self-control and self-direction in the service of objectives to which he is committed. 3. Commitment to objectives is a result of the rewards associated with their achievement. The most significant of such rewards is the satisfaction of ego and self-development needs. They can be a direct product of effort directed towards organizational objectives. 4. The average human being, under proper conditions, does not shun responsibility. He is ready not only to accept responsibility but also seek it. Avoidance of responsibility, lack of ambition, etc., are generally consequences of experience rather than being inherent in human nature. 5. The capacity to exercise a relatively high degree of imagination, ingenuity and creativity in the solution of organizational problems is widely, not narrowly, distributed in the population. 6. Under the conditions of modern industrial life, the intellectual potentialities of the average human beings are only partially utilized. In reality people have unlimited potential.

theories of X and Y. Theory X is a traditional theory of Human behaviour. McGregor has also recognised certain needs that Theory X fails to take into account. These are relating to self fulfillment, ego satisfaction and social needs of individual employees. To meet these human needs in business, McGregor suggested a counter approach to the management which he called theory Y. Theory Y has been considered as a Modern Theory. McGregor has identified the following assumptions of Theory X and Y.

CASE STUDY

Self-Actualization Even Before Physiological Needs

Mr. Joga Ram, 28 years old, joined Loyola College, Bina, a small town in Madhya Pradesh, as an Attender in 1981. He is married and has three children. His salary, inclusive of all allowances, is just Rs.425 per mensum as he is posted in a non-grant-in-aid job. His salary is less than the statutory minimum wage and it is not sufficient even to meet the bare necessities. He does not have any other source of income.

Mr. Joga Ram's self-actualization need is to be respected as the best actor in the town. He spends nights in practicing the action. He also spends major part of his salary for organizing dramas. He mobilizes funds from the lecturers of the college and the elites of the town to organize functions. These functions include inauguration of his cultural organisation and his own felicitation by the prominent public servants. But his wife complains to the principal of the college about his activities and inadequacy of the salary even to meet the bare necessities of their family.

Questions

1. What is the peculiar situation in this case?
2. To what extent Maslow's theory is applicable to Mr. Joga Ram.

(***Source:*** P.Subba Rao, *Essentials of Human Resources Management and Industrial Relations,* Himalaya Publishing House, Mumbai, 1999.)

CASE STUDY ON MOTIVATION

Pat Riverer is vice president of manufacturing and operations of a medium-size pharmaceutical firm in the Mid-west. Pat has a Ph.D. in chemistry but has not been directly involved in research and new-product development for 20 years. From the "School of hard knocks" when it comes to managing operations, Pat runs a "tight ship." The company does not have a turnover problem but it is obvious to Pat and other key management personnel that the hourly people are putting in only their eight hours a day. They are not working anywhere near their full potential. Pat is very upset with the situation because, with rising costs, the only way that the company can continue to prosper is to increase the productivity of its hourly people.

Pat called the human resource manager, Carmen Lopez, and laid it on the line: "What is it with our people, anyway? Your wage surveys show that we pay near the top in this region, our conditions are tremendous, and our fringes choke a horse. Yet these people still are not motivated. What in the world do they want?" Carmen replied: "I have told you and the president time after time that money, conditions, and benefits are not enough. Employees also need other things to motivate them. Also, I have been conducting some random confidential interviews with some of our hourly people, and they tell me that they are very discouraged because, no matter how hard they work, they get the same pay and opportunities for advancement as their co-workers who are just scraping by." Pat then replied: "Okay, you are the motivation expert; what do we do about it? We have to increase their performance."

1. Explain the "Motivation problem" in this organisation in terms of the content models of Maslow, Alderfer, and Herzberg. What are the "other things" that the human resources manager is referring to in speaking of things besides money, conditions, and fringe benefits that are needed to motivate employees?
2. Explain the motivation of the employees in this company in terms of one or more of the process models. On the basis of the responses during the confidential interviews, what would you guess are some of the expectancies, valences, and inequities of the employees in this company? How about Pat?
3. How would you respond to Pat's last question and statement if you were the human resources manager in this company?

CASE STUDY ON MOTIVATION

You are in charge of a small department and have three subordinates – Tom, Dick, and Harry. The key to the success of your department is to keep these employees as motivated as possible. Here is a brief summary profile on each of these subordinates.

Tom is the type of employee who is hard to figure out. His absenteeism record is much higher than average. He greatly enjoys his family (a wife and three small children) and thinks they should be central to his life. The best way to describe Tom is to say that he is kind of a throwback to the hippie generation and believes deeply in the values of that culture. As a result, the things that the company can offer him really inspire him very little. He feels that the job is simply a means of financing his family's basic needs and little else. Overall, Tom does an adequate job and is very conscientious, but all attempts to get him to do more have failed. He has charm and is friendly, but he is just not "gung-ho" for the company. He is pretty much allowed to "do his own thing" as long as he meets the minimal standards of performance.

Dick is in many respects opposite from Tom. Like Tom, he is a likable guy, but unlike Tom, Dick responds well to the company's rules and compensation schemes and has a high degree of personal loyalty to the company. The problem with Dick is that he will not do very much independently. He does well with what is assigned to him, but he is not very creative or even dependable when he is on his own. He also is a relatively shy person who is not very assertive when dealing with people outside the department. This hurts his performance to some degree because he cannot immediately sell himself or the department to other departments in the company or to top management.

Harry on the other hand is a very assertive person. He will work for money and would readily change jobs for more money. He really works hard for the company but expects the company also to work for him. In his present job, he feels no qualms about working a 60-hour week, if the money is there. Even though he has a family and is supporting his elderly father, he once quit a job when his employer didn't give him a raise on the premise that he was already making too much. He is quite a driver. A manager at his last place of employment indicated that, although Harry did do an excellent job for the company, his personality was so intense that they were glad to get rid of him. His former boss noted that Harry just seemed to be pushing all the time. If it wasn't for more money, it was for better fringe benefits; he never seemed satisfied.

1. Can you explain Tom's, Dick's and Harry's motivations by one or more of the work-motivation models discussed in this chapter?
2. Using Alderfer's ERG theory, what group of core needs seems to dominate each of these three subordinates?
3. How, if at all, would equity theory apply to the anlysis of the motivation of Tom, Dick, and Harry?

EXERCISE ON MOTIVATION

Gauge your ability on motivational factors by responding to the following statements, and mark the options closest to your experience. Be as honest as you can; if your answer is never, mark option 1; if it is always, mark option 4; and so on. Add your scores together, and refer to the Analysis to see how you scored. Use your answers to identify the areas that need improving.

Options

1. Never
2. Occasionally
3. Frequently
4. Always

1. I avoid office politics and discourage others from politicking.

   1 2 3 4

2. I involve people in issues at the earliest possible opportunity.

   1 2 3 4

3. I thank people for good work face to face or by handwritten note.

   1 2 3 4

4. If I feel it is necessary, I bend the rules and avoid working by the book.

   1 2 3 4

5. I look out for and move people who are not using their full potential.

1 2 3 4

6. I seek opportunities for radical change and take them where possible.

1 2 3 4

7. I reward, recognize, and promote on merit alone.

1 2 3 4

8. I give reasons for my actions and for any disagreements with people.

1 2 3 4

9. I seek consensus and encourage others to do the same.

1 2 3 4

10. I react to failure not by blame but by analysis and correction.

1 2 3 4

11. I try to persuade and influence staff rather than force them to do what I want.

1 2 3 4

12. I try to ensure that work is enjoyable for my staff.

1 2 3 4

13. I interview people who leave to find out their reasons for going.

1 2 3 4

14. I use my knowledge of non-verbal communication to influence discussions.

1 2 3 4

15. I am honest with my staff and keep them as informed as possible.

1 2 3 4

16. If I enquire into staff attitudes, I make a point of acting on what I find.

1 2 3 4

17. I seek a balance between firm control and giving people independence.

1 2 3 4

18. I make conscious efforts to improve on my motivational skills.

1 2 3 4

19. I change benchmarks to keep targets at stimulating heights.

1 2 3 4

20. I revise the system in order to remove obstacles to performance.

1 2 3 4

21. I look at more than just financial results when assessing staff performance.

1 2 3 4

22. I encourage people to be open about how much they and others are paid.

1 2 3 4

23. In appraisal interviews, I request and receive appraisals of myself.

1 2 3 4

24. I get full, clear feedback from people whose behaviour I have had to criticize.

1 2 3 4

25. I organize work so that one person can own and complete an entire task.

1 2 3 4

26. I look at assignments and move as ways to develop people.

1 2 3 4

27. I encourage people to act on their own initiatives.

1 2 3 4

28. I delegate work that does not have to be done by me.

1 2 3 4

29. If difficult "people decisions' are needed, I take them without hesitation.

1 2 3 4

30. I act to avert or settle disputes and personality clashes.

1 2 3 4

31. I make changes only after full consultation with those affected.

1 2 3 4

EXERCISE ON SUBJECT KNOWLEDGE OF MOTIVATION

General Motives	nAch
Secondary Motives	ERG Theory
McClelland	Expectancy Theory
Herzberg	Status, Security
Alderfer	Curiosity, Competence
Vroom	Two-factor Theory
Adam	Attribution Theory
McGregor	Goal-Setting Theory
Maslow	Equity Theory
Heider	Theory X, Theory Y
Locke	NEED Hierarchy
Recognition	Hygiene Factor
Salary	Motivator
Internals	Pawns of Fate
Externals	Masters of Fate

Exercise on Management By Objectives (MBO)

This exercise will help you learn how to write tangible, verifiable, measurable and relevant goals as might evolve from an MBO program.

Time: Approximately 20 to 30 minutes.

1. Break into group of three of five.
2. Spend a few minutes discussing your class instructor's job. What does he or she do? What defines good performance? What behaviour will lead to good performance?
3. Each group is to develop a list of five goals that, although not established participatively with your instructor, you believe might be developed in an MBO program at your college. Try to select goals that seem most critical.
4. Each group will have a leader who will share his or her group's goals with the entire class. For each group's goals, class discussion should focus on their (a) Specificity, (b) ease of measurement, (c) importance, and (d) motivational properties.

(***Source:*** Stephen P. Robbins, *Organisational Behaviour*).

REFERENCES

1. Hackman J.R. and Oldham G.R., "The Job Diagnostic Survey. An Instrument or the Diagnosis of Jobs and the Evaluation of Job Redesign Projects", Yale Uni. Technical Report No.04, 1975.
2. These results of Hall's Research are discussed in ron Zemke, "What are High Achieving Managers Really Like", Training/HRD, February 1979.
3. Hamner, W.C. and D.W.Organ, "Organisational Behaviour", Business Publications, Dallas, Texas, 1968.
4. Dunham, R.D., "Organizational Behaviour", Richard D.Irwin, Illinois, 1984.
5. Rotter, Julian B., Shepherd Liverant, and Douglas, P. Crowne, "The Growth and Extinction of Expectancies in Chance – Controlled and Skilled Tasks", *The Journal of Psychology*, July 1961.
6. Gannon, Martin, J., "Management : Managing for Results", Allyn and Bacon Inc., Boston, 1988.
7. Locke E., and Latham G., "Goal Setting: A Motivational Technique That Works", Prentice – Hall, Englewood – Cliffs,
8. Likert, Rensis, "Motivation: The Core of Management".
9. Luthans, Fred, "Organisational Behaviour".
10. Maslow, A.H., "Motivation and Personality".
11. J.L. Gray and F.A. Starke, "Organisational Behaviour – Concepts and Applications", Merrill Publishing Co.,
12. Larry A.Hjella and Daniel J.Ziegler, "Personality Theories: Basics Assumptions, Research and Application", McGraw-Hill.

13. Steven L.Mcshane and Mary Ann Vanglinow, "Organisational Behaviour", Tata McGraw-Hill, 2000.
14. Nigel Nicholson, "How to Motivate Your Problem People". *Harvard Business Reviews*, January 2003.
15. Steven L.McShane and Mary Ann Von Glinow, "Organizational Behaviours", TMH, 2000.
16. Frederick Herzberg, et al, " The Wise Old Tusk", *Harvard Business Reviews*, Sept. – Oct., 1974.
17. Robert Ford, "Job Enrichment Lessons for AT&T", *Harvard Business Review*, Jan. – Feb., 1973.
18. John Ivanesvich and Michael T.Matteson, "Organisational Behaviour and Management", Irwin McGraw-Hill, 1999.

CHAPTER

9

Training and Development

Meaning of Training – Difference between Training and Development – Need for Training – Objectives of Training – Types of Training – On the Job Training Methods – Off the Job Training Methods – Management Development Programs – Techniques of Management Developing Programs – On the Job Techniques – Off the Job Techniques – Exercise – Case Studies.

Learning Objectives of this Chapter are:

- To know the meanning and definition of training.
- To study the importance and needs of training.
- To analyse the types of training.
- To evaluate the methods of training.
- To identify meaning of management development program.
- To know the objectives of management development programs.
- To analyse the techniques of management development programs.

MEANING OF TRAINING

After employees are selected, placed and introduced in the organisation they must be provided with training facilities in order to adjust them to the jobs. Training is the systematic process of changing behaviour, knowledge, skills, abilities and attitudes of employees. It is the process of improving the minds of employees to do their jobs in an effective manner. Every organisation needs well trained and experienced employees to perform the activities. Training helps to raise the employees skill and knowledge. It is an act of increasing the knowledge and skills for doing a particular job in an organisation. Training improves knowledge, skills and moulds the employee behaviour and attitude based on the organizational requirement. Training is a learning process which brings relatively permanent change in an individual that will improve his or her ability to perform on the job. Training can involve in changing skills, knowledge, and attitudes of employees.

Definitions of Training

Training can be defined according to Dale S. Beach, "The organized procedure by which people learn knowledge and/or skill for a definite purpose'.

According to Edwin B. Flippo, "Training is the act of increasing the knowledge and skills of an employee for doing a particular job."

DIFFERENCE BETWEEN TRAINING AND DEVELOPMENT

Employee training is distinct from management development or executive development. While the former refers to training given to employees in the areas of operations, technical and allied areas, the latter refers to developing an employee in the areas of principles and technique of management, administration, organisation and allied areas. The difference between training development is presented in the following box:

Training	Development
1. Technical skills and knowledge	1. Managerial and behavioural skills and knowledge
2. Specific job-related	2. Conceptual and general knowledge
3. Short-term	3. Long-term
4. Mostly technical and non-managerial personnel	4. Mostly for managerial personnel

Importance of Training

The importance of training as a means of improving productivity is increasingly recognized. Changing technology and patterns of work mean that training must be a continuous process throughout a working life. Skills acquired for one job may also be transferred, modified and supplemented for other jobs. Training makes the employees more effective and productive. Training is an important activity of Human resource management. It constitutes a significant part of management control. Training enhances six C's, and Six E's they are

1. Competence	1. Efficiency
2. Commitment	2. Effectiveness
3. Creativity	3. Etiquette
4. Confidence	4. Emotional Stability
5. Contribution	5. Emotional Intelligence
6. Communications	6. Empowerment

NEED FOR TRAINING

Training is necessary both for organisation and employee because of the following reasons:

1. Technological Changes

Technology is changing at a fast pace. The workers must learn new techniques to make use of advance technology. Thus, training should be treated as a continuous process to update the employees in new methods and procedures.

2. Changing Tasks of Customer

The task and needs of the customer are changing. They have become quality conscious. In order to satisfy the customer the quality and features of the products must be continuously improved which needs training of employees.

3. To Match the Employee with Organisation

An employee's specification may not exactly suit to the requirements of the job and the organisation irrespective of his past experience, qualifications, skills, knowledge, etc. Thus, management may find deviations between employee's present specification and the job requirements and organisation needs. Training is needed to fill these gaps by developing and moulding the employee's skill, knowledge, attitude, behaviour etc. to the tune of job requirements and organisation needs.

4. To Increase the Productivity

It is essential to increase productivity and reduce cost of production for meeting competition in the market. Effective training can help to increase productivity of the workers.

5. Complexity of Organisation

The mechanization and automation, manufacturing of multiple products and by-products of dealing in services of diversified lines, extension of operations to various regions of the country or in overseas countries, made organisations become completed. This leads to growth in number and kind of employees and layers in an organizational hierarchy. This in turn, creates the problems of co-ordination and integration of activities at various levels. This situation calls for training the skills of co-ordination, integration and adaptability to the requirements of growth, diversification and expansion. Companies constantly search for opportunities to improve organizational effectiveness. Training is responsible for much of the planned change and effectiveness in an organisation as it prepares the people to be the change agents and to implement the programmes of effectiveness.

6. Employee Promotion

Training is necessary when the existing employee is promoted to the higher level in the organisation and when there is some new job or occupation due to transfer. Training is also necessary to equip with the advanced disciplines, techniques or technology.

OBJECTIVES OF TRAINING

The objective of the training are as follows:

1. To impart new abilities and skills to the employees in a systematic way so as to learn quickly.
2. To impart new employees the basic knowledge and skills they need for good performance of a given job.
3. To increase the knowledge of the employees in doing specific job.
4. To prepare employees for promotion to higher level jobs
5. To bring about change in the attitudes of the employees towards co-workers, supervisors and organisations.
6. To improve the performance of employees.
7. To help employees to function more effectively in their present job by exposing them to the latest concepts, information and techniques and developing the skills they need in their field.
8. To broaden the outlook and minds of senior managers.
9. To make the employees to handle materials, machines and equipment efficiently and thus to check wastage of time and resources.
10. To prevent obsolescence.

TYPES OF TRAINING

Training is required for several purposes. Accordingly, training programmes may be of the following types:

1. Orientation Training : Induction or orientation training seeks to adjust newly appointed employees to the work environment. Every new employee needs to be made fully familiar with his job, his superiors and subordinates, and with the rules and regulations of the organisation. Orientation training creates self – confidence in the employees. It is brief and informative. It is also known as "pre-job training."

2. Job Training : Job training refers to the training with a view to increase the knowledge and skills of an employee for improving performance on the job. Employees may be taught the correct methods of handling equipment and machines used in the job.

3. Safety Training : Training provided to minimize accidents and damage to machinery is known as "safety training". It involves instruction in the use of safety devices and in safety consciousness.

4. Promotional Training : Promotional training involves training of existing employees to enable them to perform higher level jobs. Employees with potential are selected and they are given training before their promotion. Such training enables them to shoulder higher responsibilities of the new position to which they are promoted.

5. Refresher Training : When existing techniques become absolete due to the development of better techniques, employees have to be trained in the use of new methods and techniques. With the passage of time employees may forget some of the methods of doing work. Refresher training is designed to revive and refresh the knowledge and to update the skills of the existing employees. Short – term refresher courses have become popular on account of rapid change in technology and methods of work. Refresher or re-training programmes are conducted at avoid obsolescence of knowledge and skills.

6. Remedial Training : Remedial training is arranged to overcome the shortcomings in the behaviour and performance of old employees. Some of the experience employees might have picked up in appropriate methods and styles of working. Such employees are identified and correct work methods and procedures are taught to them. Remedial training is usually conducted by psychological experts.

Methods of Training

Training methods are broadly divided into two types. They are (1) On the job training program methods (2) Off the job training program methods. They can be analyzed as follows:

On the job training methods	Off the job training methods
1. Job rotation	1. Vestibule training
2. Under study	2. Role playing
3. Coaching	3. Lecture method
4. Committee assignments	4. Conferences
	5. Programmed Instructions
	6. Group Discussion
	7. Case study
	8. Simulation

ON THE JOB TRAINING METHODS

1. Job Rotation

The purpose of job rotation is to broaden the background of the trainee in various positions. The trainee is periodically rotated from job to job instead of sticking to one job so that he acquires a general background of different jobs. However, rotation of an employee from one job to another should not be done frequently. He should be allowed to stay on a job for a sufficient period so that he may acquire the full knowledge of the job.

2. Understudy

The superior gives training to a subordinate as his assistant. The subordinate learns through experiences and observation. It prepares the subordinate to assume the responsibilities of the superior's job, in case the superior leaves the organisation.

3. Coaching

In this method, the supervisor imparts job knowledge and skills to his subordinate. The emphasis in coaching or instructing the subordinate is on learning by doing. This method is very effective if the superior has sufficient time to provide coaching to his subordinates.

4. Committee Assistant

In this method five or six employees are formed as a trainee group. They are given a problem and asked to work on it and solve the problem. The trainees solve the problem and develop team work.

OFF-THE JOB TRAINING METHODS

1. Vestibule Training : In this method, actual work conditions are simulated in a class room. Material, files and equipment those are used in actual job performance are also used in training. This type of training is commonly used for training personnel for electrical and semi-skilled jobs. The duration of this training ranges from a few days to a few weeks. Theory can be related to practice in this method.

2. Role playing : It is defined as a method of human interaction that involves realistic behaviour in imaginary situation. This method of training involves action, doing and practice. The participants play the role of certain characters, such as the production manager, mechanical engineer, superintendents, maintenance engineers, quality control inspector, foreman, workers and the like. This method is mostly used for developing interpersonal interaction and relations.

3. Lecture Method : The lecture is a traditional and direct method of instruction. The instructor organizes the material and gives it to a group of trainees in the form of a talk. To be effective, the lecture must motivate and create interest among the trainees. An advantage of lecture method is that it is direct and can be used for a large group of trainees. Thus, cost and time involved are reduced. The major limitation of the lecture method is that it does not provide for transfer of training effectively.

4. Conferences : In this method, the trainer delivers a lecture and involves the trainee in a discussion so that his doubts about the job get clarified. When big organisations use this method, the trainer uses audio – visual aids such as blackboards, mockups and slides; in some cases the lectures are video taped or audio taped. Even the trainee's presentation can be taped for self – confrontation and self-assessment. The conference is, thus, a group – centred approach where there is clarification of ideas, communication of procedures and standards to the trainees. Those individuals who have a general educational background and whatever specific skills are required – such as typing, shorthand, office equipment operation, filing, indexing, recording, etc., may be provided with specific instruction to handle their respective jobs.

5. Programmed instruction: In recent years this method has become popular. The subject – matter to be learned is presented in a series of carefully planned sequential units. These units are arranged from simple to more complex levels of instructions. The trainee goes through these units by answering questions or filling the blanks. This method is, thus, expensive and time–consuming.

6. Group Discussion : In this method, a group of employees who pose ideas, examine and share facts, ideas and data, test assumptions, and draw conclusions, all of which contribute to the improvement of job performance. Discussion has the distinct advantage over the lecture method, in that the discussion involves two-way communication and hence feedback is provided. For this method small group discussion is better, because the participants feel free to speak and interact well.

7. Case Study : Cases are prepared on the basis of business situations that happened in various organisations. The trainees are given cases for discussing and deciding upon the case. Then they are asked to identify the apparent and hidden problems for which they have to suggest solutions. The situation is generally described in a comprehensive manner and the trainee has to distinguish the significant facts from the insignificant, analyse the facts, identify the different alternative solutions, select and suggest the best. This whole exercise improves the participant's decision-making skills by sharpening their analytical and judging abilities.

8. Simulation : Under this technique, the situation is duplicated in such a way that it carries a closer resemblance to the actual job situation. The trainee experience a feeling that he is actually encountering all those conditions. Then he is asked to assume a particular role in the circumstances and solve the problems by making a decision. He is immediately given a feedback of his performance. One of the limitations of this method is that it is very difficult to duplicate the situation to the extent of making the trainee feel the pressures and realities of actual decision-making on the job. The very fact that the trainee knows that it is an artificial situation prevents him from experiencing all that he experiences in a real job situation.

MANAGEMENT DEVELOPMENT PROGRAMS

Meaning of Management Development Program

The basic purpose of management development programme is to improve managerial performance by imparting knowledge, changing attitudes or increasing skills. Companies spend lavishly on such programmes with a view to attract and retain the best brains in the industry. Management development is a systematic process of growth and development by which the managers develop their abilities to manage. It is the result of not only participation in formal courses of instruction but also of actual job experience. It is concerned with improving the performance of the managers by giving them opportunities for growth and development.

Need for Management Development Program

Managers are basic pillars in any organisation. Without highly competent executive team members, no organisation is expected to hold a place of prominence despite having other valuable resource such as capita, technology and various other factors. It is the managers who plan organize, direct and control all the resource and activities in every organisation. Recognise the importance of developing managerial skills and knowledge from time to time, most organisations spend lavishly on management development programs. Thus, management development program is important and they are necessary to development the managerial talents based on the following reasons:

1. Executive development program is necessary, based on the changing trends and practices. Dale Yoder strongly remarks "without training, the executives lose their punch and drive and they die on the vine. Training and development are the only ways of overcoming the executive drop-outs."
2. Basic change in the style of management and the posture of managers of today give rise to the training and development of the traditional managers. For instance, the new manager is much more a diagnostician – he is a bridge builder linking the theory with practice.
3. Manpower obsolescence turns out to be a costly game, as in the present era of stifling competition, the survival and success of the firm is increasingly depending on the manpower and especially the managerial quality.
4. A major tool for the organisations for harnessing knowledge is "executive talent". Today's tool functionally – oriented executives is ill-equipped with the methods of handling the jobs.
5. Many managers exhibit fear for handling computers. The computer revolution is frightening for them and it needs no reiteration that they require development and training.
6. Apart from the technical skills, the managers are required to learn the techniques of dealing with people. In the present day hyper- industrialized society, the methods of dealing with human resources are radically different from the past.
7. Development programmes designed for executives are not new, even though most of them are of recent origin.

Objectives of Management Development Program

1. To provide opportunities for development of managers.
2. To update the managerial skills and knowledge
3. To prepare the lower level managers for promotions.
4. To improve the performance of the managers.
5. To develop the broad view on all functional areas of an organisation.
6. To increase the morale of the members of the management group.
7. To keep the managers abreast with the changes and developments.
8. To create the management succession.
9. To broaden the outlook of executive position and responsibilities.
10. To understand the problems of human relations.

Steps to Develop Management Development Programs

The importance steps in developing management development program are as follows:

1.	Identification of developmental needs.
2.	Accessing the present management talents.
3.	Identify the strength of managers.
4.	Designing management development program.
5.	Organizing the development programs.
6.	Evaluation of the programs.

Need for Management Development Program

1.	Rapid changes in the technology.
2.	Changes in the socio-cultural environment.
3.	Competitive changing environment in the present market.
4.	Increased recognition of social responsibility.
5.	Today's worker's social awareness and participation in the management.
6.	Frequent labour management conflicts.
7.	Changing trends in the business.
8.	Changing practices and policies.

TECHNIQUES OF MANAGEMENT DEVELOPING PROGRAMS

There are two types of techniques of management development. (1) On the job techniques (2) Off the job techniques. They are as follows:

On the Job Techniques	Off the Job Techniques
1. Coaching 2. Job rotation 3. Understudy 4. Multiple management	1. Role playing 2. Case study 3. Incident method 4. Simulation 5. Sensitivity training 6. Lecture method 7. In–basket method 8. Conference 9. Business game 10. Managerial grid

ON THE JOB TECHNIQUES

1. Coaching

In this method, the supervisor imparts job knowledge and skills to his subordinate. The emphasis in coaching or instructing the subordinate is on learning by doing. This method is very effective if the superior has sufficient time to provide coaching to his subordinates.

2. Job Rotation

The purpose of job rotation is to broaden the background of the trainee in various positions. The trainee is periodically rotated from job-to-job instead of sticking to one job, so that he acquires a general background of different jobs. However, rotation of an employee from one job to another should not be done frequently. He should be allowed to stay on a job for a sufficient period so that he may acquire the full knowledge of the job.

3. Understudy

The superior gives training to a subordinate as his assistant. The subordinate learns through experiences and observation. It prepares the subordinate to assume the responsibilities of the superior's job in case the superior leaves the organisation.

4. Multiple Management

Multiple management is a system in which permanent advisory committees of managers study problems of the company and make recommendation to higher management. It is also called Junior-board of executive system. These committees discuss the actual problems and different alternative solutions after which the decisions are taken.

The technique of multiple management has certain advantages over the other techniques. Dale S. Beach described them as follows:

1. Members have the opportunity to acquire the knowledge of various aspects of business.
2. It helps to identify the members who have the skills and capabilities of an effective manager.
3. Members have the opportunity to participate in the group interaction and thereby gain the practical experience of group decision-making,
4. It is relatively inexpensive method, and
5. Considerable number of executives can be developed in a short span of time.

OFF THE JOB TECHNIQUES

1. Role playing

It is defined as a method of human interaction that involves realistic behaviour in imaginary situation. This method of training involves action, doing and practice. The participants play the role of certain characters, such as the production manager, mechanical engineer, superintendents, maintenance engineers, quality control inspector, foreman, workers and the like. This method is mostly used for developing interpersonal interaction and relations.

2. Case Study

Cases are prepared on the basis of business situations that happened in various organisations. The trainees are given cases for discussing and deciding upon the case. Then they are asked to identify the apparent and hidden problems for which they have to suggest solutions. The situation is generally described in a comprehensive manner and the trainee has to distinguish the significant facts from the insignificant, analyse the facts, identify the different alternative solutions, select and suggest the best. This whole exercise improves the participant's decision-making skills by sharpening their analytical and judging abilities.

3. Incident Method

Paul Rigors developed this method. It aims to develop the trainee in the areas of intellectual ability, practical judgement and social awareness. Incidents are prepared on the basis of actual situations which happened in different organisations. Each employee in the training group is asked to study the incident and to make short-term decisions in the role of a person who has to cope with the incident in the actual situation. Later, the group studies and discusses the incident and takes decision relating to incident, based on the group interaction and decisions taken by each member. Thus, this method is similar to a combination of case method and in-basket method.

4. Simulation

Under this technique, the situation is duplicated in such a way that it carries a closer resemblance to the actual job situation. The trainee experience a feeling that he is actually encountering all those conditions. Then he is asked to assume a particular role in the circumstances and solve the problems by making a decision. He is immediately given a feedback of his performance. One of the limitations of this method is that it is very difficult to duplicate the situation to the extent of making the trainee feel the pressures and realities of actual decision-making on the job. The very fact that the trainee knows that it is an artificial situation prevents him from experiencing all that he experiences in a real job situation.

5. Sensitive Training

Sensitivity training is called as T-group training. It is also known as laboratory training as it is conducted under controlled conditions. It means the development of awareness and sensitivity to behavioural patterns of oneself and others. 'T' groups are helpful in unlearning and learning certain things. They help the participants to understand how groups actually work and give them a chance to discover how they are interpreted by others. It also aims at increasing tolerance power of the individual and his ability to understand others. The sensitivity training programmes are generally conducted under controlled laboratory conditions. The two functions of a T-group or sensitivity development group are: (i) To help its members learn how groups actually work, (ii) To give each member of the group a chance to discover how other people interpret and are affected by his own behaviour.

The activity to T-group consists mainly of sitting around a table discussing for hours. A trainer usually is a psychologist. Trainer at the group's first meeting simply states that idea of a T-group is to help its members learn about their own behaviours and also learn from other's behaviours. As the members of a T-group discuss what they should talk about and how their discussion should be structured, conflicts obviously arise. Members criticize freely the behaviour of each other thereby giving feedback, which may be positive or negative.

Sensitivity training is an important tool of helping managers to win the co-operation of people working with them. There is no doubt that the T-group is one of the sufficient educational innovations of this century. It has been experienced that about two-thirds of the participants who have undergone laboratory training display change in behaviour of positive type.

6. Lecture Method

Lecture method is the best technique to present and explain series of facts, concepts and principles. The lecturer organizes the material and gives it to a group of trainees in the form of talk. The main uses of lectures in executive development are :

1. It is direct and can be used for a larger group of trainees.
2. It presents the overview and scope of the subject clearly.
3. It presents the principles, concepts, policies and experience in the shortest time. Thus, it is a time saving technique.

The lecture method do not give scope for trainee participation and may sometimes be boring which in turn hinders learning. Skills can be learnt only by doing and therefore lectures are of little use for technical skills.

7. In-Basket Method

In this method the trainees are put in an artificial situation, i.e., in an executive position. The trainee will take various decisions as if he is a real executive in that situation. It goes like this. The trainees are first given background information about a simulated company, its products, key personnel, various memoranda, requests and all data pertaining to the firm. The trainee has to understand all this, make notes, delegate tasks and prepare memos within a specified amount of time. Abilities that this kind of exercise develops are: (1) Situational judgement being able to recall details, establish priorities, interrelate items and determine need for more information, (2) Social sensitivity in exhibiting courtesy in written notes, scheduling meetings with personnel involved and explaining reasons for actions taken, and (3) Willingness to make decision and take action.

8. Conferences

In this method, the trainer delivers a lecture and involves the trainee in a discussion so that his doubts about the job get clarified. When big organisations use this method, the trainer uses audio-visual aids such as blackboards, mockups and slides; in some cases the lectures are video tapped or audio taped. Even the trainee's presentation can be taped for self-confrontation and self-assessment. The conference is, thus, a group-centred approach, where there is a clarification of ideas, communication of procedures and standards to the trainees. Those individuals who have a general educational background and whatever specific skills are required – such as typing, shorthand, office equipment operation, filing, indexing, recording, etc., may be provided with specific instruction to handle their respective jobs.

9. Business Games

Managers are presented with information about a company's – financial position, products, markets, etc. They are given different management roles to perform. One group may be concerned with sales, another with production and so on. The main difficulty is in assessing the probable results of the decisions made. Sometimes, a computer is used for this purpose. The managers may reject the whole of the learning if they feel the assessment of the probable outcome of their decisions is unrealistic.

Under this method, the trainees are divided into groups of different teams. Each team has to discuss and arrive at decisions concerning such subjects as production, pricing, research expenditure, advertising etc. assuming itself to be the management of a simulated firm. The other teams assume themselves as competitors and react to the decision. This immediate feedback helps to know the relative performance of each team. The team's co-operative decision promotes greater interaction among participants and gives them the experience in co-operative group processes.

10. Managerial Grid

This is also called as leadership grid. This is one of the well-known leadership styles developed by Blake and Mouton. It consists of two factors such as task oriented and relation oriented behaviour. This style is related to concern for people and concern for production, concern for people includes the degree of personal commitment, maintaining self esteem of workers, responsibility, interpersonal relationship, etc., towards goal achievement. Concern for production means the attitude of supervisor/leader, quality of decision, work efficiency, volume of output, quality of staff service etc. The managerial grid has identified five styles based on two factors. They are: (1) Concern for production (2) Concern for employees.

1. The style 1.1 is impoverished management – low concern for both people and production. This is similar to *Laissez faire* leadership style.
2. This style 1.9 is country club management – high concern for employees, but low concern for production.
3. The style 9.1 is task oriented – high concern for production and low concern for employees.
4. The style 5.5 is middle of the road of Management both production and employees concern medium which means intermediate stage.
5. The style 9.9 is team management – both production and employees are the highest concern. This is similar to democratic style. Blake and Mouton strongly argued that 9.9 style is the effective leadership style. Hence, management may use this style for effective goal attainment.

Suitability of Various Techniques of Management Development

(i) Job Rotation	This is particularly useful in the development of diversified skills and to give executives a broader outlook, which are very important to the upper management levels.
(ii) Understudy	An understudy is normally chosen with forethought of making available to the organisation a subordinate who is equal to his superior in the event of retirement, illness or death of the supervisor. The subordinate will be able to take over his position and manage as effectively as his boss could.
(iii) Multiple Management	This technique is mainly useful in bringing the managers out of their narrow shells and help them gain a broader outlook and knowledge in different functional areas.
(iv) Case study	In the development of executive and analytical and decision – making skills, this technique is particularly useful.
(v) Incident Method	This technique improves one's intellectual ability, practical judgement and social awareness.
(vi) Role playing	Role playing helps executives in understanding people better by giving them vicarious experiences.
(vii) In-Basket	Situational judgement and social sensitivity are the two important qualities that can be developed with the help of this method.
(viii) Business Games	This technique may be used in order to develop organizational ability, quickness of thinking and leadership.
(ix) Sensitivity Training	This helps one know more about himself and the impact of his behaviour on others, which are important to manage people better.
(x) Simulation	Problem solving through decision-making can be developed quite well with the help of simulation.
(xi) Managerial Grid	To develop leadership qualities in executives over a long period of time, this technique is adopted.
(xii) Conferences	The most difficult thing for any one is to change his own attitude. This technique develops the ability of the executives to modify their attitudes, when needed in the interest of the organisation.
(xiii) Lectures	This is the best technique to give more knowledge in a short period of time to a large number of participants.

EXERCISE AND CASE STUDY

EXERCISE ON CREATIVITY

This test does not measure your intelligence, your fluency with words, and certainly not you mathematical ability. It will, however, give you some gauge of your mental flexibility and creativity. Examine each of the following and identify what each acronym, phrase or abbreviation shows.

1. 26 = L of the A **** Sample ***** 26 = Letters of the Alphabet.
2. 7 = W of the A W ____________________
3. 1,001 = A N ____________________
4. 12 = S of the Z ____________________
5. 54 = C in a D (with the J' s) ____________________
6. 9 = P in the S S ____________________
7. 88 = P K ____________________
8. 13 = S on the A F ____________________
9. 32 = D F at which W F ____________________
10. 18 = H on a G C ____________________
11. 90 = D in a R A ____________________
12. 200 = D for P G in M ____________________
13. 8 = S on a S S ____________________
14. 3 = B M (SHTR) ____________________
15. 4 =- Q IN A G ____________________
16. 24 = H in a D ____________________
17. 1 = W on a U ____________________
18. 5 = D in a ZC ____________________
19. 57 = H V ____________________
20. 11 = P on a F T ____________________
21. 1,000 = W that a P is W ____________________
22. 29 = D in Finaly ____________________
23. 64 = S on a C ____________________
24. 40 = D and N of the G F ____________________

For Answer Key & More Details contact at – email: dracmohan_mannava@yahoo.com

(***Source:*** Fred Luthans, *Organisational Behaviour*, McGraw-Hill)

EXERCISE ON DISVOWELED TERMINOLOGY:

DISVOWELED TERM

TRAINING TERMS

1. NDS
2. VLTN
3. BJCTVS
4. PRTST
5. LRNNG

MOVIE TITLES

1. DLVRNC
2. STRWRS
3. DRN
4. STRSBRNTRGRT

ORGANIZATIONAL TITLES

1. FRMN
2. CHRMNFTHBRD
3. MNGMNTTRN
4. SPRVSR
5. SCRTRY

AMERICAN PRESIDENTS

1. NXN
2. DMS
3. SNHWR
4. CLDG
5. MNR

For Answer Key & More Details contact at – email: dracmohan_mannava@yahoo.com

Team Exercises on Assessing Occupational Status

1. Air Traffic Controller
2. Coach of an Indian cricket team
3. Mayor of the large city
4. Minister of the Central Government

5. Physician
6. Professor of Top B. School
7. Indian Army Chief
8. Criminal Lawyer
9. Manager of Maruthi Automobile Industry
10. Star Sales Executive of MNC.

Rank the above 10 occupations from most prestigious 1 to least prestigious 10 and answer the following questions. Now form into groups of every three members of each, Answer the following questions:

a. How closely did your top five choices (1-5) match?
b. How closely did your bottom five choices (6-10) match?
c. What occupations were generally easiest to rate? Which were most difficult? Why?
d. What does this exercise tell you about the criteria for assessing status?

For Answer Key & More Details contact at – email: dracmohan_mannava@yahoo.com

Each block represent a saying or well-known phrase. Please write your answer.

1 POCHICKENT POCHICKENT POCHICKENT POCHICKENT	2 ECAP PACE	3 GUN, JR	3 PARKEDPARKED
5 CHECK CHECK CHECK	6 HEAWENS - PENNIES	7 COUNTRY COUNTRY	8 CR ☹ WD
9 DANGER	10 FISHING C	11 B A E D U M R	12 TAKE 1 MEAL TAKE 1 MEAL TAKE 1 MEAL TAKE 1 MEAL
13 VIOLETS	14 ROAD	15 PEP PEP PEP PEP PEP PEP PEP PEP PEP PEP PEP PEP PEP	16 agb

For Answer Key & More Details contact at – email: dracmohan_mannava@yahoo.com

CASE STUDY

1. Is Rajat in Need of Remedial Training?

Rajat Sharma has been employed for six months in the accounts section of a large manufacturing company in Faridabad. You have been his supervisor for the past three months. Recently, you have been asked by the management to find out the contributions of each employee in the Accounts Section and monitor carefully whether they are meeting the standards set by you.

A few days back you have completed your formal investigation and with the exception of Rajat, all seem to be meeting the targets set by you. Along with numerous errors, Rajat's work is characterized by low performance – often he does 20 percent less work than the other clerks in the department.

As you look into Rajat's performance review sheets again, you begin to wonder whether some sort of remedial training is needed for people like him.

Questions

1. As Rajat's supervisor can you find out whether the poor performance is due to poor training or due to some other cause?
2. If you find Rajat has been inadequately trained, how do you go about introducing a remedial training programme?
3. If he has been with the company six months, what kind of remedial programme would be best?
4. Should you supervise him more closely? Can you do this without making it obvious to him and his co-workers?
5. Should you discuss the situation with Rajat?

CASE STUDY

1. Unwanted Promotion

Kartar Singh joined Lakshmi Bank, Meerut branch as a clerk after obtaining the post graduate degree in chemistry from Delhi Unviersity in 1986. He did his work with due diligence and was generally rated as a hard-working, ambitious young man. He obtained the professional qualification, CAIIB, in 1992. Thereafter, he has applied for the officer's post under the promotion quota. He could not get the promotion as his scores in the written test were low. Meanwhile, he is transferred to the Delhi university campus branch, Delhi. His attempts to scale the career ladder did not succeed and after several frustrating trials, he consciously decided to join the ranks of the union as an active member. He became the president of the local branch of Bank employee's Union in 1995. Through his interpersonal skills, he moved closer to most employees in the bank and is able to put out the fires between people quickly. Of late, he is considered a tough union activist to bargain with and management has developed a kind of negative attitude towards his career moves.

In 1996, when the opportunity came, he was not considered for promotion as his interview scores, this time were found to be not satisfactory. The branch managers' confidential report about his union activities, it is rumoured, is said to be the major obstacle to his promotion. Meanwhile, Kartar Singh started a business of dealership in automobiles using a dummy name. He has also succeeded, to a large extent, in delivering the deposits of nearby business community to other banks. Based on the recommendation of the new branch manager, management has decided to promote Katar Singh to the officer cadre in 1999. Kartar received the oppointment order for the oficer's post from the head office recently. The colleagues, along with the Branch Manager planned on evening tea party, congratulating his achievement. To their surprise, Kartar expressed his unwillingness to accept the offer and refused the promotion straight away, citing medical reasons.

Questions

1. Comment on the promotion policy of the bank, using inputs from the above case.
2. Do you think management's action of selecting Kartar as an officer after 13 years of service is in the right direction? Why? Why not?
3. Why did Kartar refuse promotion?

2. The Supervisor's Dilemma

I am a supervisor at a modern soap factory built about ten years ago at Ghaziabad, which is a fast developing town is Uttar Pradesh and lies about 18 miles away from Delhi, the capital city. The factory is situated in a beautiful and what one might call rural surroundings. The factory is itself surrounded by cultivable land and many of the factory workers own ancestral property here. The pattern of living of the workers, in most cases, conforms to the joint family system.

I feel that production at our factory has never come upto management's expectations for several reasons. One of these is heavy absenteeism, for during the agricultural season the factory workers stay at home to cultivate their own land. Since the worker is also a farmer, they do not depend upon factory wages alone, the factory worker takes things easy, which results in a situation of chronic absenteeism in the factory.

About six years ago, within the same factory compound, a fruit processing unit was also added by the company. The job in this unit are seasonal; that is, only during the fruit-growing season it does work to its full capacity. The unit employs 22 workers. All of them are given semi-skilled grade E jobs.

During the season, besides the bottling of fruit products, fruit juices are also filled in wooden casks and stored up, so that in lean periods, they could be bottled: some of the jobs done in the unit are peeling fruit, extracting juice, boiling juice and other ingredients into syrups or jams, bottling, capping, labelling, storing, and keeping the premises clean.

During the lean period the major portion of all these jobs come to an end and therefore, part of the workforce is transferred to the soap plant and allied sections, to make a good labour shortages which occur there. However, a small portion of workers who remain in the fruit processing plant are given light jobs, such as keeping the premises clean, rolling the barrels, and so on. The only exceptions are the two workers who are engaged in filling and capping bottles. They have an obvious job title: Bottle Filler and Capper. All workers in the fruit processing unit are permanent employees. When these two workers – Bottle Filler and Capper – see others having an easy time they become disgruntled and demand higher wages or that others do the filling and capping jobs as well. They cannot be given higher grades because in the soap factory people doing almost similar jobs are in E grade and they too, would then claim higher grades. The other workers cannot be made to do these jobs because production would suffer. The bottle filler and capper have done the job for years and have attained great speed in doing it. Others cannot match that speed.

I first cajoled those two workers and also counselled them but without success. Finally, I threatened them with punitive action. This has only resulted in a 'go-slow' response from them. I am faced with a dilemma. I am convinced that so far as my unit is concerned these two workmen's demands are just and fair since the workload on them is definitely more than the others in the unit, and also their jobs are more skilled than that of the rest of the workers there. However, in the context of the entire factory, their demands cannot be conceded.

Questions

1. What is the main problem in this case?
2. What are your views about the problem of the supervisor?
3. What would have been your way of handling the problem as supervisor and as part of the management? Explain the possible consequences of the action taken to restore productivity in the food processing unit.
4. Suggest possible measures to resolve the major problem faced by the organisation.

CASE STUDY

Training Expenditure: Cost or Investment

KPMG-one of the major accounting firms - provides accounting, auditing and tax services. Majority of its rare Chartered Accountants and CPAs. The company has ambitious plans for expansion in view of boom in consultancy industry consequent upon globalisation. Company's policy is promoting within and therefore, most of its senior level employees are promoted from entry-level accountants. In view of its promotion policy , the company invests heavily on training of employees in the form of development of in-house educational and training facilities. Most of its employees receive training at frequent intervals in the company's training colleges.

Majority of training investment of the company is on technical and procedural training for entry-level accountants in the areas of accounting, finance, tax, auditing, project reports and report writing. However, KPMG has problems in attracting dynamic and energetic young graduates from the colleges and universities. This situation, sometimes, discourages clients to continue with KPMG in case of existing clients. This situation to some extent is due to the 'fast-in, fast-out style of big time consulting'. Employees of the company gradually learn to interpret the subleties of clients needs and sometimes employees have been let go due to the absence of interpersonal skills.

The training colleges of the company, therefore suggested to provide training in interpersonal skills. But the line managers point out that the company has conducted training in client and customer relations, just two years back. They added that there is no improvement in customer relations and the return on money spent on training can't be justified. The senior managers of the company feel that much investment in training is unnecessary as some of the trained employees join other organizations.

However, most of the managers feel that investment in training is essential, but the dilemma is that which part of the skill should receive more attention and investment.

Questions

1. Will training correct the problem of interpersonal relations?
2. Is training cost effective?
3. Is KPMG provide the right knowledge and skill?

Suitability of the Technique

The IDBI Bank Ltd., has been facing problems relating to deposit mobilisation and loan recovery. The bank appointed a number of Committees to go into the problems and find out the root cause for these problems. All the committees pointed out that the delay in decision-making and faulty decisions made by the executives at different levels are responsible for the state of affairs in the bank. Mr. Raman, the Chairman of the bank, on 18 April 2010, asked the Chief HR Manager of the bank to develop various techniques and organise the executive development programmes in order to improve the decision -making skills of the bank executives from the level branch manager to the general manager.

The Chairman of the bank attended an executive development programme during December, 2009 conducted by the Administrative Staff College of India for Chairmen of all Banks. He was very much impressed by two techniques in the entire programme. They are role playing and sensitivity training. He thought that he should educate his HR manager about these techniques and these techniques should be used in the proposed executive development programme of the bank. He called on the Chief HR Manager of the bank and told him about his experiences and ideas. But the Chief HR Manager responded negatively. Mr. Raman tried his level best to convince the Chief HR Manager and similarly the Chief HR Manager also tried to persuade chairman about the nature of those techniques and the naure of the proposed development programme. At last Mr. Raman vexed with the behavior of the Chief HR Manager ordered him to use role playing and sensitivity training techniques.

Questions

1. Do you find any justification in the argument of Mr. Raman?
2. Why did Mr. Raman form such an opinion?
3. What do you feel about the suitability of technique for the executive development programme in this case?

REFERENCES

1. Jucius, M.J., "Personnel Management", Richard D.Irwin, Illinois, Homewood, 1973.
2. Yoder, Dale., "Personnel Management and industrial Relations", Prentice Hall of India, New Delhi, 1972.
3. Peter F. Drucker, "The Practice of Management", Harper and Brothers, New York, 1954.
4. Rudrabasavaraj M.N., "Personnel Administration Policies in India", V.M.N. Institue of Co-operative Management, Pune, 1969.
5. Robbins, Stephen P., "Personnel – The Mangement of Human Resources", Prentice Hall Inc., New Jersey, 1978.
6. Flippo Edvin B., "Principle of Management", 1976.
7. Subba, Rao, P., "Essentials of Human Resource Management and Industrial Recoliar", Himalaya Publishing House, Mumbai
8. V.S.P. Rao, "Human Resource Management", Excel Books, New Delhi, 2000.
9. Anjali Ghanekar, "Human Resource Management", Everest Publishing House, Pune, 2004.
10. C.B. Mamoria and S.V. Gankar, "Human Resource Management", Himalaya Publishing House, Mumbai, 2005.
11. Bernadin, J.H., "Human Resource Management: An Experimental Approach", Tata McGraw-Hill, New Delhi,
12. French, W., 1970, "The Personnel Management Process: Human Resources Administration", Houghton Mifflin Company, Boston.
13. Jyothi, P., "Training of Trainers: Material Composed for Training Programme", Institute of Public Enterprise, Hyderabad,
14. Rudrabasavaraj, N.M., 1969, "Personnel Administration Practice in India", Vaikunthalal Mehta Institute of Co-operative Management, Pune.
15. Peper, A., "Managing the Training and Development Function", Gower Publishing, Aldershott.

CHAPTER

10

Wage and Salary Administration

Introduction – Different Terms of Wage and Salary Administration – Factors Affecting Wage and Salary Administration – Wage Boards and Pay Commissions – Principles of Wage and Salary Administration – Wage incentives – Objectives of wag incentives – Types of Wage Incentive Schemes – Non-financial Incentives – Case Study – Exercise

Learning Objectives of this Chapter are:

- To know meaning and definitions of wage and salary
- To understand the difference between wage and salary terms.
- To study the factors affecting wage and salary administration
- To study wage boards and pay commission.
- To know the principles of wage and salary administration.
- To identify wage incentives.
- To understand the types of wages and incentives schemes.
- To study the financial and non-financial incentieves.

INTRODUCTION

One of the most important functions of human resource management is to provide equitable compensation to employees for their contributions. The factors affecting the determination of equitable compensation are many, varied and complex, and management has to arrive at some decision concerning the basic wage or salary. The strength of compensation management depends upon the amount of wage and salary paid to an employee for a fair day's work. Development of a sound wage and salary policies is a significant managerial function. Majority of the union-management conflicts are due to remuneration. The employee bargains for higher wages as it increases his financial status. On the other hand, management bargains for lower wages as it cuts the expenditure and thereby increases the profit. In view of this, wage and salary decisions and its administration are very important.

Compensation means different things to different people; it depends on a person's perspective. From employee's point of view, compensation may be considered as a return for their efforts or a reward for satisfactory or outstanding work. It may indicate the value the employer attaches to their skills and abilities – the return on their investment in education and training. In the case of most of the employees, their pay matters a lot in determining their socio-economic well-being. McBeath and Rands said that wage and salary administration is essentially the application of a systematic approach to the problem of ensuring that employees are paid in a logical, equitable and fair manner. Wage and salary are often used interchangeably. But they are two different terms.

Box 10:1

Definitions of Different Terms

We come across different terms relating to wage and salary administration. The definition of the terms are given below:

Wage: International Labour Organisation (ILO) defined wage as "the remuneration paid by the employer for the services of hourly, daily, weekly and fortnightly employees."

Salary: Salary can be defined as the remuneration paid to the clerical and managerial personnel employed on monthly or annual basis.

Earnings: Earnings are the total amount of remuneration received by an employee during a given period. These include salary (pay), dearness allowance, house rent allowance, city compensatory allowance, other allowances, overtime payments, etc.

Nominal wage: It is the wage paid or received in monetary terms. It is also known as money wage.

Dearness allowance: It is an allowance paid to the employees to enable them to face the growing dearness of essential commodities.

Fringe benefits: These represent supplemental forms of payments beyond stated wage or salary rates, either in money or financial rights, e.g. payment of bonus, profit-sharing, pension or insurance, etc., that form part of the organization's manpower costs. These refer to compensation given to employees, over and above wages, that often is not directly related to output, performance, or time worked.

Real wage: Real wage is the amount of wage arrived after discounting nominal wage by the living cost. It represents the purchasing power of money wage.

Take home salary: It is the amount of salary left to the employee after making authorized deductions like contribution to the provident fund, life insurance premium, income tax and other charges.

Minimum wage: It is the amount of remuneration which could meet the "normal needs of the average employee regarded as a human being living in a civilized society." It is defined as the amount or remuneration, "which may be sufficient to enable a worker to live in reasonable comfort, having regard to all obligations to which an average worker would ordinarily be subjected to."

Statutory minimum wage: It is the amount of remuneration fixed according to the provisions of the Minimum Wages Act, 1948.

Wage Structure: It signifies the relationship of wage rates for all the jobs within the organisation, industry or labour market area. Organisations may maintain two parallel wage/salary structures, one for hourly rated and the other for salaried employees. Job evaluation data is used for setting up wage/salary structures.

Wage Surveys: These are conducted within the industry or in the geographical locality and the information thus obtained helps in determining the wage-level of an organisation.

Wage Scale: It means putting together all properly evaluated standard wage rates arranged in sequence according to evaluation of the job and size of the rate.

OBJECTIVES OF WAGE AND SALARY ADMINISTRATION

Box 10:2

1. To acquire qualified competent personnel
2. To retain the present employees
3. To secure internal and external equity
4. To ensure desired behaviour
5. To keep labour and administrative costs
6. To protect in public as progressive employers
7. To pay according to the content and difficulty
8. To facilitate pay roll
9. To simplify collective bargaining
10. To promote organisation

FACTORS AFFECTING WAGE AND SALARY ADMINISTRATION

Box 10:3

- Remuneration in comparable industries
- Demand for and supply of labour
- Labour market condition
- Prevailing market rates
- Ability to pay
- Cost of living
- The living wage
- Labour productivity
- Bargaining power

- Attraction and retention of employees
- Goodwill of the organisation
- Government policy
- Job requirements
- Socio psychological factors.

WAGE BOARDS AND PAY COMMISSIONS

Wage policies are formulated by the following institutions in India. They are. (i) Collective Bargaining and Adjudication (ii) Wage Boards and (iii) Pay Commissions.

(i) Collective Bargaining and Adjudication: Collective bargaining is a procedure in which compromise is reached through balancing of opposed strengths. It is a means through which employee problems relating to various issues including wages are settled. If these problems are not settled through collective bargaining, they may be settled through voluntary arbitration or adjudication. The awards are given or reached by or through the arbitrator or adjudicator or collective bargaining agreements from the basis for fixing wages in various organisations.

(ii) Wage Boards: This is one of the important institution set up by the Government of India for fixation and revision of wages. Separate wage boards are set up for separate industries. Government of India started instituting Wage Boards in accordance with the recommendation of the Second Five Year Plan, which were reiterated by the Third Five Year Plan. Wage Boards are not governed by an legislation but are appointed on *ad-hoc* basis by the Government.

Each Wage Board consist of one neutral chairman, two independent members and two or three representatives of workers and management. The Wage Boards have to study various factors before making its recommendation. The recommendation of the Wage Board is first referred to the Government for its acceptance. The Government may accept with or without modification or reject the recommendation of the Wage Board. The recommendation accepted by the Government are enforceable by the parties concerned.

The Wages Boards take the following factors into consideration for fixing or revising the wages in various industries:

1. Job evaluation
2. Wage rates for similar jobs in comparable industries
3. Employee's productivity
4. Firm's ability to pay
5. Various wage legislations
6. Existing level of wage differentials and their desirability
7. Government's objectives regarding social justice, social equality, economic justice and economic quality
8. Place of industry in the economy and society of the country and the region
9. Need for incentives, improvement in productivity, etc.

The Wage Boards fix and revise various components of wages like basic pay, dearness allowance, incentive earnings, overtime pay, house rent allowance and all other allowances.

(iii) Pay Commissions: This is another institution which fixes and revises the wages and allowances to the employees working in government and government departments. Pay commissions are separately constituted by Central and State Governments. Central Governments so far have appointed five Pay Commissions as follows:

Box 10:4
The First Pay Commission appointed in 1946
The Second Pay Commission appointed in 1957
The Third Pay Commission appointed in 1970
The Fourth Pay Commission appointed in 1983
The Fifth Pay Commission appointed in 1996
The Sixth Pay Commission appointed 2006

PRINCIPLES OF WAGE AND SALARY ADMINISTRATION

Wage and Salary Administration should be guided by the following generally accepted principles:

1. Wage policies should be carefully developed keeping in view the interests of employers, employees, consumers and the community.
2. Wage policies should be clearly expressed in writing to ensure uniformity and stability.
3. Wage decisions should be checked against the carefully formed policies.
4. Wage policies should be evaluated from time to time to ensure their adequacy for current needs.
5. Job descriptions and performance ratings should be checked periodically to keep them up-to-date.
6. Differences in pay for jobs should be based upon variation in job requirements such as skill, effort, responsibility and working conditions.
7. Wage and salary levels should be matching with those that prevail in the labour market.
8. 'Equal pay for equal work' should be given for the same job regardless of any gender differences.
9. Adequate information about the procedure used to establish wage rates should be given to the employees and their unions.
10. The wage should be adequate to make certain that the worker and his family can get reasonable standard of living.
11. Clearly established procedure should exist for minimizing and reducing wage disputes.
12. Wage and salary structure should be flexible so that changing conditions can be easily met.

WAGE INCENTIVES

The term wage incentives has been used both in the restricted sense of participation and in the widest sense of financial motivation. It has been defined differently by different authors. They are as follows:

Box 10:5

According to Nickerson "it refers to all the plans that provide extra pay for extra performance in addition to regular wages for a job.

According to Florence: "it refers to increase willingness as distinguished from capacity. Incentives do not create but only aim to increase the national momentum towards productivity."

According to the National Commission Labour, "wage incentives are extra financial motivation. They are designed to stimulate human effort by rewarding the person over and above the time rated remuneration, for improvements in the present or targeted results."

OBJECTIVES OF WAGE INCENTIVES

Box 10:6

I. To improve the profit

II. To avoid additional capital investment for expansion

III. To increase the worker's earnings

IV. To use wage incentives as a useful tool for securing better utilization.

TYPES OF WAGE INCENTIVE SCHEMES

Box 10:7

1. Halsey Premium Plan
2. Rowan Premium Plan
3. The 100 per cent Premium Plan
4. The Bedeax Point Plan
5. Taylor's Differential Piece Rate Plan
6. Merric's Multiple Piece Rate Plan
7. Gantt Task Plan
8. Emerson Efficiency Plan
9. Co-partnership system
10. Accelerating Premium Systems.

1. Halsey Premium Plan: This is a time-saving bonus plan which is ordinarily used when accurate performance standards have not been established. Under this plan, it is optional for a workman to work on the premium plan or not. His day's wage is assured to him whether he earns a premium or not, provided that he is not so incompetent as to be useless. A standard output within a standard time is fixed on the basis of previous experience. The bonus is based on the amount of time saved by the worker. He is entitled to a bonus calculating on the basis of 33 1/3 per cent of the time saved. He thus gets wages on the time rate basis. If he does not complete the standard output within the stipulated time, he is paid on the basis of a time wage. The plan is a combination of the day wage and the piece wage is a modified form.

2. Rowan Premium Plan: This plan differs from the Halsey Plan only in regard to the determination of the bonus. In all other respects, the two are the same. In the Rowan Plan, the time saved is expressed as a percentage of the time allowed and the hourly rate of pay is increased by that percentage so that total earnings of the worker are the total number of hours multiplexed by the increased hourly wages. The plan aims at ensuring the permanence of the premium rate, which is often cut by the employer when the worker's efficiency increases beyond a certain limit. The premium is calculated on the basis of the proportion which the time saved bears to standard time.

3. The 100 Per Cent Premium Plan: Under this plan, task standards are set by time study or work sampling, and rates are expressed in time rates rather than in money. A definite hourly rate is paid for each task-hour of work performed. The plan is identical with the straight piece-rate except for its higher guranteed hourly rate and the use of task time as a unit of payment instead of a price per price. The worker is paid the full value of the time saved. If he completes the tasks of 10 hours in 8 hours and if the hourly rate is ₹ 0.50, his total earnings will be ₹8 × 0.50 + (10 – 8) × 0.50 = ₹ 4.00 + 100 = ₹ 5.00.

4. The Bedeaux Point Plan: This plan is used when carefully assessed performance standards have been established. It differs from the 100 percent plan, in that the basic unit of the time is the minute termed as B. Every job is expressed in terms of Bs (after Bedeaux), which means that a job should be completed in so many minutes. Suppose a worker earns 600 Bs in a day; if the rate per point is ₹ 0.01, his total earning would be:

₹ 4.80 × 0.01 + ¾(600 – 480) × 0.1

= ₹ 480 + ₹ 0.90 = ₹ 5.70.

The chief advantage of this plan is that is can be applied to any kind of job. It is particularly suitable for plants in which workers are assigned diverse kinds of jobs, shifted from one job or department to another. All the points which a worker earns in a day are recorded and the bonus is calculated on that basis.

5. Taylor's Differential Piece – Rate Plan: This system was introduced by Taylor with two objectives : first, to give the sufficient incentive to workmen to induce them to produce upto their full capacity; and second, to remove the fear of wage cut. There is one rate for those who reach the standard; they are given a higher rate to enable them to get the bonus. The other is the lower rate for those who are below the standard, so that the hope of receiving a higher rate (that is, a bonus) may serve as an incentive to come up to the standard. Workers are expected to do certain units of work within a certain period of time. This standard is determined on the basis of time and motion studies. Such scientific determination ensures that the standard fixed is not unduly high and is within the easy reach of the workers. On a proper determination of the standard depends the success of the scheme.

This system is designed to encourage the specially efficient worker with a higher rate of payment and to penalize the inefficient by a lower rate of payment. In practice, this plan is seldom used now.

6. Merrie's Multiple Piece Rate system: This system too is based on the principle of a low piece rate for a slow worker and a higher piece rate for higher production; but the plan differs from Taylor's plan, in that it offers three graded piece rate instead of two : (i) Upto, say 83% of standard output a piece-rate + 10% of time rate as bonus; (ii) Above 83% and upto 100% of standard output – same piece rate + 20% of time rate and (iii) Above 100% of standard output – same piece rate but no bonus.

Such a scheme is usually introduced in an organisation where the performance level is already high and management is aiming at 100% effieciency. Management has some discretion in distributing the 20% of time rate, over 17% of production above 83%.

7. The Gantt Task and Bonus Plan: This plan has been devised by H.L. Gantt and is the only one that pays a bonus percentage multiplied by the value of standard time. Under this system, fixed time rates are guaranteed. Output standards and time standards are established for the performance of each job. Workers completing the job within the standard time or in less time, receive wages for the standard time plus a bonus which ranges from 20 per cent to 50 per cent of the time allowed and not time saved. When a worker fails to turn out the required quantity of a product, he simply gets his time rate without any bonus.

Under this plan, there are also three stages of payment : (i) below the standard performance, only the minimum guaranteed wage is to be paid; (ii) at the standard performance, this wage + 20% of time – rate will be paid as a bonus and (iii) When the standard is exceeded, a higher piece rate is paid but there is no bonus.

8. Emerson Efficiency Plan: Under this system, a standard time is established for a standard task. The day wage is assured. There is no sudden rise in wages on achieving the standard of performance. The remuneration based on efficiency rises gradually. Efficiency is determined by the ratio between the standard time fixed for a performance and the time actually taken by a worker. Thus, if the period of 8 hours is the standard time for a task and if a worker performs it in 16 hours, his efficiency is 50 per cent. He who finishes the task in 8 hours has 100 per cent efficiency. No bonus is paid to a worker unless he attains 66 $^{2}/_{3}$ per cent efficiency, at which stage he receives a nominal bonus. This bonus goes on increasing till the time he achieves 100 per cent efficiency, the bonus comes to 20 per cent of the guranteed wages. At 120 per cent efficiency, a worker receives a bonus of 40 per cent and at 140 per cent efficiency the bonus is 60 per cent of the day wage.

9. Co–partnership System: This system tries to eliminate friction between capital and labour. Under this system, not only does a worker share in the profits of the undertaking but he also takes part in its control and, therefore, shares responsibilities. There are different degrees of this partnership and control allowed to the operatives in different cases; but in a complete co-partnership system, the following factors are present:

a. The payment of the existing standard wages of labour;
b. The payment of a fixed rate or interest on capital;
c. The division of the surplus profit between capital and labour in an agreed proportion;
d. The payment for a part of the worker's labour by the allotment of a share in the capital;
e. The sharing in the control of the business by the representatives of labour.

10. Accelerating Premium Systems: There are the systems which provide for a guaranteed minimum wage for output below standard.

For low and average increases in output above the standard, small increment in earnings are allowed. Increasingly, large earnings are conceded for above average output, the increment being different for each 1% increase in output. Very significant increases in earnings are given for really high output.

In this system, the production is pushed up higher and higher by discouraging low output and rewarding at an increasingly effective rate of higher outputs.

Such schemes are generally adopted when much higher outputs than what are currently obtained are to be achieved.

NON-FINANCIAL INCENTIVES

Main task of human resource manager is to motivate the employees to contribute their best towards accomplishment of work. Generally, employees produce only 60-70% of their capacity to work but if given some inducement, or additional attraction, they work more. Incentives and work results have direct positive correlation with each other. While financial incentives play an important role in motivating employees, many factors unrelated to money can also serve as encouragers of action. It is a well established fact now that an individual does not work for money alone. He requires certain non-financial incentives also which satisfy his social, psychological and personal growth needs. Many people choose to work when the work is made more pleasant and enjoyable. This is a non-financial incentive. Non-financial incentives can be divided into personal as well as group incentives. They are as follows:

Box 10:8

Personal Incentives	Group Incentives
1. Status of an employee	1. Social importance
2. Responsibility and challenges	2. Team spirit
3. Pleasant and interesting work	3. Health competition
4. Recognition of work	4. Leadership
5. Job security of an employee	5. High morale
6. Pride in the job	6. Open and honest communication

CASE STUDY ON PAY SCALE

Mr. C.S Sharma joined the Indian Institute of Technology in 2000 – a premier educational institution in the country imparting higher level education in technology. His job demands higher level and latest knowledge, higher level teaching skill, and other skills in introducing and practicing different teaching methods and bringing co-ordination between the institute and industry. The Institute implemented the pay scales in 1996, recommended by the University Grants Commission which were at par with the pay scales of teachers in Universities and Colleges. The demands of the jobs in Universities and Colleges are quite at low compared to those of the Institute.

The pay of Mr. Sharma has been fixed at that level of Mr. Singh who joined the institute in 2004 as the University Grants Commission, did not recommend any weightage for the teachers who put up less than five years experience. Mr. Sharma was quite unhappy over the parity of salary of the teachers of the Institute with those of University teachers and college teachers on the one hand and equalising his pay with his junior Mr. Singh on the other hand.

The institute again revised the pay scale of the teachers in 2006, based on the pay scales recommended by the University Grants Commission in 2006. University Grants Commission again maintained parity in pay scales of Institute teachers, University teachers and College teachers. The pay scale of Mr. Sharma was revised and it was fixed at ₹ 29,400 which was equal to the pay of Mr. Singh, Mr. Kulkarni who joined the Institute in 2006 and Mr. Prasad who joined the Institute in 2007.

Mr. Sharma rushed to the chambers of the Director of the Indian Institute of Technology on 20th July, 2007 and told him he was quiting the job in the Institute and he was going to join Degree College, at Rajahmundry. He further said that he was going to get the same salary in a small town. The Director was shocked after listening to Mr. Sharma.

Questions

1. Do you justify the decision made by Mr. Sharma?
2. Do you suggest any measures to stop Mr. Sharma from quiting the job?
3. Do you think?
4. At there is something wrong with the Institute pay practices and the University Grants Commission's recommendations? If yes, what are they? How do you rectify?

WHICH IS A COMPARABLE INDUSTRY

A financial institution has just decided to open a Branch at Bhimunipatnam, an exclusive resort located about 20 miles from Waltair, a large city. There is no bank at present in Bhimunipatnam.

The financial institution is anxious to determine the appropriate wage for the clerical staff it expects to hire. Clerks in the city office at Waltair receive a starting wage of ` 1,000 per month. As a matter of company policy, these wage rates have been set at mid-point of the range for financial institutions in Waltair.

A survey at local business at Bhimunipatnam indicates that the 'going rate' for qualified clerical personnel varies between ₹ 1,200- ₹ 1,400 a month. This higher rate in Bhimunipatnam be attributed, in part, to the substantially higher cost of living in this resort town, the limited number of young people seeking employment and the fact that there are no other financial institutions in Bhimunipatnam. Banks in Waltair have traditionally paid lower wages than other businesses, on the ground that banks offer better working conditions and higher prestige.

Questions

1. What amount, the financial institution should fix as its hiring rate for clerical personnel? What factors should be considered in making the decision?

CHAPTER

11

Performance Appraisal

Performance Appraisal – Meaning – Definitions- Importance- Objectives – Techniques of Performance Appraisal – Quality of Work life –Definition of Quality of work life – Dimensions of Quality of Work life - Qualities Circles –Definition and Objectives of Quality Circles – Case Study – Exercise.

Learning Objectives of this Chapter are:

- To know meaning and definitions of performance appraisal.
- To study the importance of performance appraisal.
- To identify the objectives of performance appraisal.
- To analyse the techniques/methods of performance appraisal.
- To know the definitions and concept of quality of work life.
- To explain the definition and objective of quality circles.

INTRODUCTION

Once the employee has been selected, trained and motivated, he is then appraised for his performance. Performance appraisal is the step where the management finds out how effective it has been at hiring and placing employees. If any problems are identified, steps are taken to communicate with the employee and to remedy them. Performance appraisal is a process of evaluating the behaviour of an employee in doing a particular job in the organisation. It is a continuous process in every organisation to know the behaviour of an employee while doing his/her job. Performance is the evaluation of present performance and future capabilities of an employee or a group of employees. It is regarded as the process of estimating or judging the value, excellence, qualities or status of some object, or person. It is a part of all the other staffing process, namely, recruitment, selection and placement. Employee assessment should not be confirmed to past performance alone. Potentials of the employee for future performance must also be observed.

DEFINITION OF PERFORMANCE APPRAISAL

According to Flippo, "Performance appraisal is the systematic, periodic and an impartial rating of an employee's excellence in matters pertaining to his present job and his potential for a better job."

It can be defined as, " Performance appraisal is a method of evaluating the behaviour of an employee in doing a particular job in the organisation, both qualitative and quantitative aspect of the job of an employee."

IMPORTANCE OF PERFORMANCE APPRAISAL

Performance appraisal has been considered as a most significant and indispensable tool for an organisation, for the information it provides is highly useful in making decisions regarding various personal aspects such as promotions and merit increases. Performance measures also link information gathering and decision-making process which provides a basis for judging the effectiveness of personnel sub-divisions such as recruiting, selection, training and compensation. Accurate information play a vital role in the organisation as a whole. They help to pinpoint weak areas in the primary systems.

Performance appraisal has been considered as a most significant and indispensable tool for an organisation, for the information it provides is highly useful in making decisions regarding various personnel aspects. It can be put to several uses concerning the entire spectrum of human resource management function. Broadly, performance appraisal serves four purposes of objectives, namely, (1) Developmental uses, (2) Administrative uses for decision (3) Organisational maintenance, and (4) Documentation purposes. The importance or uses of performance appraisal are given below:

Objectives of performance appraisal: The main objectives of performance appraisal are as follows:

1. To assess the worth of employees in relation to job requirements.
2. To provide a valid data base for personnel decision concerning placements, play, promotion, transfer and punishment.
3. To assess the good and bad points in working of employees and then making suggestions for improvement.
4. To test the effectiveness of recruitment, selection, placement and induction programmes.
5. To evaluate skill and training capabilities of employees and helping in planning suitable training and development programmes.
6. To know the problems faced by employees while doing various jobs.
7. To provide a basis for comparison to segregate efficient and inefficient employees.
8. To help management in fixing employees according to their capacity, interest, aptitude and qualifications.
9. To help supervisors to know their subordinates more closely for increasing their efficiency. To facilitate research in human resource management.

What is to be Appraised?

Every organisation has to decide upon the content to be appraised before the programme is approved. Generally, the content to be appraised is determined on the basis of job analysis. The content to be appraised may be in the form of contribution to organizational objectives (measures) like production, saving in terms of cost, return on capital, etc. Other measures are based on: (1) behaviours which measure observable physical actions, movements, (2) Objectives which measure job related results like amount of deposits mobilized, and (3) traits which are measured in terms of personal characteristics are observable in employee's job activities. The content to be appraised may vary with the purpose of appraisal and type and level of employees. The appraisal factors used in some leading Indian industries are shown in the table below.

Indian Tabacco Company	*A.C.C. Ltd*	*I.O.C. Ltd*	*Sandoz (India) Ltd.*	*Union Carbide of India Ltd.*
1. Ability to plan delegate, control and co-ordinate	1. Ability to take decision	1. Job knowledge	1. Quantity of work	1. Job Knowledge
2. Knowledge of job	2. Leadership	2. Quality and dependability	2. Availability of work	2. Work output
3. Clarity about objectives	3. Organising ability	3. Quantity of work	3. Ability to learn	3. Drive
4. Cost consciousness and result	4. Understanding and conformity with policy	4. Planning, organizing and controlling	4. Knowledge of work	4. Ability to handle people
5. Power of expression, written and verbal	5. Judgement	5. Developing people	5. Initiative	5. Judgement
6. Decision making	6. Employee relationship	6. Cost consciousness	6. Dependability	6. Ability to communicate
7. Comprehension	7. Delegation	7. Intelligence and decision-making	7. Personality	7. Creativity
8. Use of discretion and judgement	8. Ability to communicate	8. Leadership	8. Tidiness	8. Organising ability
9. Resourcefulness and industry	9. Sociability	9. Initiative and original thinking	9. Attendance	
10. Co-operation	10. Ability to run meetings.	10. Attitude and co-operation		
11. Manner and general bearing	11. Knowledge and execution of responsibilities	11. Integrity		
12. Dealings and relations with seniors & juniors	12. Attitude to work			
13. Leadership	13. Loyalty			
14. Courage to disagree & to reason tactfully	14. Initiative			

CONTENTS TO BE APPRAISED FOR AN OFFICER'S JOB

1. Regularity of Attendance
2. Self Expression: Written and Oral
3. Ability to Work with Others
4. Leadership Styles and Abilities
5. Initiative
6. Technical Skill
7. Technical Ability/Knowledge
8. Ability to Grasp New Things
9. Ability to Reason
10. Originality and Resourcefulness
11. Creative Skills
12. Area of Interest
13. Area of Suitability
14. Judgement Skills
15. Integrity
16. Capability for Assuming Responsibility
17. Level of Acceptance by Subordinates
18. Honesty and Sincerity
19. Thoroughness in Job and Organisational Knowledge
20. Knowledge of Systems and Procedures
21. Quality of Suggestion Offered for Improvement.

ESSENTIAL ELEMENTS OF AN AFFECTIVE PERFORMANCE APPRAISAL:

1. Mutual Understanding
2. Clear Objectives
3. Standardisation
4. Training
5. Job-relatedness
6. Documentation
7. Feedback and participation
8. Individual differences
9. Post-appraisal interview
10. Review and appeal

METHODS OF PERFORMANCE APPRAISAL

Performance appraisal methods are classified broadly into two types: They are as follows:

1. Traditional Methods
2. Modern Methods

Traditional Methods	*Modern Methods*
1. Graphic Rating Scales	1. Assessing Centre
2. Ranking Method	2. Human Resource Accounting
3. Paired Comparison Method	3. Appraisal by Results
4. Forced Distribution Method	4. Psychological Appraisal
5. Checklist Methods	5. Behaviorally Anchored Rating Scales
6. Free Form Appraisal	6. 360° Appraisal Method
7. Group Appraisal	
8. Confidential Reports	
9. Critical Incident Method	
10. Field review method	

TRADITIONAL METHODS

Traditional methods of performance appraisal can be presented as follows:

Graphic Rating Scales: This method is the oldest and widely used method. This method is also known as "linear rating scale" or "simple rating scale". In this method, a printed appraisal form is used for each employee to be rated. The form contains several characteristics relating to the personality and performance of employees. Intelligence, quality of work, leadership skills, judgement, etc., are some of these characteristics. The rater records his judgement on the employee's trait on the scale. The numerical points given to an employee are added up to find out his overall performance standing in the group. The numerical points added up may be expressed by numbers as 5,4,3,2 and 1. These numbers can also be expressed in terms of descriptions like excellent, very good, average, poor and very poor, good or bad and so on. The rating scale method is widely used as it is easy to understand and use. It allows a statistical tabulation of scores and a ready comparison of scores among the employees is possible. It is economical to design and administer rating scales. The approach is multi-dimensional as several significant dimensions of the job can be considered in evaluation. But there are some defects in this method. They are:

I. The rating is generally arbitrary and subjective because specific job related performance criteria are not considered.

II. It is assumed that each trait is equally important for all jobs.

III. This method imposes a heavy burden on the rater.

IV. The descriptive words often used in such scales may have different meanings to different raters.

Ranking Method

This is method is also called as "Order of Merit Method". Under this method, the employees are ranked from best to worst on some characteristics. The rater first finds the employee with the highest performance and the employees with the lowest performance in that particular job category and rates the former as the best and the latter as the poorest. Then the rater selects the next highest and next lowest and so on until he rates all the employees in that group. Consider all of your 20 employees in terms of their total performance. Then select the one you would consider as having the best total performance. Put his name in Column I below, on the first line, numbered (1) Next pick out the person having the worst total performance, put his name at the bottom of Column II, on the line numbered 20. Now from the remaining names, select the one having the best total performance. Put his name in the first column on line. (2) Keep up this process until all names have been placed on the scale. The relative position of an employee is reflected in his numerical rank. For example, if Six employees A,B,C,D,E and F are to be ranked, the ranking may be as follows:

Employee	Rank	Employee	Rank
A	6	D	2
B	1	E	4
C	5	F	3

Paired Comparison Method: This method is a modified form of man to man ranking. In this method, each employee is compared with all the others in pairs, one at a time. Usually only one trait, overall suitability to perform the job, is considered. The rater or evaluator is provided with a bunch of slips, each containing a pair of names. The rater puts a tick mark against the person whom he considered the better of the two and final ranking is determined by the number of times that person is judged better than others.

Forced Distribution Method

The rater may rate his employees at the higher or at the lower end of the scale under the earlier methods. Forced distribution method is developed to prevent the raters from rating too high or too low. Under this method, the rater after assigning the points to the performance of each employee has to distribute his ratings in a pattern to conform to normal frequency distribution. Thus, similar to the ranking technique, forced distribution requires the raters (supervisor) to spread their employee evaluations in a prescribed distribution.

Checklist Methods

The checklist is a simple rating technique in which the supervisor is given a list of statements or words and asked to check statements representing the characteristics and performance of each employee. There are three types of checklist methods, *viz.* simple checklist, weighted checklist and forced choice method.

Free Form Appraisal

This method requires the manager to write a short essay describing each employee's performance during the rating period. This format emphasizes evaluation of overall performance, based on strengths/weaknesses of employee performance rather than specific job dimensions. By asking supervisors to enumerate specific examples of employee behaviour, the essay technique minimize supervisory bias and the halo effect. The time involved in writing separate essays about each employee can be formidable. Essays are not amenable for evaluation and analysis; fifty essays describing different employee's performance cannot be tied to merit increases and promotion possibilities because there is no common standard.

Group Appraisal Method: Under this method, a group of evaluators assesses employees. This group consists of the immediate supervisor of the employee, other supervisor having close contact with the employee's work, head of the department and personnel expert. This group determines the standards of performance for the job, measures actual performance of an employee, analyses the causes of poor performance and offer suggestion for improvement in future. The advantage of this method is that it is simple, yet more thorough. Due to multiple evaluators personal bias is minimized. But it is a very time consuming process. This method is widely used for purposes of promotion, demotion and retrenchment appraisal.

Confidential Reports: Assessing the employees performance confidentially is a traditional method of performance appraisal. Under this method, superior appraises the performance of his subordinates based on his observation, judgements and intuitions. The superior keeps his judgement and report confidentially. In other words, the superior does not allow the employee to know the report and his performance. Superior writes the report about his subordinate's strengths, weaknesses, intelligence, attitude of work, sincerity, commitment, punctuality, attendance, conduct, character, friendliness, etc. Though confidential report is a traditional method, most of the public sector organisations still follow this method in appraising employee's performance. But this method suffers from some limitations.

This method involves a lot of subjectivity because appraisal is based on impressions rather than on data. No feedback is provided to the employees being appraised and therefore, its credibility is very low. This method focuses on evaluating rather than developing the employee. In recent years, a negative confidential report is required to be communicated to the employee. If the employee disagrees, a noting to that effect has to be made in the report. This has been made necessary by trade unions and courts. The traditional methods discussed above all focus more on the traits of an employee than on his job performance. These methods are based on judgement role of the supervisor.

Critical Incidents Methods: In this method, the supervisor keeps a written record of critical events, either good or bad, and how different employees behaved during such events. The ratings of an employee depends on his positive or negative behaviours during these events. These critical incidents are identified after thorough study of the job and discussion with the staff. For example, a fire, a sudden breakdown of machinery, a serious accident, etc., may be identified as critical incidents for the working of a factory. Critical incidents method helps to avoid vague impressions and general remarks as the rating is based on actual records of behaviour or performance. The feedback from actual events can be discussed with the employee to allow improvements. The rater can fully defend his ratings on the basis of his records.

Field Review Method: In this method, a trained officer from the human resource department interviews line supervisor to evaluate their respective subordinates. The interviewer prepares in advance the questions to be asked. By answering these questions, a supervisor gives his opinions about the level of performance of his subordinate, the subordinate's work progress, his strengths and weaknesses, promotion potential, etc. The evaluator takes detailed notes of the answers which are then approved by the concerned supervisor. These are then placed in employee's personal service file. This system relieves the supervisor of the need for filling in appraisal forms. The supervisor's personal bias is reduced due to the active involvement of the evaluator. The ratings are usually classified into three categories, namely, outstanding, satisfactory and unsatisfactory. This method is, however, a time–consuming method. The success of this method depends upon the competence and sincerity of the interview.

MODERN METHODS

The Modern Methods of performance appraisal can be presented as follows.

Assessment Centre Method: This method of appraising was first applied in German Army in 1930. Later, business and industrial houses started using this method. This is not a technique of performance appraisal by itself. In fact, it is a system or organisation, where assessment of several individuals is done by various experts by using various techniques.

In this approach, individuals from various departments who are brought together spend two or three days on an assignment similar to the one they would be handling when promoted. Observers rank the performance of each and every participant in order of merit. They use simulation techniques like role – playing, business games and in – basket exercises. The observers or evaluators observe and evaluate employees as they perform jobs. Assessments are done generally to determine employee potential for promotion. Since assessment centres are basically meant for evaluating the potential of candidates to be considered for promotion, training or development, they offer an excellent means for conducting evaluation process in an objective way. All assesses get an equal opportunity to show their talents and capabilities and secure promotion based on merit. The evaluators prepare a summary report and feedback is administered on a face-to-face basis to the employees who ask for it. An assessment centre generally measures interpersonal skills, communicating ability to plan and organize, etc. Personal interview and projective tests are used to assess work motivation, career, orientation and dependence on others. Paper and pencil test are used to measure intellectual capacity.

Human Resource Accounting Method: Human resources are a valuable asset of any organisation. This asset can be valued in terms of money. When competent and well-trained employees leave an organisation, the human asset is decreased and *vice versa*. Under this method, performance is judged in terms of costs and contribution of employees. Costs of human resources consist of expenditure on human resource planning, recruitment, selection, induction, training, compensation etc. Contribution of human resources is the money value of labour productivity or value added by human resources. Difference between cost and contribution will reflect the performance of employees. This technique has not developed and still it is in the transitionary stage. Therefore, it is not popular at present.

Appraisal by Results: This is also called as MBO. The concept of "management by objectives" was developed by Peter Drucker in 1954. It was described only recently as the "large range" in performance appraisal. MBO is a process whereby the superior and subordinate managers of an organisation jointly identify its common goals, define each individual's major areas of responsibilities in terms of results expected to him, and use these measures or guides for operating the units and assessing the contribution of its members. Thus, MBO focuses attention on participatively set goals that are tangible, verified and measurable. The emphasis is on what must be accomplished.

Psychological Appraisal

Psychological appraisals are conducted to assess the employee potential. They consist of (a) in-depth interviews, (b) psychological tests (c) consultation and discussions with the employee, (d) discussions with the superiors, subordinates and peers, and (e) review of other evaluations.

Evaluation is conducted in the areas of : (a) employee's intellectual abilities (b) emotional stability (c) motivational responses, (d) reasoning and analytical abilities, (e) sociability (f) interpretation and judgement skills, and (g) ability to foresee the future. The psychological results are useful for decision–making about employee placement, career planning and development, and training and development.

Behaviourally Anchored Rating Scales (BARS): This method combines graphic rating scales with critical incidents method. Bars are descriptions of various degrees of behaviour relating to specific performance dimensions. Critical areas of job performance and the most effective behaviour for getting results are determined in advance. The rater records the observable job behaviour of an employee and compares these observations with BARS. In this way an employee's, actual job behaviour is judged against the desired behaviour.

360° Degree Appraisal : This technique has been introduced very recently to appraise the employee performance by different appraisers. When appraisal is made by superiors, peers, subordinates, customers, consultants and self appraisal. It is called the "360- degree system of appraisal". In the 360–degree method, besides assessing performance, other attributes of the assessee, such as talents, behaviour, values, ethical standards, tempers and loyalty are also appraised. Thus, 360 – degree system involves evaluation of a manager by everyone above, alongside and below him. The 360–degree performance appraisal has six integral components: They are as follows:

1. Appraisal by superiors
2. Appraisal by peers
3. Appraisal by subordinates
4. Appraisal by customers
5. Appraisal by consultants
6. Appraisal by self

ETHICS OF PERFORMANCE APPRAISALS

Marion S. Kellog suggests the following ten points as ethics of appraisals:

1. Don't appraise without knowing why the appraisal is needed.
2. Appraise on the basis of representative information.
3. Appraise on the basis of sufficient information.
4. Appraise on the basis of relevant information.
5. Be honest in your assessment of all the facts you obtain.
6. Don't write one thing and say another.
7. In offering an appraisal, make it plain that this is only your personal opinion of the facts as you see them.
8. Pass along appraisal information only to those who have good reasons to know it.
9. Don't imply the existence of an appraisal that hasn't been made.
10. Don't accept another's appraisal without knowing the basis on which it was made.

QUALITY OF WORK LIFE

Human Resource Development techniques include human resource planning, training and development, career planning and development, performance appraisal, potential appraisal, organizational change and development, human relations , Quality circles and quality of work life. Quality of work life deals with various aspects of working conditions and environment. It provides the human resource development efficiently therefore quality of work life helps for development of human resources. Quality of work life motivates the employee to learn future new roles of an employee job. The term quality of work life has appeared in research journals and the press in USA only in 1970s.

DIMENSIONS OF QUALITY OF WORK LIFE

J. Richard and J. Loy define QWL as "the degree to which members of a work organisation are able to satisfy important personnel needs through their experience in the organisation."

Richard E. Walton explains quality of worklife in terms of eight broad dimensions of employment that constitute desirable quality of worklife. He proposed the same criteria for measuring QWL. They can be presented as follows:

1. Adequate and Fair Compensation
2. Safety and Healthy Working Conditions
3. Opportunity to Use and Develop Human Capacities
4. Opportunity for Career Growh
5. Social Integration in the Work Force
6. Constitutionalism in the Work Organisation
7. Work and Quality of Life
8. Social Relevance of Work.

Factors Involved in Quality of Work Life

There are number of factors involved in quality of work life. These factors can be grouped into three categories (a) individual factors, (b) job factors, and (c) organisational factors. In improving QWL all these factors have to be taken into account. The various factors involved in QWL are given below:

1. Flexibility in work schedules
2. Autonomous work group
3. Job enrichment
4. Opportunity for growth
5. Participation
6. Communication

Principles of Quality of Work Life

Quality of work life means the relationship between employees and their total working conditions. QWL affects job involvement, sense of competence, job satisfaction and job performance. The following are the basic principles of quality of work life:

1. The Principle of security
2. The principle of equity
3. The principle of individualism
4. The principle of democracy

Measurement Techniques of Quality of Work Life

The techniques to measure the quality of work life can be presented as follows:

1. Job Involvement
2. Job satisfaction
3. Sense of competence
4. Job performance
5. Productivity

Techniques for Improving the Quality of Work Life

The quality of work life movement is of recent origin and has a long way to go. Individuals as well as organized efforts are required to improve the quality of work life for millions in the country. Some of the techniques used to improve QWL are given below:

1. Job redesign
2. Career development
3. Autonomous work groups
4. Flexible work schedules
5. Participative management
6. Job security and Fair treatment

Responsibilities of Different Parties Concerned with Quality of Work Life

National productivity council has organized a national seminar on quality of work life in 1981. The seminar made several suggestions and recommendations to improve the quality of work life. They have strongly pointed out the responsibilities of members in improving the qualities of work life. The importance parties in improving qualities of work life are as follows:

1. Responsibilities of Employees
2. Responsibilities of Unions and Workers
3. Responsibilities of Professional organisations
4. Responsibilities of Government.

QUALITY CIRCLES

In today's LPGS (Liberalization, Privatization, Globalization and Stabilization) economy, Education of workers and their constructive participation in the management has become an important aspect in human resource management. Willing participation of workers exactly enhances the production level of workers and induces motivational spirit among them. Workers participation indicates Industrial Democracy, which in turn assures team building and thus co-operation of all parties involved in the organization. The changing economic policies and changing trends in human resource management have given rise to positive and constrictive way of co-operation from workers for better performance of organisation than the negative approach and punishment. One of the most effective form of worker participation is Quality Circles. The concept of Quality Circles was initiated for the first time by a Japanese professor, Dr. Kaoru Ishikawa of Muushashi Institute of Technology, Tokyo, in 1961. Later, the scope and coverage of Quality Circles has tremendously increased.

Quality Circle is formation of small group of employees in the same organisation with similar interests and work objectives. These circles are mainly formed to solve work related as well other worker related problems. The basic idea is to make use of available brainpower of employees by tapping them for solving problems. One important feature of QCs is that it is voluntary in nature. There should not be any influence or pressure from any quarter to form into Quality Circles. But the management can educate them and motivate them towards formation of such groups. For successful implementation of quality circles, important key factors have to be remembered.

Definition of Quality Circles

Quality circles are a small group of employees in a small work area or otherwise doing similar kind of work, who voluntarily meet regularly every week, for identifying, analyzing, and resolving work-related problems. More importantly, they look at imperative issues such as quality improvement and organizational performance. The employees come together voluntarily to form associations to contribute to the organisation.

Objectives of Quality Circles

1. To utilize the human resources effectively
2. To improve the quality of products and services and to reduce the cost of production.
3. To motivate the employees among the various groups working in the organisation.
4. To satisfy the psychological needs of the employees.
5. To develop the leadership skills and human relations skills.
6. To develop problem solving skills and innovative techniques for effective utilization of human resources.
7. To develop the supervisory skills of various employees.
8. To improve the co-ordination and co-operation among the working groups.

Principles of Quality Circles

1. Principle of motivation
2. Principle of Co-operation and Co-ordination
3. Principle of Morale and Job Satisfaction

4. Principle of Human Relations
5. Principle of Productivity
6. Principle of Quality of product and services
7. Principle of Effective utilization of Human resources
8. Principle of Innovative and creative thinking.

Key Factors of Quality Circles:

1. Support and commitment of the management. Though Quality Circles are basically voluntary in nature, top management support and commitment throughout is very important. To start with, the management has to educate the employees regarding the nature and significance of QCs and encourage them to form into circles. It is common that the managements initiate such programmes with great enthusiasm and loses steam as soon as it started. As such, the management has to take care to see that not only QCs are formed but also they are continued for longer times.

2. Education and training. The most important factor for the success of QCs lies in the commitment of its members. The members are fully committed, only when they understand the true nature and significance of the circles. The management has to therefore take care to see that the employees are properly educated and trained to understand the nature and functioning of the circle. Especially, the grass root level workers need particular concentration because QCs start at grass root levels of the organisation.

3. People building philosophy. QC mainly stands on the building up philosophy. The main strength of QC is its people. Through QC, organisations sought to build up people. Problems are solved through co-ordinated, concerted efforts of its people. This would enhance the feeling of togetherness and develop interpersonal relation among employees.

4. Voluntary participation. Another important factor is voluntary participation. The management has to educate employees, encourage them and support them by providing various facilities. But their role ends there. Once circle is formed it is the individual employee who has to decide whether to join such Circle or not. They cannot be forced to become members.

5. Team work through small group working. Quality Circles encourages formation of small groups, Starting from grass root levels, employees in different departments or work areas form into groups and try to solve problems which may arise in the course of their work. Because of their familiarity with such problems and knowledge about the particular area it is expected that they can solve problems with greater efficiency and speed. This in turn also encourages group work, which is mostly becoming extinct in today's work organisation.

6. Problem solving at grass root level. The main aim of QCs is to provide chance to even employees at lowest levels with an opportunity to solve their problems. Given a chance they prove to be efficient problem shooters. For this, complete commitment on part of the employees is needed. This can be achieved by eliminating any misconception that they may have regarding the nature and philosophy of Quality Circles. Educating and training them regarding these issues may be helpful in this direction.

EXERCISE

Exercise on Problem Solving and Judgement Skills

Part 1: Connect the following nine dots without lifting your pen or pencil by using 4 straight lines on a sheet of your own paper or board.

Part 2: Connect the following sixteen dots without lifting a pen or pencil by using six straight lines on a sheet of your own paper or board.

Part 3: Identify the maximum triangles in the following figure. Triangles must be exceeded to Thirty -five. Highest Scorers are winners.

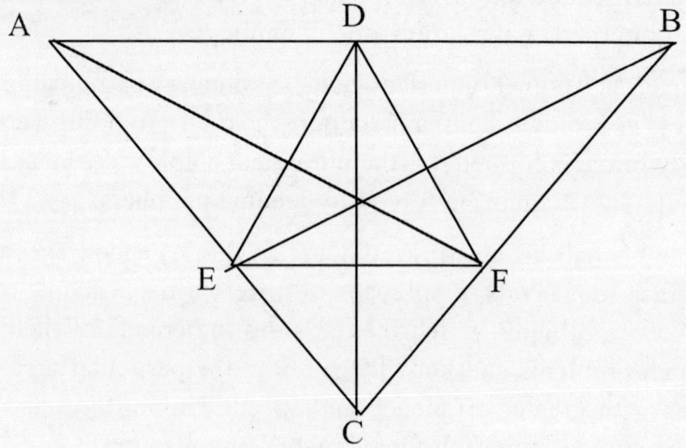

Part 4: Participants are provided with a visual drawing of a large square, divided as shown below. They are then directed to quickly count the total number of squares seen, and report that number orally. Correct answer is 30.

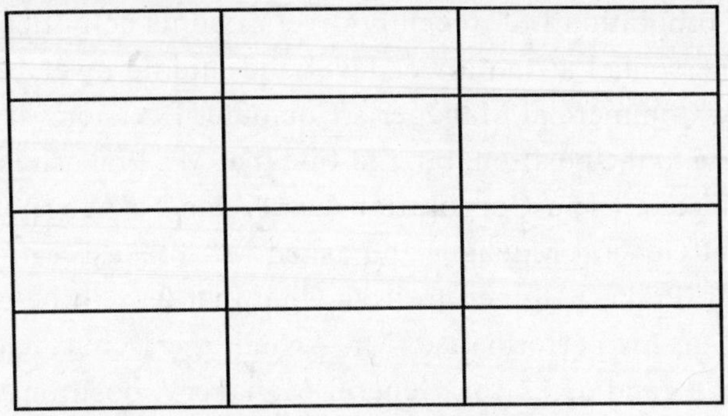

For answer key and more detail contact at: email: dracmohan_mannava@yahoo.com

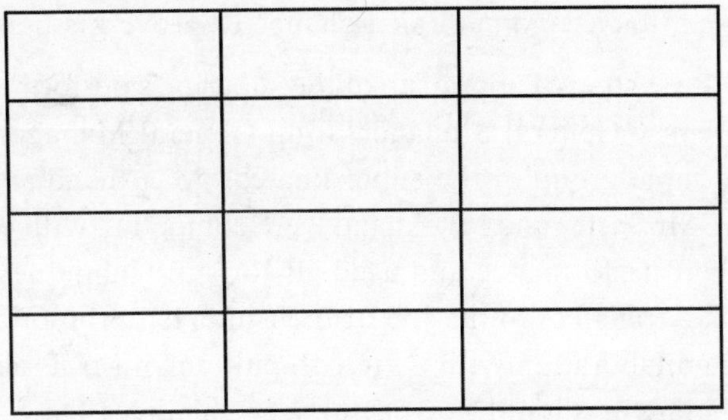

CASE STUDY

1. Politics and Performance Appraisal

Kalyani Electronic Corporation Ltd, recently diversified its activities and started producing computers. It employed personnel at the lower level and middle level. It has received several applications for the post of Commercial Manager – Computer Division. It could not decide upon the stability of the candidate to the position, but did find that Mr. Prakash is more qualified for the position than other candidates. The Corporation has created a new post below the cadre of General Manager i.e., joint General Manager and asked Mr. Prakash to join the Corporation as Joint General Manager. Mr. Prakash agreed to it viewing that he will be considered for General Manager's position based on his performance. Mr. Anand, the Deputy General Manager of the Corporation and one of the candidates for General Manager's position was annoyed with the management's practice. But, he wanted to show his performance record to the management at the next appraisal meeting. The management of the Corporation asked Mr Sastry, General Manager of Television's Division to be the General Manager in-charge of Compute Division for sometime, until a new General Manager is appointed. Mr.Sastry wanted to switch over to Computer Division in view of the prospects, prestige and recognition of the position among the top management of the Corporation. He viewed this assignment as a chance to prove his performance.

The Corporation has the system of appraisal of the superior's performance by the subordinate. The performance of the Deputy General Manager, Joint General Manager and General Manager has to be appraised by the same group of the subordinates. Mr. Anand and Mr. Sastry system as well as its *modus operandi*. Mr Sastry and Mr. Anand were competing with each other in convincing their subordinates about their performance and used all sorts of techniques for pleasing them like promising them a wage hike, transfers to the job of their interest, promotion etc. However, these two officers functioned in collaboration with a view to pull down Mr. Prakash. They openly told their subordinates that a stranger should not occupy the 'chair'. They created several groups among employees like pro – Anand's group, pro – Sastry's group, Anti – Prakash and Sastry group, Anti – Anand and Prakash group.

Mr. Prakash has been watching the proceedings calmly and keeping the top management in touch will all these developments. However, Mr. Prakash has been quite work–conscious and top management found his performance under such a political atmosphere to be satisfactory. Prakash's pleasing manners and way of maintaining human relations with different levels of employees did, however, prevent the emergence of an anti – Prakash wave in the company. But in view of the political atmosphere within the company, there is no strong pro – Prakash's group either.

Management administered the performance appraisal technique and the subordinates appraised the performance of all these three managers. In the end, surprisingly, the workers assigned the following overall scores. Prakash: 560 points, Sastry: 420 points, and Anand: 260 points.

Questions

1. How do you evaluate the worker's appraisal in this case?
2. Do you suggest any technique to avert politics creeping into the process of performance appraisal by subordinates? Or do you suggest the measure of dispensing with such appraisal systems?

2. MACHINIST'S INDISCIPLINED BEHAVIOUR

Dinesh, a machine operator, worked as a machinist for Ganesh, the supervisor. Ganesh told Dinesh to pick up some trash that had fallen from Dinesh's work area, and Dinesh replied, "I won't do the janitor's work".

Ganesh replied, " when you drop it, you pick it up". Dinesh became angry and abusive, calling Ganesh a number of names in a loud voice and refusing to pick up the trash. All employees in the department heard Dinesh' comments.

Ganesh had been trying for two weeks to get his employees to pick up trash in order to have cleaner workplace and prevent accidents. He talked to all employees in a weekly departmental meeting and to each employee individually at least once. He stated that he was following the instruction of the general manager. The only objection came from Dinesh.

Dinesh has been with the company for five years, and in this department for six months. Ganesh had spoken to him twice about excessive alcoholism but otherwise his record was good. He was known to have quick temper.

The outburst by Dinesh hurt Ganesh badly. Ganesh told Dinesh to come to the office and suspended him for one day for insubordination and abusive language to a supervisor. The discipline was within company policy, and similar behaviours had been punished in other departments.

After Dinesh left Ganesh's office, Ganesh phoned the HR manager, reported what he had done, and said that he was sending a copy of the suspension order for Dinesh's file.

EXPERIENTIAL LEARNING ON SELF APPRAISAL

This exercise has been designed to know about your skills, success and failures, what kind of person you are. This helps to improve your talents after you have analysed each of the following statement.

Time : 20minutes

Procedure : Individual discussion/Opinion-if Yes/No please specify reason.

1. Do I need to improve Communication Skills. Yes/No
2. Am I reliable and Trustworthy person. Yes/No
3. Do I need to develop Human Relations Skills. Yes/No
4. Does my appearance reflects an image which will help me to reach my Objectives. Yes/No

5. Do I use my Time Management Skills. Yes/No
6. Do I have positive attitude about people and environment. Yes/No
7. Do I need to break some habits to develop my career Yes/No
8. Do I use my Money Management Techniques. Yes/No
9. Do I treat others respect. Yes/No
10. Do I have creative mind/Innovative approach Yes/No

For Answer Email: dracmohan_mannava@yahoo.com

REFERENCES

1. V.S.P. Rao, Human Resource Management, Excel Books, New Delhi, 2000.
2. K. Aswathappa, "Human Resource and Personnel Management", Tata McGraw-Hill Publishing Company Limited, New Delhi, 1999.
3. Yoder, Dale. "Personnel Management and Industrial Relations", Prentice Hall of India, New Delhi, 1972.
4. Peter F. Drucker, "The Practice of Management", Harper and Brothers, New York, 1954.
5. Rudrabasavaraj M.N., "Personnel Administration Policies in India", V.M.N. Institue of Co-operative Management, Pune, 1969.
6. Robbins, Stephen P., "Personnel – The Mangement of Human Resources", Prentice Hall Inc., New Jersey, 1978.
7. Flippo Edwin B., "Principles of Management", 1976.
8. Subba, Rao, P., "Essentials of Human Resource Management and Industrial Relations", Himalaya Publishing House, Mumbai.
9. Anjali Ghanekar, "Human Resource Management", Everest Publishing House, Pune, 2004.
10. C.B. Mamoria and S.V. Gankar, "Human Resource Management", Himalaya Publishing House, Mumbai, 2005.
11. Axline, L.L. 1994, "Ethical Considerations of Performance Appraisals", Management Review, March.
12. Bernardin, H.J. and Beatty, R.W., 1984, "Performance Appraisal: Assessing Human Behaviour at Work", Kent Publishing, Boston.
13. Coleman, D. and Borman, W.C., 2000, "Investigating the Underlying Structure of the Citizenship Performance Domain", Human Resource Management Review.
14. Findley, H.M. Moss holder, K.W. and Glies, W.F., 2000, "Performance Appraisal Process and System Facets", Applied Psychology,
15. Segal, J.A., 1999, "Performance Management for Jekyll and Hyde", HR Magazine.

CHAPTER

12

Employee Morale, Attitude and Job Satisfaction

Meaning - Definition of Morale - Characteristics of Morale - Factors Determining Morale - Caueses of Low Morale - Measures to Improve Morale - Importance of Attitude- Definition of Attitude- Components of Attitude - Functions of Attitude - Types of Attitude - Attitude Formation - Attitude Change - Theories of Attitude Formation and Changes - Importance of Job Satisfaction - Definition of Job Satisfaction - Factors Determinants of Job Satisfaction - Causes of Job Satisfaction - Consequences of Job Satisfaction - Benefits of Job Satisfaction – Exercises – Case Study.

Learning Objectives of this Chapter are:

- To understand the Meaning and Definition of Morale
- To study the Characteristics of Morale
- To identify the Factors Determining Morale
- To analyze the Causes of Low Morale
- To examine the Measures to Improve Morale
- To know the Importance of Attitude
- To understand the Meaning and Definition of Attitude
- To study the Cmponents of Attitude
- To know the Functions of Attitude
- To learn the Types of Attitude
- To examine the Attitude Formation
- To analyze the Attitude Change
- To describe the Theories of Attitude Formation and Changes
- To know the importance of Job Satisfaction
- To understand the definition of Job Satisfaction
- To examine the factors determining Job Satisfaction

- To identify the causes of Job Satisfaction
- To know the consequences of Job Satisfaction
- To study the benefits of Job Satisfaction

EMPLOYEE MORALE

INTRODUCTION

Motivation and morale are interrelated and they are different each other. The term Morale is used to armed forces during the war time to sports and military teams. It refers team spirit and cooperation of people for common purpose. Recently Its importance has been realized by the management. It is felt by the management that if employee morale is high production would be high and othe other hand if morale is low, production would be also low. Thus morale of the employee depends upon the motivation of an employee because both are interrelated.

Morale represents the attitudes of individuals and groups in the organization towards their work environment and towards voluntary co-operation to the full extent of their capabilities for the fulfillment of organizational objectives. Morale is the indicator of the attitude of an employee towards job.It is mental process to develop good relationship and feelings towards working environment.

DEFINITION OF MORALE

According to Theo Haimann; Morale is the state of mind and emotions affecting the attitude and willingness to work,which in term affects individual and organizational objectives.

In the simple terms Morale is level of job satisfaction within a group.

CHARACTERISTICS OF MORALE

- Morale is psychological process
- Morale is relative concept which is related to the attitude of the worker
- It reflects the degree of willingness of an employee to do the work
- Morale is related the employees feelings and sentiments
- Morale is dynamic in nature,it cannot be developed overnight.
- Morale is multi-dimensional process which represents human needs and motivational factors.
- Morale is intangible which means difficult to measure accurately

FACTORS DETERMINING MORALE

- Confident in leadership
- Job satisfaction
- Confidence in the co-workers
- Sound and efficient organization
- Fair remuneration
- Security of job
- Opportunity to rise
- Working conditions
- Physical and mental heath
- Relationship and cooperation of employees

POSSIBLE COMBINATIONS OF MORALE

Morale is one of the important factors to increase the productivity of an organization. Many other factors like technology,style of supervision and employee training, etc. also influence the productivity. There are four possible combinations of morale and productivity. They are as follows

Box 12.1

- High morale and high productivity
- High morale and low productivity
- Low morale and low productivity
- Low morale and high productivity

CAUSES OF LOW MORALE

Box 12.2

- High rate of labor turnover
- High rate of absenteeism
- Excessive complaints and grievances
- Frustration among the employees
- Resistance to change
- Lack of discipline
- Low quantity and quality of output
- Antagonism towards management
- Lack of co-operation among the employees

MEASURES TO IMPROVE MORALE

Box 12.3

- Fair system of wage payment
- Sense of job security of employee
- Sound promotion policy
- Competent supervisors should be appointed
- Communications should be effective from top to bottom
- Free and frank consultation with employees
- Employee should develop loyalty
- Employees' Welfare facilities should be provided at satisfactory level
- Proper training programs should be organized for employees
- Employees should develop positive attitude towards job

ATTITUDE

IMPORTANCE OF ATTITUDE

Attitude of an employee is very important to perform his/her job in the Organisation. Attitude plays an important role to develop good human relations and better understanding among the people. Attitude is an individual characteristic way of responding consistently in a favorable or unfavorable manner to objects, people and environment. In simple terms attitudes are evaluate statement towards object people and environment. Attitude is interpretations and behavior of the person towards environment and people. Employees develop their own attitude towards organization and people. They have positive attitude and negative attitude. Attitude reflects the behavior and feeling of the person towards job and organization. Beliefs, values and sentiments are also influenced to develop the positive attitude of employee in the organization.

Definition of Attitude

Evaluate statements or judgments concerning objects, people and environment.

A learned disposition to respond in a consistently favourable manner with respect to a given object.

CHARACTERISTICS OF ATTITUDE

- Attitudes are evaluate statements to judge the people
- Attitudes are feelings and beliefs of individuals and group of people
- Attitudes are predispositions of individual towards given aspects of world

- Attitudes are organized and core to individual
- Attitudes are feelings of an individual about people and environment
- Attitudes are positive and negative

COMPONENTS OF ATTITUDE

Cognitive component of attitude: The beliefs, opinion, knowledge, or information held by the individual. Example: my superior is not fair.

Affective component of attitude: The feelings, sentiments, moods and emotions about some idea, person, event or object. Example: I don't like my superior because he never encourages me.

Behavioral component of attitude: The predispositions to get on a favorable or unfavorable evaluation of something. Example: I would like to request to transfer me to another department.

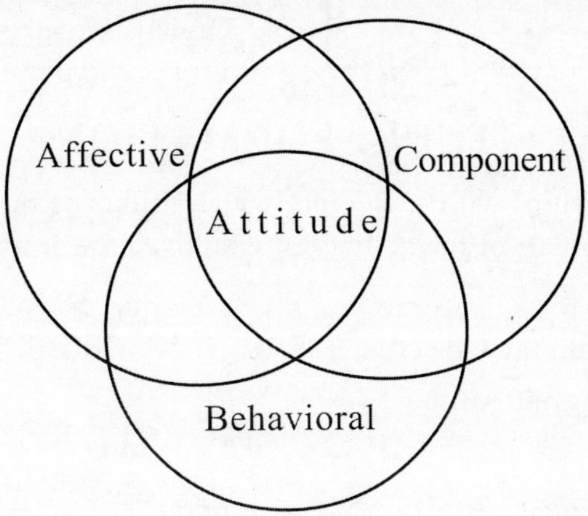

FUNCTIONS OF ATTITUDE

- Value expressive function
- Ego-defensive function
- Adjustment function
- Knowledge function

BOX 12.4

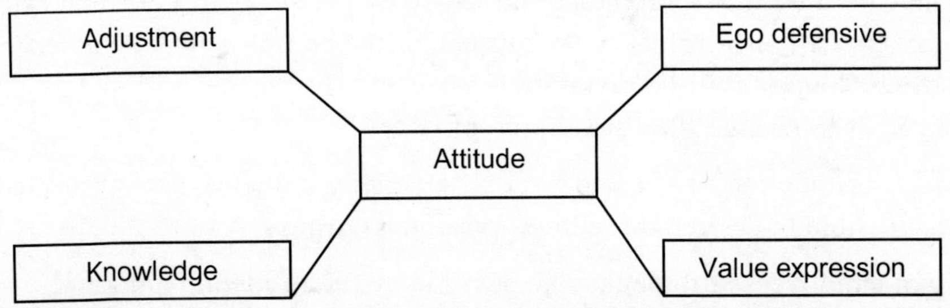

TYPES OF ATTITUDE

Job satisfaction & Job involvement

Organizational commitment

BOX 12.5

Job Satisfaction & Job Involvement	***Organisational Commitment***
1. Wage and Salary of an employee	1. Turnover and Productivity
2. Promotions of an employee	2. Improvement of Quality of Work
3. Relationships with Supervisors and other employees	3. Commitment towards organizational objectives
4. Working conditions	4. Organisational effectiveness

ATTITUDE FORMATION

Employees form relationships with each other which influence the attitude to maintain and develop the association. It is a part of the activity of employee to form three main sources. They are as follows:

- Direct Experience with the Objective
- Classical conditioning and Attitudes
- Vicarious Learning
- Family and Peer groups
- Operant conditioning and Attitude acquisition
- Economic Status and Occupation
- Mass Communication
- Neighbourhood

ATTITUDE CHANGE

Attitude is very important component of an employee in the organization. Attitudes are very difficult to change because many people are influence by people, affiliation and esteem. Friends, parents and teachers will also influence the attitude of the an individual. Another reason is prior commitments of employees will be given preference and they are unwilling to change. In short attitudes are difficult to change they are source of reward.

Occasionally attitude can be affected through the highly influenced and respected individuals. Sometimes it is possible in desired direction for training purpose.

Changing of employees attitude may be possible by the following hints.

Box 12.6

1. Feedback of employees
2. Positive role model
3. Providing new information
4. Use of fear
5. Influence of friends and peers
6. Co-opting approach
7. Influence of media
8. Influence of family members

JOB SATISFACTION

IMPORTANCE OF JOB SATISFACTION

Employee Job satisfactions is an important to achieve individual as well as organizational objectives. It is Interlinked with productivity and turnover of the organization. Employee morale and job satisfaction both are interrelated but they different. Both are interchangeably used in an organizational environment. Job satisfaction of an employee plays an important role to achieve individual as well as organizational goals. Job satisfaction refers feeling of an employee how he/ she is doing job. It is influenced various factors such as wages, working conditions, relationships and fair treatment by the employer. Thus it is set of various factors relating job.

DEFINITION OF JOB SATISFACTION

A positive feeling about one's job resulting from an evaluation of its characteristics.

A set of favourable or unfavourable feelings of an employee towards his/her job.

FACTORS DETERMINANTS OF JOB SATISFACTION

1. Personal Individual Factors
2. Group Factors
3. Social Factors
4. Organisational Factors

Box 12.7

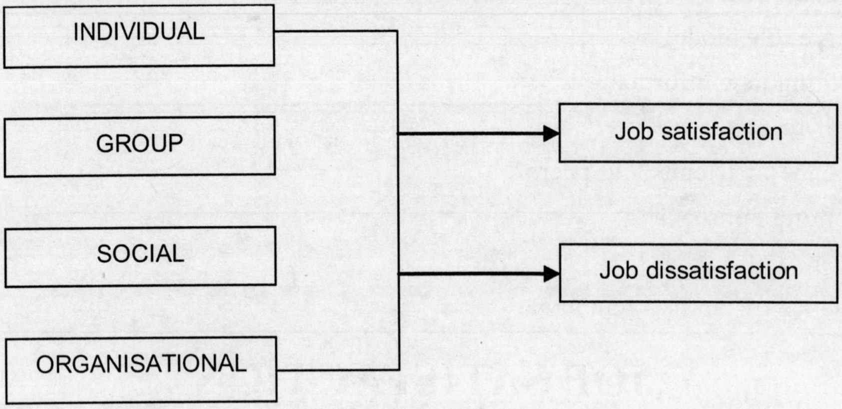

CAUSES OF JOB SATISFACTION

Box 12.8

- Wage and salaries of employees
- Promotions of employees
- Nature of work
- Organizational policies and procedures
- Working conditions
- Relationship of employees with peers and supervisors
- Size of the group members
- Quality of supervision

CONSEQUENCES OF JOB SATISFACTION

Box 12.9

- Increase of productivity
- Increase of turnover
- Improvement of attendance
- Reduced accidents
- Less job stress
- Lower unionism

BENEFITS OF JOB SATISFACTION

Box 12.10

- Employees' surveys
- Improved communication
- Attitude improvement
- Improved quality and productivity
- Assessment of training needs
- Effectiveness of reward system
- Impact of evaluation of attitude

EXPERIENTIAL LEARNING ON ATTITUDE OF MANAGERS

This exercise has been designed to analyse the attitude of Indian Manager. It is useful to compare Indian Manager and Foregin Manager to know on Indian Manager. Please Mark Yes/No and support your statement in the discussion.

Time : 1 Hour

Procedure : Form a group of 4 members and analyse about each statement.

1. Indian Managers are highly motivated and hardworking. Yes/No
2. Indian Managers are poorly motivated and lazy persons. Yes/No
3. The people I have associated and worked with hardworking Yes/No
4. Comparatively Foreign Manager, Indian Managers are more Resourceful Yes/No
5. Comparatively Foreign Managers, Indian Managers are more productive Yes/No
6. Comparatively Foreign Managers, Indian Managers are less productive Yes/No
7. Over the past two decades Indian Mangers have improved in overall quality of Job performance. Yes/No
8. Most of Indian Managers are Autocratic that is why they are successful in the Corporate world. Yes/No
9. Most of the Indian Managers are democratic that is why they are successful in the corporate world. Yes/No
10. India Managers are punctual in Time Management strategy. Yes/No

For Answer Email: dracmohan_mannava@yahoo.com

EXERCISE ON ATTITUDE

This exercise has been designed to understand the following statements and to give ratio of all the statements. It helps to understand your opinion about work place.

Time : 1 Hour

Procedure : Add your scores and discuss about each statement.

1. Strongly disagree 2. Disagree 3. Undecided 4. Agree 5. Strongly Agree

1. The Company/Institute is a good place for my career development.
2. I can get good opportunity in this Company/Institute
3. This Company/Institute's image is Good and Competitive to develop my career.
4. People treated fairly in the Organisation/Institution.
5. I understand the various facilities are provided to develop every individual.
6. My Job makes the best use of Talents and skills.
7. My Job is Challenging but not burdensome.
8. I have trust and confidence in my boss
9. I have freedom to tell my boss whatever I think to tell.
10. I can understand what my superior expects from me

For Answer Email: dracmohan_mannava@yahoo.com

EXERCISE ON ATTITUDES AND TRUSTWORTHY LEADER

INSTRUCTIONS Listed below are behaviors and attitudes of leaders who are generally trusted by their group members and other constitutents. After you read each characteristic, check to the right whether this is a behavior or attitude that you appear to have developed already, or whether it does not fit you at present.

	Fits Me	Does Not Fit Me
1. Readily accepts feedback on behavior from others	☐	☐
2. Maintains eye contact with people when talking to them	☐	☐
3. Appears relaxed and confident when explaning his or her side of a story	☐	☐
4. Individualizes compliments to others rather than saying something like "You look great" to many people	☐	☐
5. Minimizes telling people what they want to hear	☐	☐
6. Is described by others as "walking the talk"	☐	☐

7. Delivers consistent messages to others in terms of matching words and deeds ☐ ☐
8. Does what he or she expects others to do ☐ ☐
9. Minimizes hypocrisy by not engaging in activities he or she tells others are Wrong ☐ ☐
10. Tells the truth consistently ☐ ☐
11. Is good at keeping secrets and confidences ☐ ☐
12. It is described by others as being reliable ☐ ☐
13. Tells people he or she is going to do something, and then always follows through and gets it done. ☐ ☐
14. Does not expect lavish perks for himself or herself while expecting Others to go on an austerity diet ☐ ☐
15. Readily shares financial information with others ☐ ☐
16. Communicates information to people at all organizational levels ☐ ☐
17. Collaborates with others to make cooperative decisions ☐ ☐
18. Does not tell others a crisis is pending (when it is not) just gain their cooperation ☐ ☐

For Answer Email: dracmohan_mannava@yahoo.com

EXERCISE ON THE ASSERTIVENESS SCALE

INSTRUCTIONS Indicate whether each of the following statements is mostly true or mostly false as it applies to you. If in doubt about your reaction to a particular statement, thick of how you would generally respond.

	Mostly True	Mostly False
1. People would describe me as too outspoken.	☐	☐
2. I am quite willing to have the store take back a piece of furniture that was scratched upon delivery.	☐	☐
3. I dread having to express anger toward a co-worker.	☐	☐
4. People often say that I am too reserved and emotionally controlled	☐	☐
5. I have told friends and work associates exactly what it is about their Behavior that irritates or displeases me	☐	☐
6. It is extremely difficult for me to turn down a sales representative When he or she is a nice person	☐	☐

7. I express criticism freely ☐ ☐
8. If another person is being very unfair, I bring it to that person's attention ☐ ☐
9. Work is no place to let your feelings show ☐ ☐
10. It is no use asking for favors; people get what they deserve ☐ ☐
11. Business is not the place for tact; say what you think
12. If a person looks as if he or she is in a hurry, I let that person in front of me in a supermarket line. ☐ ☐
13. A weakness of mine is that I am too nice a person ☐ ☐
14. If my restaurant bill is even 50 paise more than it should be, I demand that the mistake be corrected ☐ ☐
15. If the mood strikes me, I will laugh out loud in public. ☐ ☐
16. I fight for my rights down to the last detail. ☐ ☐
17. I have no misgivings about remaining an overcoat to the store if it does not fit me right. ☐ ☐
18. After I have an argument with a person, I try to avoid him or her ☐ ☐
19. I insist that my spouse (or roommate or partner) do his or her fair Share of undesirable chores. ☐ ☐
20. It is difficult for me to look directly at another person when the two of us are in disagreement ☐ ☐
21. I sometimes show my anger by swearing at or belittling another person ☐ ☐
22. It is in poor taste to express what you really feel about another individual ☐ ☐
23. I am able to turn down social engagements with people I do not particularly care for. ☐ ☐
24. If someone near me at a movie keeps up a conversation with Another person, I ask him or her to stop. ☐ ☐
25. I have cried among friends more than once. ☐ ☐

KEY

- 0-15: Nonassertive
- 16-20: Assertive
- 20+ :Aggressive

For Answer Email: dracmohan_mannava@yahoo.com

CASE ON ATTITUDE AND JOB SATISFACTION

November 30, 1997 goes down in the history of a Bangalore based electric company as the day nobody wanting it to recur but every one recollecting it with a sense of pride.

It was a festive day for all the 700 – plus employees. Festoons were strung all over, banners were put up, banana trunks and leaves adored the factory gate, instead of the usual red flags; and loud speakers were blaring Kannada film songs.

It was the day the employees chose to celebrate Kannada Rajyothsava, annual feature of all Karnataka based organisations. The function was to start at 4 p.m. and everybody was eagerly waiting for the big event to take place.

But the event, budgeted at ₹ 1,00,000 did not take place. At around 2 p.m., there was a ghastly accident in the machine shop. Murthy was caught in the vertical turret lathe and was wounded fatally. His end came in the ambulance on the way to hospital.

The management sought union help, and the union leaders did respond with a positive attitude. They did not want to fish in troubled waters.

Series of meetings were held between the union leaders and the management. They centered around two major issues – (i) restoring normalcy, and (ii) determining the amount of compensation to be paid to the dependants of Murthy.

Luckily, for the management, the accident took place on Saturday. The next day was a weekly holiday and this helped the tension to diffuse to a large extent. The funeral of the deceased took place on Sunday without any hitch. The management hoped that things would be normal on Monday morning.

But the hope was belied. The workers refused to resume work. Again the management approached the union for help. Union leaders advised the workers to resume work in all departments except in the machine shop, and the suggestion was accepted by all.

Two weeks went by, nobody entered the machine shop, though work in other places resumed. Union leaders came with a new idea to the management – to perform a pooja to ward off any evil that had befallen on the lathe. The management accepted the idea and homa was performed in the machine shop for about five hours commencing early in the morning. This helped to some extent. The workers started operations on all other machines in the machine shop expect on the fateful lathe. It took two full months and a lot of persuasion from the union leaders for the workers to switch on the lathe.

The crisis was blown over, thanks to the responsible role played by the union leaders and their fellow workers. Neither the management nor the workers wish that such an incident should recur.

As the wages of the deceased grossed ₹ 6,500 per month, Murthy was not covered under the ESI Act. Management had to pay compensation. Age and experience of the victim were taken in account to arrive at ₹ 1,87,000 which was the amount payable to the wife of the deceased. To this was added ₹ 2,50,000 at the intervention of the union leaders. In addition, the widow was paid a gratuity and the monthly pension of ₹ 4,300. And nobody's wages were cut for the days not worked.

Murthy's death witnessed an unusual behaviour on the part of the workers and their leaders, and magnanimous gesture from the management. It is a pride moment in the life of the factory.

Questions

1. What made employee union respond positively towards solving the crisis?
2. Apply the following concepts to the case and write a note on each:
   (a) Attitudes, (b) Job satisfaction

CHAPTER

13

Teams and Teamwork

Importance of Teams - Difference between Groups and Teams - Definations of Team – Definition of Group – Features of Team – Types of Teams - Teamwork - Team Building - Roles of Team Member - Team Effectiveness - Building Trust - Team Development – Case Study – Exercise.

Learning Objectives of this Chapter are:

- To study the importance of Teams
- To understand the difference between Groups and Teams
- To identify the types of Teams
- To know the concept of Teamwork
- To examine the Team Building
- To identify the role of Team Member
- To know the Team Effectiveness
- To describe Building Trust
- To understand Team Development

IMPORTANCE OF TEAMS

Nowadays the world is changing fast and Trends are changing. It is true that the world has been evolving and changing since time began, but what is so different today is both the pace and effects of change, which impinge on everyone's life. Competition is hotting up. New products, new technologies, new processes hit the markets with frustrating regularity. In order to surive corporate are virtually compelled to economies on every front after modern technology, restructure operations, explore new market, find new uses of existing products, innovate, experiment and find new ways of living and most importantly use human resources productively. While fighting with the various forces of change, corporations have realized the importance of teams which are more flexible and responsive to changing events than are traditional departments or other forms of permanent groupings.

DIFFERENCES BETWEEN GROUPS AND TEAMS

A group consists of two or more individuals, interacting and interdependent, who have come together to achieve a common goal. Members interact, share information and help each other in order to realize the goals. On the other hand, a work team generates positive synergy through coordinated effort. The individual efforts result in a level of performance that is greater than the sum of those individuals inputs.

DEFINITION OF TEAM

A team may be ***defined as a small group of people with complimentary skills who work actively together to achieve a common purpose for which they hold themselves collectively accountable.***

DEFINITION OF GROUP

Group can be defined "It is combination of two or more persons to interact to achieve common objectives".

Box 13.1 Features of a Team
Members
➢ Commited to goas they helped define. ➢ Possess complementary skills. ➢ Support one another willingly. ➢ Hold themselves collectively accountable for results. ➢ Trust and support other members. ➢ Offer suggestions and give feedback to other members. ➢ May disagree but work to resolve differences and reach consensus. ➢ In short teams create the potential for an organization to generate greater outputs with no increase in inputs.

- A work team produces positive synergy through coordinated effort.
- Members put their (abilities, skills and knowledge) to best use in producing an overall level of performance that is greater than the sum of the individual inputs.
- Teams focus on individual and mutual accountability-that is, they work together to produce an outcome (e.g. product, service or decision) that represents their joint contributions , and each member shares responsibility for that outcome.
- Team members also share a common commitment to purpose-typically positioning a firm at the top or serving customers in the best possible way, or producing quality products better than rivals, etc.

- Teams usually set their goals and choose the approach that helps them realize those goals without interference from management.
- The differences between the two concepts may be summarized thus

Box 13.2 Comparing Work Group and Work Teams

Group	*Point*	*Team*
A function of what its members individuals	Performance	Performance includes individual do as efforts and collective work products which are the result of joint, coordinated efforts.
Strong, clearly focused leader	Leader	Shared Leadership roles
Individual Accountability	Accountability	Individual and mutual accountability
Runs efficient meetings	Meetings	Encourages open-ended active, problem-solving meeting
Random and varied	Skills	Complementary
Neutral (sometime negative)	Synergy	Positive
Discusses, decides and delegates	Functioning	Discusses, decides and does real work together

Teamwork has a synergistic effect in that the individuals working together achieve more than they could alone. Members share a common purpose which is clear to each team member. Teamwork, in any case does not just happen, it needs continuous effort. The effort should also be enjoyable, full and should result in a feeling of personal satisfaction for every team member. Much of his job is done by the the team leader who makes them realize that team interests are above personal aspirations. Another feature of the team is that it has a 'feel' about it, a sort teamness. Members exchange feelings, opinions ideas freely discuss openly and try to learn from each other.

TYPES OF TEAMS

Teams are classified into four. They are as follows:

Problems Solving Teams

It is a group of 5 to 10 employees from the same department, who voluntarily meet for a few hours each week to discuss and solve quality, cost, ways of improving efficiency and other work-related problems. The recommendations of the team, emerging out of such regular meetings, are put forward before management for approval. Problem solving teams normally are the first step in a company's move toward great employee participation. As the company matures, problems-solving teams can take the shape of self-directed teams.

Self-managing Teams

Self-managing teams typically consist of 6 to 15 multi-skilled workers who rotate jobs to produce an entire product or service or at least one complete aspect or portion of a product or service such as engine assembly, insurance claim processing, etc. These groups are empowered to make the decisions required to manage themselves on a day-to-day basis.

Self-directed teams typically include the following elements:

- The team includes employees with several skills and functions and the combined skills are sufficient to perform a major organizational task. A team may include members from the foundry, machining, grinding fabrication and sales departments, with each member cross-trained to perform one another's job.
- The team is given access to resources such as information, equipment, machinery and supplies required to perform the complete task.
- The team is empowered with decision-making authority which means that members have the freedom to select new members, solve problems, spend money, monitor results, adapt to changing conditions and plan for the future.
- It also has a strong commitment to the organisation's mission, the autonomy needed to control its own activities, belief in itself and a chance to see directly the impact of its efforts.

Self-directed teams have proved to be effective. Several companies such as Federal Express and IDS have boosted productivity upto 40 percent by adopting self-directed teams.

Cross-functional Teams

It consists of a group of employees from about the same hierarchical level, but from different work areas who come together to accomplish a task. A task force or a project team comes under this category· These teams are created to deal with a specific problem and are usually disbanded when the task is completed or the problem is solved. A committee is (another cross-functional team) a formal organizational team usually relatively long lived, created to carry out specific organizational teams to speed the process of bringing new drugs to the market place. Major automobile manufacturers including Toyota, Honda, BMW, Ford, GM, Daimler Chrysler, Mahindra & Mahindra, Tata Motors have relied on cross-functional teams to create and manufacture new models.

However, cross-functional teams are not easy to manage. Members from various fields with diverse backgrounds may find it difficult to get along, especially during the formative stages of the team.

- Work to see that each member belives that he or she has the opportunity to influence the goups's decision making (stake building)
- Try to make sure that members' expectations and personal agendas are brought before the team and deliberated upon freely (transparency)

- Ensure that all divergent points of views are explicitly recognised and examined acilitate the building of much trust as possible within the group, so that no one feels that someone else will try to take advantage of them.

Virtual Teams

IBM began to use virtual teams in early 1970s. Currently, about one out of three IBM employees participate as a member of atleast one virtual team. Members need not be working in close proximity and may often be geographically dispersed-cross-organizationally or cross-nationally. Almost all meetings could take place via electronic communication (including wide area networks, video conferencing, fax, e-mail, etc.) Sometimes a company may also virtual teams in partnership with suppliers or in many cases with competitors brains to complet to pull together the best brains to comple to a project or speed a new product to market. Leadership among team members is shared or altered depending on the area of expertise required to each stage of the project.

Virtual teams bring cost effectiveness and speed to teamwork where members are unable to meet easily face-to-face. There is the added advantage of objective information sharing and decision making based on facts. Where members are well trained in the use of computers and are able to process and interpret data without any emotional considerations, virtual teams may yield positive gains.

On the negative side, virtual teams suffer from lack of social rapport and direct interaction. The information exchange may take place speedily but in the absence of direct contact, even straight forward ideas may be misinterpreted.

- Careful selection of partners and team members; encourage team members to interact one to one, without feeling obliged to copy every email message to the entire team; encourage team members to discuss cultural differences freely.
- Strong management support of the team and its goals; be sure that someone is responsible for facilitating the communication process.
- Utilization of best communication tools and procedures, better to use a variety of communication technologies; pay special attention to the quality of the communication transmission (like low quality voice transmissions, poor video images, etc.).
- Development of trust among all members; to achieve this, it is better to hold an initial meeting on a face to face basis; whenever possible individual team members could pay a visit and meet members who are easily accessible; periodic meetings with members of course minimize the dangers emanating “out of site, out of mind” attitudes.
- Information sharing; also train team members to match their choice of technology to the task.

TEAMWORK

Teamwork occurs when group members work together in ways that utilize their skills to accomplish a common purpose. (Philips) In such a scenario, members are prepared to listen and respond constructively to views expressed by others. Team work of this nature, of course, does not just happen. You cannot simply expect people to do a great hob by assigning members to a group.

High performance teams thus have strong core values, clear performance goals, the right mix of skills and creativity. Members in a homogeneous group (when members are alike in respect of age, gender, race, ethnicity experience, etc.) may score better than others in most cases because they find it easy to build social relationship quickly and begin interactions needed to work harmoniously together. Team diversity (in terms of demography, experiences, cultures) may create performance difficulties initially.

TEAM BUILDING

Team building is a broad title for activities designed to construct, develop and sustain groups of people who are working together to achieve common goals with a commitment to taking collective responsibility. (Watson) The process begins collective efforts.

1. **Size:** High performing teams tend to be small (generally 5 to 12). Large groups do not allow members to develop close understanding and rapport easily.
2. **Skills:** Members must possess three kinds of skills. The most important one is the technical competence, followed by problem solving and interpersonal skills.
3. **Role:** For a team to be successful over the long run, it must be structured so as to both maintain its members social well being and accomplish its task. Two types of roles are worth highlighting here.

Box 13.3 Roles of Team Member

Task Specialist Role	Socio-economic Role
People who play the task specialist role display the following behaviours. ➢ **Initiation:** Purpose new solutions to team problems. ➢ **Give opinions:** Offer opinions on task solutions; give candid feedback on others' suggestions ➢ **Seek information:** Ask for task relevant facts. ➢ **Summarise:** Relate various ideas to the problem at hand; pull ideas together into a summary perspective. ➢ **Energizer:** Stimulate the team into action when interest drops.	People who support team members' emotional needs play the following roles: ➢ **Encourage:** Warm and receptive to others' ideas; praise and encourage others to draw forth their contributions. ➢ **Harmonise:** Reconcile group conflicts; help disagreeing parties reach agreement. ➢ **Reduce tension:** May tell jokes or in other ways draw off emotions when group atmosphere is tense. ➢ **Follow:** Go along with the team; agree to other team members' ideas. ➢ **Compromise:** Will shift own opinions to maintain team harmony.

Some may even play a role, where the member contributes to both the team's task and supports members' emotional needs. Members who do not take an active part (playing a non-participative role) are held in low esteem by the team as a whole. Effective teams must have people in both task specialist and socio-emotional role.

1. **Behaviours:** Team members must exhibit certain behaviours which help in developing close ties with others (S.R. Lloyd). These are listed below:

Box 13.4 Team Members: Ground Rules

- Speak respectfully to one another and about one another.
- Listen without interrupting
- Express opinions, feelings openly, honestly
- Make 'I' statements and not 'you' statements.
- Ask for help when needed, offer help when possible.
- Make commitments seriously and keep them.
- Support the team and each other.
- Focus on problems and solutions, not blame and accusations.

Box 13.5

People related factors

- Personal work satisfaction →
- Mutual trust and team spirit
- Good communications
- Low unresolved conflict and power struggle
- Low threat, fail-safe, good job security

Organisation-related factors

- Organizational stability and job security →
- Involved, interested, supportive management
- Proper rewards and recognition of accomplishments
- Stable goals and priorities

Task-related factors

- Clear objectives, directions, and project plans
- Proper technical direction and leadership →
- Autonomy and professionally challenging work
- Experienced and qualified project/team personnel
- Team involvement and project visibility

Effective team performance

1. Innovative ideas
2. Goal(s) accomplished
3. Adaptable to change
4. High personal/team commitment
5. Rated highly by top Management

Rewards

Members who indulge in social loafing (the tendency of individuals to extend less effort when working collectively than when working individually), as stated above, are not held in high esteem in a group setting.

Leaders

The successful functioning of a team depends to a large exten on the 'soft skills' exhibited by the leader in the frm of communication, conflict resolution, motivation, sharing and trust building. They can be mentioned in the

Box 13.6

- First, the leader should know his own strengths and how those strengths and how those strengths can help the entire group.
- Second, the leader should share power and information in order to empower team members and reach goals.
- Third, team leaders should enable members to find answers for themselves by asking questions and encouraging balanced participation.
- Fourth, team leaders should coordinate team activities and avoid wasting time on details that can be better handled through transfer of responsibility to the team.
- Fifth, leaders should accept the concept of continuous, on-the-job learning.

BUILDING TRUST

The mere presence of a good leader does not guarantee the success of a team automatically unless members trust the leader. Trust, a belief in the integrity, character or ability of others, is essential if people are to achieve anything together in the long run.

The primary responsibility of creating trust in the minds of members rests with the leader/ manager. The manager by virtue of his hierarchical advantage has greater access to key information. If the manager tries to get results through intimidation, members join together incohesive resistance.

Box 13.7 Trust and Effective Group Interaction

Trust	:	A personal commitment to openness and trust A willingness to change if necessary.
Information	:	Full disclosure of relevant information, feelings and opinions
Control	:	Reliance on self-control rather than procedural control Confidence that others will perform as agreed Mutual commitment to success
Influence	:	A willingness to be influenced by others concerning goals, Procedures, and performance evaluation.

Ways to Build Trust

Trut is a fragile thing and it grows slowly. A thoughtless remark, sometimes, may destroy years of hard work. According to Bartolome, managers need to concentrate on the following points (Bartolome) mentioned in

Box 13.8

- Demonstrate that you are working for others' interests as well as your own.
- Support your work team wholeheartedly. When the team is under attack, you must demonstrate your loyalty to the team through your words and actions.
- Keep people fully informed about what is going on. Explain your decisions. Let them know the problems. If you hold back any of these, members begin to suspect your moves and withdraw support.
- Rewards must equal contributions. Learn to appreciate and give credit to people who show performance.
- In addition to cold facts, you need t share your feelings with team members. Such an interchange of opinions, helps you move closer to your teammates.
- If people share their concerns and feelings with you, do not try to betray their confidence by leaking it to affected parties.
- Learn to guide others through technical competence, team building and interpersonal skills.

TEAM DEVELOPMENT

How to create and develop effective teams? The following tips should help managers in answering this question. (Hayward)

Box 13.9 Team Development

Tips

1. Create a balanced set of roles.
2. Develop communication and process awareness.
3. Diagnose and manage teams.
4. Understand team preferences.
5. Define team goal.
6. Establish review mechanisms.
7. Share leadership and create equality of contribution
8. Develop facilitation skills for effective meetings.
9. Confront issues and problems.
10. Decision making based on consensus.

➢ **Balanced roles:** People with different work preferences must gain entry into teams rather than like minded people.

- **Open communication:** Communication should be open, flexible and capable of building trust between people.
- **Handling stress:** Working with others in close proximity can itself be stressful. Aditionally, we tend to react differently to various work pressures.
- **Team choices:** These choices must be made explicit. Once the range is known, alternatives could be ascertained. Support someone from the team says. "I think teams are good in principle, but in practive they can be a complete waste of time". Once a response like this comes out, the team can begin to deal with it.
- **Team goals:** Teams make sense only when there is a common goal which requires colletive action. Defining the team's purpose is vital.
- **Shared leadership:** Teams need different frms of leadership at different times. Both the leader and the members must be willing to exchange roles, depending on the situation.
- **Facilitation skills:** Ensure that team meetings are well organized, allowing enough roomd for all to express their feelings and thoughts properly.
- **Shake of constraints of the past:** All relevant issues affecting the functioning of a team must be discussed, debated and resolved.
- **Consensus:** Team decisions need to be based on consensus, so that all members can agree with - and be committed to – implementing important decisions.

CASE ON TEAMS AND TEAMWORK

On November 17, 1998, Daimler Benz and Chrysler finalised a $35 billion transatlantic merger. The merger made sense economically and provided a number of advantages for both of the previous companies. Chrysler wanted to improve its image as a maker of luxury automobiles; Daimler wanted to improve the marketability of its cars and expand into the light truck segment. Although Daimler Benz has always been known for its German craftsmanship and meticulous attention to detail, Chrysler added its expertise in using the platform team as a method of putting cars together.

The platform team is one thing that did not change with the merger and continues to add considerable value to the production process as its application is expanded.

Actually, the platform team, long the standard way of putting cars together among Japanese automakers, was officially embraced by Chrysler executives several years ago as superior to the compartmentalised functional system still prevalent throughout the US auto industry. Simplification is the goal of the platform team. When designers, product engineers, manufacturing engineers, purchasing agents, suppliers and line workers make decisions together from the beginning, it saves time, money, and untold hassles when the car finally goes into production.

A typical example of how teams can contribute to productivity occurred at Chrysler's assembly plant at Brampton, Ontario. Don Callahan and Brian Large huddled around a half-built Dodge intrepid; trying to figure out why the warning light on the instrument panel was on even though the air-conditioner was working fine. Both men were members of the LH car's "platform team".

Callahan, an hourly assembly-line worker, and Large, a product engineer, have worked together since the intrepid prototype was first built. In a few hours, they managed to fix the electrical glitch and send their car down the line.

If Chrysler had developed the LH like most US vehicles have been developed. Callahan wouldn't have contacted Large about the problem because the two would never have met. And the early production cars would likely have reached customers' hands with the electrical system still on the fritz. But the workers, designers, and engineers who collaborated in developing the first test batch of cars thrashed out the final stages of vehicle development process that sought to blur the traditional lines between people in different functional work units – all in the name of building a better car.

The team approach paid off in a number of ways for former Chrysler. The LH team, for example, shaved a full year off Chrysler's average vehicle – development cycle, historically 4 ¼ years. This was an attractive lure for executives at Daimler who sensed that they could learn a lot from Chrysler about how to get a wider variety of cars to market more quickly. And team member did it with 40 per cent fewer engineers than a typical product program budget came in well under those of two other well-known team efforts. Ford's $3 billion Taurus/Sable and GM's $3.5 billion Snifegip

Questions

1. How did teams benefit Chrysler?
2. Relate the principles you have learnt about teams in this chapter to this case.

CHAPTER 14

Personality and Perception

Meaning of Personality – Definition of Personality – Nature and Significance of Personality – Determinants of Personality – Measurement of Personality – The Big Five Model – Traits of Personality – Type A and Type B Personalities – Meaning of Perception – Elements of Perception – Definition of Perception – Sensation vs. Perception – Characteristics of Perceiver – Halo- effect and Stereo Type – Exercises – Case Study.

Learning Objectives of this Chapter are:

- To understand the meaning and definition of Personality
- To study the nature and Significance of Personality
- To examine the Determinants of Personality
- To analyze the Measurement of Personality
- To know the Big five Model
- To identify the Traits of Personality
- To know the types of Personality
- To understand the meaning and definition of Perception
- To study Sensation vs. perception
- To know the Characteristics of the Perceiver
- To understand Halo-effect and Stereo type

INTRODCTION

The term Personality has been derived from the latin word "personare" which means to speak through. The concept of personality has been identified by behavioral scientists to understand the uniqueness of the individuals and their characteristic patterns of behavior. Personality indicates relatively stable and enduring aspects of individual which is different from other people. Personality is a comprehensive concept and rather an all embrassing one. Personality corporate how person thinks, how person solves problems and how person relates to others.

Personality means how an individual influences others through external appearances which means actions. Every Individuals interacts with other people in different situations. Personality is a dynamic concept which represents some of the total characteristics of the individual to interact, attract and react based on the situation. Personality is a set of relatively stable characteristic, individual thoughts, feelings of a person based on the situation.

Definition of Personality

Personality can be defined as some total of ways in which an individual interact and reacts with other people.

According to Mc Clelland the most adequate conceptualization of an individual's behavior in all its details which the scientist can provide at a moment in time.

Nature and Significance of Personality

Peersonality factors are most crucial and they are important in an organizational environment. Personality properties are also belived to produce varied emotional reactions to test. Personality characteristics are atmost significance from the stand point of interpersonal relations and human behavior in an organizational environment. Personality is very diverse and psychological concept to understand the various characteristics and qualities of a person in different situations.

Determinants of Personality

1. **Biological factors**

   Biological factors can be studied through several approaches such as Heredity, the Brain, and Physical Characteristics of a person.

2. **Physical Characteristics**

   An individual physical appearance is a vital ingredient of Personality and it is essentially determined by biologically. It is tall or short, fat, skinny, handsome, ugly, black, white will influence the personality.

3. **Cultural factors**

   Cultural factors are usually considered to make more significant contribution to Personality than Biological factors. Culture largely determines the contents of learning it indicates what individual will learn. It also determines attributes such as Independence, Competition and Co-operation.

4. **Family and Social factors**

   Family has the most significant impact on Personality development. In India Men and Women are socialized in different manner to follow traditional and modern culture based on the situation. The parents play an important part in the identification process which is important to the individual early development. Besides family background, social factors like Social Class and Social status also influences individuals personality and perception in general.

Measurement of Personality

Personality inventories are printed forms containing questions, objectives and statements about human behavior. The individual is required to indicate reactions to different items. In the initial stage there are only single trait inventories such as introversion and extroversion. But nowadays there are multiple trait inventories are available which are relatively less time consuming and easy to operate. Some of the important traits are as follows:

1. **The Myers Briggs type indicator:**

   This is a 100 question personality test asking the respondents how they usually feel or act in particular situations . This is one of the most widely used Personality tests.

   According to the answers given by individuals they are classified as :

   - **E**xtroverts or **I**ntroverts (E or I)
   - **S**ensitive or **I**ntutive
   - **T**hinking or **F**eeling (T or F)
   - **P**erceiving or **J**udging (P or J)

These arrangements are classified into 16 personality traits (as show in Table No. 14.1)

People with **INTJ viz**., introverted, intuitive, thinking and judging have original minds, and great drive for their own ideas and purposes. Their characters are sceptical, critical, independent, determined and often stubborn.

ESTJs are: organizers, realistic, logical, analytical, decesive and have a natural inclination towards business/mechanics.

ENTPs are: conceptualisers, innovative, individualistic and versatile entrepreneurs, resourceful in solving challenging problems.

2. The Big Five Model

Personality traits of an executive influences the behavior of employee in an organization. The major Personality traits which influence the job behaviours and job performance are called as the big five Personality Traits. These traits can be studied in Box No. 14.1

Box 14.1

1. **Extroversion**: Sociable, talkative and assertive.
2. **Aggreeableness**: Good natured, co-operative and trusting.
3. **Conscientiousness**: Responsible, dependable, persistent and achievement-oriented.
4. **Emotional Stability**: Calm, self-confident, secure, tense, insecure and nervous.
5. **Openness to Experience**: Imaginative and artistically sensitive.

Box 14.2 Traits of Personality

1. Reserved vs Outgoing
2. Less Intelligent vs-More Intelligent
3. Affected by feeling vs-Emotionally stable
4. Submissive vs-Dominant
5. Serious vs Happy-go-lucky
6. Expedient vs. Conscientious
7. Timid vs. Venturesome
8. Tough-minded vs./Sensitive
9. Trusting vs. Suspicious
10. Practical vs. Imaginative
11. Forthright vs. Shrewd
12. Self-assured vs. Apprehensive
13. Conservative vs. Experimenting
14. Group-dependent vs. Self-sufficient
15. Uncontrolled vs. Controlled
16. Relaxed vs. Tense

TYPE "A" AND TYPE "B" PERSONALITIES

Type A personality is "aggressively involved in a chronic, incessant struggle to achieve more and more in lesser and lesser time, and, if required to do so, against the opposing efforts of other things or other persons." This type of personality is treated as positive personality in North American culture and an undesirable personality in the Indian culture.

Profile of Type A Personality is :

Box 14.3

- Always moving, walking rapidly, talking and eating rapidly
- Impatient
- Doing two things at the same time
- Not coping up with leisure time
- Obsessed with numbers
- Measuring success with quantity
- Aggressive and competitive and
- Always under time pressure.

Type B Personality

Type B personalities are exactly opposite to Type A. These personalities are "rarely harried by the desire to obtain a widely increasing number of things or participate in an endless growing series of events in ever-decreasing amount of time."

Profile of Type B personality:

Box 14.4
➢ It is not concerned about time, patient, mild mannered and never in a hurry
➢ Does not brag
➢ Plays for fun and not to win
➢ Relaxes without guilt
➢ Has no pressing deadlines

PERCEPTION

Meaning of Perception

Perception is an important cognitive process in understanding human behaviour in an organization. Perception is the process by which the people become aware of internal and external feelings and interpret these feelings in different situations. Every individual perceives, the world through his senses such as hearing, touching, smelling, and awareness of activities etc. Every Indivduals approaches life differently. Perception is a Psychological process by which people organize and interpret their sensory impressions. Perception is different from one person to another person. Perception is a feeling of a person or thinking of a person based on the situation. Identify how many squares are there in the following figure.

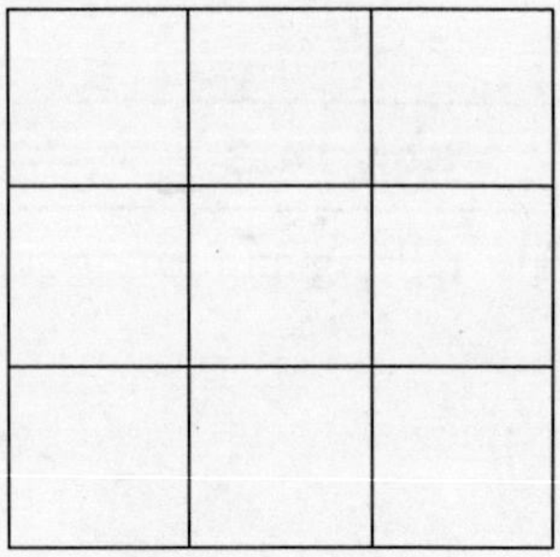

Fig. 14.1

Some people will identify there are nine figures in the box on the other hand others will identify there are 10, 12,13, 14 and 18. It means what you are thinking, what you are looking, what you are feeling, what you are looking, what you are identifying, what you are understanding and analyzing, it is called Perception.

ELEMENTS IN PERCEPTION

This can be shown in the following box.

Box 14.5
➢ Involvement of an individual ➢ Psychological process ➢ Receiving, Selecting, and Organizing Sensory Impressions ➢ Picture of environment

DEFINITION OF PERCEPTION

Perception can be defined as "Psychological process by which individuals organize and interpret their sensory impressions in order to give meaning to their environment."

Perception may also be defined as "A process of receiving, selecting, organizing, interpreting, checking and reacting to sensory stimuli or data so as to form a meaningful and coherent picture of the world."

SENSATION VS. PERCEPTION

Sensory organs like eyes and ears collect the data from the environment. The physical senses are vision, touch, smell, taste and hearing. These are the five senses. Some of us believe in the sixth-sense "intuition". The physical senses are bombarded by numerous external and internal stimuli.

Stimuli

Stimuli is an enabling or disabling factor to act within an individual. Stimuli is of two types viz., external stimuli and internal stimuli.

External Stimuli include heat waves in the summer, cold waves in the day time, sound waves of a factory, smell from the kitchen/garden.

Internal Stimuli include food passing through the digestive system, internal comfort or discomfort and actions and reactions caused by the psychological functioning. Sensation is the experience we get by touching a baby, seeing a picture or an incident, listening to a conversation, smelling a flower or tasting food.

CHARACTERISTICS OF PERCEIVERS

Knowing oneself makes it easier to see others accurately. One's own characteristics affect the characteristics likely to see in others. An individual who accepts himself is more likely to be able to see favourable aspects of the other individuals. Accuracy in perceiving others is not a single skill. It depends upon the various factors. Characteristic of perceiver as follows:

Box 14.6

1. Needs
2. Experiences
3. Expectations
4. Values
5. Attitudes
6. Personality

HALO-EFFECT AND STEREO TYPE

Halo-effect is the tendency of perceiving a person or situation on the basis of single characteristic of a person. For example, Mr. Karthik of ABC Company attends the office on time everyday. While other colleagues attend the office atleast 10 minutes late. But Mr. Karthik is not efficient in performing the job. Branch Manager ranked his performance as the best simply based on punctuality in attending the office. The Halo-effect is likely to be related to our own self image.

The Halo-effect plays the significant role in rating employee performance. Those employees with some favorable features may be rated highly on other characteristics also. An employee who has an excellent attendance record is often judged as highly productive, though facts may not be shown. On the other hand with poor attendance record a person may be rated as less productive though that may not be the case in fact. Sometimes Halo-effect is also known as Halo error because it causes the entire appraisal to be biased. According to Bruner, Halo effect is marked

1. When the traits to be perceived or unclear in behavioral expressions.
2. When the traits are not frequently used by the perceiver.
3. When the traits have moral implications.

Halo effect has most profound impact and implication on an individual's perception and in the behaviour in the working environment. The reality of the Halo effect was confirmed in classic study where subjects were given list of traits like intelligence innovative, creative, practical, industrious and determined to evaluate the person to whom these traits applied. Based on the above trait the person who are judged to be a popular, humorous, wise and imaginative. Thus the subjects are allowing a single trait to influence the overall impressions of the person being judged.

Stereotype

We normally tend to classify and categories' people and events into already known or perceived catergories. Such tendency is called as Stereo typing. We have certain pre established with certain attributes based on the professional characteristics. We approach teachers, doctors, judges with most positive and obedient attributes, whereas we approach policeman with fear and submissive attributes.

Age is one of the stereo types which influences the organizational environment. We presume the physical qualities, psychological qualities and intellectual qualities based on the age factor. The stereotypes of young people comparatively old people are different. Young people have a qualities of dynamic and dashing, quick decision, highly interested in new techniques. On the other hand the stereotypes of the older people to have more resistant to organizational change, less creative and innovative, more conservative in nature and lower in physical capabilities and less interested in new techniques. Stereotypes of men and women are also different. The stereotypes of men includes tough leadership, high self confidence, high competitiveness and detailed analytical ability. On the other hand Stereo type of women employees have highly emotional, highly submissive, more commitment and highly tolerant.

EXERCISE 1

1 **Sir** **Food**	2 **IMPROVEMENT** **IMPROVEMENT** **IMPROVEMENT** **IMPROVEMENT**	3 **FA TH**	4 **BRTH 1111 DEATH**
5 **COF FEE**	6 **IKD**	7 **ENTURY**	8 **E** **L** **K** **C** **U** **B**
9 **SKATING** IIiiii	10 **person / ality**	11 **I** ――― **8**	12 **Schedule Bit**
13 C U M	14 NAWHAT'SME	15 **D Movie** **D Movie** **D Movie**	16 **p** **a** **y** **m** **e** **n** **t**
17 Hard <u>x Ahead</u>	18 **GOOD LAST** **GOOD LAST**	19 **COW**	20 **Jan.Feb.Mar.** ―――― DUE

EXERCISE 2

1 Over Over	2 π **EAR**	3 **HANDS HANDS** **HANDS HANDS** **HANDS HANDS** **DECK**	4 **PALS** **CENTURIONS** **YOKELS**
5 **Schedule Mon.Tues.Wed**	6 **PIKE'S PEAK** **MIDNIGHT** **ROBERT** **REDFORT**	7 **WORRY** **Me Quit**	8
9 **FINAL**	10 **R R R R** **U U U U** **O O O O** **H H H H**	11 HiOiWiEiR	12 **O** **R** **N** **E** **R** **Y**
13 **Heaven** **x Pennies**	14 **RAP** **TIMBER**	15 **Standing** **MISS**	16 **D E N R U T** **S I D E**
17 **Looking All** **Bargain Bargain** **Bargain Bargain**	18 **MONEY** **BIRTH**	19 	20 **No** **No** **No** **Punch** **No** **No** **No**

EXERCISE 3

1 MAST	2 HOROBOD	3 YGETARTS	4 CC TICKET
5 JET	6 IT IT IT IT TIME IT IT IT IT	7 Soil	8 Business
9 A I 4 D	10 EAR (boxed) EAR	11 RIGHT RIGHT	12 GOL
13 1T3456	14 abcdefghij	15 O N A I P	16 HEAD
17 Yr Yr Yr Yr Bar Yr Yr Bar Yr Yr Yr Yr	18 GOOD BETTER	19 D WEST D	20 DR. DR.

EXERCISE 4

1 BENDING DRAW DRAW	2 2345 67890	3 RcAAErG	4 tion tion
5 LA B OR	6 DEAL	7 N W E S	8 wolf
9 ¢¢¢¢¢¢ – Murder	10 T T A A C C	11 10 10 The Heat 10 10	12 Decision Dec / ision
13 jury jury jury jury	14 tion tion tion tion tion GOOD tion tion tion tion tion	15 SETTLE 20 SETTLE	16 copy
17 House the Range	18 NOSLIW	19 11 TIME	20 WAD

CASE STUDY

PREJUDICES IN WORKPLACES: REAL OR PERCEIVED?

Manjula Srivastav had been head of marketing for the last four years at Blue Chips, a computer products firm. The company's turnover had increased by two-and-a-half times during this period and its market share in a number of products had also moved up marginally. What was creditable was that all this had happened in an environment in which computer prices had been crashing.

Although she had a talent for striking an instant rapport with people particularly with the company's dealers, Srivastav often found herself battling against odds, as she perceived it, as far as her relationship with her subordinates and peers in the company were concerned. Srivastav had to, all along, fight male prejudice. She found it unfair that she had to prove herself regularly at work and she used to make her displeasure known to everyone.

Six months ago, Blue Chips had been taken over by an industrial group which had a diversity of business interests and was, more importantly, flush with funds. The change of ownership had led to replacement of the managing director, but it had not affected the existing core management team. Anand Prakash, the new managing director, had his prioritites clear. 'Blue Chips will go international,' he had declared in the first executive committee meeting, 'and exports will be out first concern.'

Prakash had also brought in Harish Naik as his executive assistant with special responsibility for exports. Naik had been seconded too Srivastav for five weeks as part of a familiarisation programme. Much to her surprise, he had been appointed, within two months, as the vice president(exports), with compensation and perks higher than her own. Srivastav had made a formal protest to Prakash who had assured her that he was aware of her good work in the company and that she would have an appropriate role once the restructuring plan he was already working on was put into effect.

One morning as she entered the office and switched on her workstation, a message flashed on her screen. It was from Prakash. 'Want to see you sometime today regarding restructuring. Will 2.30 be convenient?' it said.

Later, in his office, Prakash had come straight to the point. He wanted to create a new post called general manager (public affairs) in the company. 'With your excellent background in customer relations and contact with the dealer network, you are the ideal person for the job,' he said, 'and I am offering it to you.' Srivastav was quick to react. 'There is very little I can contribute in that kind of job,' she said. 'If you continue in marketing, you will have to be reporting to Naik which I thought may not be fair to you. In any case, we need someone who is strong in marketing to handle public affairs, let me assure you that the new post I am offering will in no way diminish your importance in the company. You will in fact be reporting to me directly.'

'You are being unfair and you are diminishing my importance in the company, restorted Srivastav.' You know that I am a hardcore marketing professional and you also know I am the best. Why, then, am I being deprived of a rightful promotion in marketing? Tell me. she asked pointedly, 'would you have done this to a male colleague?'

'That is a hypothetical question,' said Prakash. 'But I can't think of any other slot for you in the restructuring plan I want to implement other than what I am offering.'

'If the reason why you are asking me to handle this fancy public affairs business of yours,' said Srivastav, 'is that you can't think of any other slot for me, then I would have second thoughts about continuing to work for this company.'

'May I reiterate,' said Prakash, 'that I value your role and it is precisely because of this that I am delegating to you the work I have been personally handling so far? May I also state that I am upgrading the job not only because it is important but also because it should match your existing stature in the organisation?'

'I need to think about this. I will let you know tomorrow,' said Srivastav and left the office.

Questions

1. What role did perception play in Prakash's treatment of Srivastav?
2. Do you think that Srivastav should continue in Blue Chips?

OVERCONFIDENE OF AN EMPLOYEE

Firms are downsizing. Consumer confidence is plunging. Given the economic environment, why should anybody give up a secure job?

It may seem odd, but competent people still do it everyday. They job-hop in search of greener pastures. Take Sridhar, a software expert in a Bangalore based firm, who scribbled the following remarks on his exit interview questionnaire.

'This job is not right for me. I would like to have more input on decisions that affect me, more chance to show what I can do. I do not get enough feedback to tell me if I am doing a good job or not, and the firm keeps people in the dark about where it is headed. Basically, I feel like a interchangeable part most of the time'.

In reply to the question whether the firm could have done anything to retain Sridhar, he replied 'probably not'.

Why do so many promising employees leave their jobs? And why do so many others stay on but perform at minimal levels for lack of better alternatives? One of the main reasons – Sridhar's reasons – can be all but invisible, because it is so common in many organisations; a systematical failure to keep good people.

Companies should worry about people like Sridhar. By investing in them they may actually help reduce turnover, save on training costs, increase productivity, improve quality and reap the benefits of innovative thinking and teamwork.

Human resource professionals and managers can contribute to corporate success by encouraging employees' empowerment, security, identity and competence. How? By recognising the essential components of keeping their best people and by understanding what enhances and diminishes those components.

Sridhar doubts that his firm will ever change, but other organisations are taking positive steps to focus on and enhance employee retention. As a result, they are reducing turnover, improving quality, increasing productivity, and saving on their training costs.

Questions

1. Do you think that Sridhar's self-esteem had anything to do with his leaving the firm?
2. What do you think were Sridhar's satisfaction with and commitment to the job and firm he is leaving?
3. What lessons can this firm learn from the case of Sridhar? What can and should it now do?
4. Which theory of personality does best describe Sridhar's behaviour?

IT'S ALL A MATTER OF PERSONALITY

Largely because of downsizing, the survivors are working harder and longer hours every year, and although some get burned out and stressed, others seem to thrive on it. At Apple Computer, for example development teams are well-known for wearing T-shirts that proclaim, '90 Hours a week and loving it!' And high-tech firms are now coaxing double and triple time out of their employees, a practice that is spreading to other sectors of the economy. One of the best examples is provided by the increasing number of telecommuters who work at home. By giving employees PCs, cellular phones, pagers and other devices, the company can stay in contact. However, many of these telecommuters are now finding that they are on call 24 hours a day. One of the rules of survival in an increasing number of workplaces appears to be. "If you don't have the personality to work round-the-clock, don't bother applying for a job here."

Of course, for some people work is extremely enjoyable, and they do not mind the new demands. Take the case of entrepreneur Wayne Huizenga, a self-made billionaire. Huizenga started out with a partner in the garbage collection business, confident that his firm could outperform the small mom-and-pop garbage companies and get their business. He was supremely confident on his own ability. It was not long before his plan started to come true. Wall Street did not think much of his ideas, however, and when he issued his first stock in 1971 it was to raise a mere 5 million. By the time Huizenga left in 1984, the market value of the firm's stock was $3 billion.

Huizenga's next move was to blockbuster entertainment. He was convinced that the movie rental business was a wave of the future. Again he was right. For a mere $18.5 million, he and his partner were able to buy the company, and soon thereafter sales took off, rising from $43 million annually to over $2 billion. By the time he sold out to Viacom in 1994, he had put another billion dollars in his pocket.

Now, Huizenga is looking into new business ventures, including a garbage collection company, a security alar firm, and a used-car operation. The latter is of particular interest to investors because it involves a novel approach to car buying. Huizenga is convinced that because the price of new cars is going up so quickly and more and more people are buying used cars, the big profit will be in the second-hand market. Whether he is right or wrong, Huizenga remains confident of his new investment decisions, and those who have bet him in the past believe he was another set of winning strategies on the drawing board.

The same can be said for Steve Wynn of Mirage Resorts. Wynn's company was recently listed as one of the Fortune's 10 most admired firms in America. Why? Part of it is a reflection of Wynn's own personality. He is eternally optimistic and wants his people to be the same. Wynn's strategy is to keep everybody happy. If any one is not, Wynn's employees are there to fix it. As he tells his people, "if you snge fpr tjeee a hotel guest with the the tiniest from on her face, don't ask a supervisor, take care of it. Erase the change, send the dinner back, don't change for the room.' In addition Wynn sponsors elaborate parties to honour staffers who have kept the most number of customers happy. At one recent party for a Vietnamese woman who was being honoured as employee of the year, Wynn brought in George and Barbara Bush to congratulate the lady. It cost a lot of money for the party, but as Wynn puts it, 'it's an investment'.

Questions

1. Why do employees at firms such as Apple Computer work so hard and put in such long hours?
2. How would you describe Wayne Huizenga in terms of the self-concept, Speciality and self-esteem?
3. Why is job satisfaction and organisational commitment so high at Mirage Resorts? How does Steve Wynn manage to keep his employees so happy?

CHAPTER

15

Human Resource Development

Significance of Human Resource Development – Difference Between HRD and Personnel Function – Features of HRD – Objectives of HRD – HRD Matrix – Techniques of Human Resource Development – The Functions of HRD Managers – HRD Tasks of Line Manager – Qualities of an HRD Manager – Case Study – Exercise.

Learning Objectives of this Chapter are:

- To know the Significance of HRD
- To study the Difference between HRD aned Personnel Function
- To examine the features of HRD
- To learn the Objectives of HRD
- To know the HRD Matrix
- To analyse the Techniques of HRD
- To identify the functions of HRD Managers
- To describe the HRD Tasks of Line Manager
- To describe the Qualities of an HRD Manager

SIGNIFICANCE OF HUMAN RESOURCE DEVELOPMENT

The efficiency of production process and various areas of management depend to a great extent on the level of human resources development. HRD assumes significance in view of the fast changing organizational environments and need of the organization to adopt new techniques in order to respond to the environmental changes. The changing environmental factors include:

1. Unprecedented increase in competition within and outside the country consequent upon the announcement and implementation of economic liberalizations.
2. The economic liberalization demands continuous improvement of human resources.
3. Trends towards market economy are more prevalent in most of the countries including the erstwhile communist countries. These trends towards market economy are resulting

in severe competition not only among the industries around the globe but also industries within the nation.

Organizations to be dynamic, growth-oriented and fast changing, should develop heir human resources. It is needless to say that the organization possessing competent human resources grow faster and can be dynamic. Though the positive personnel policies and programmes motivate the employees by their commitment and loyalty, these efforts cannot keep the organization dynamic and fast-changing. Organizations to be dynamic should possess dynamic human resources. Human resources to be dynamic should acquire capabilities continuously, adopt the values and beliefs and aptitude in accordance with changing requirements of the organization. Similarly, when employees use their initiative, take risks, experiment, innovate and make things happen, the organization may be said to have an enabling culture. The competent human resources can be dynamic in an enabling culture. Thus, the organisation can develop, change and excel, only if it possess developed human resources. Thus, HRD plays significant role in making the human resources vital, useful and purposeful.

DIFFERENCE BETWEEN HRD AND PERSONNEL FUNCTION

Personnel Functions	*HRD*
Maintenance oriented	Development oriented
An independent function with independent sub-functions	Consists of inter-dependent parts.
Reactive function, responding to events as and when they take place	Proactive function, trying to anticipate and get ready with appropriate responses.
Exclusive responsibility of personnel department	Responsibility of all managers in the organization
Emphasis is put on monetary rewards	Emphasis is on higher-order needs such as how to design jobs with stretch, pull and challenge; how to empower people in all respects, etc.
Improved performance is the result of improved satisfaction and morale	Better use of human resources leads to improved satisfaction andmorale.
Tries to improve the efficiency of people and administration	It tries to develop the organization as a whole and its culture.

FEATURES OF HRD

HRD is a process by which employees of an organisation to help themselves as well as the organisation. It has the following features:

1. HRD systems which consists of several independent parts and subsystems for the development of individual and organization.
2. HRD is a planned process which follows systematic way to develop the people. It is continuous process to achieve the common goals.

3. HRD involves development of competencies to develop four different levels such as individual level, employee level, group level and functional level.
4. HRD is a inter-disciplinary concept to implement various ideas, principles and practices.
5. HRD improves the quality of work life which enables employees to utilize the capabilities and to improve the quality of work life at various levels in an organisation.
6. HRD aims at offering motivating environment. It will help the employees to develop the potentialities for best utilization of human resources.
7. HRD also helps to develop commitment towards organisation effectiveness.
8. HRD also help the employees to introduce new trends and practices based on the changing policies in the corporate world.

OBJECTIVES OF HRD

1. Capabilities of an individual employee.
2. Capabilities of an individual employee to the present role.
3. Capabilities of an individual employee to the future role.
4. The dynamic relationship between employer and employee
5. The teamwork and team spirit among the people in the organisation.
6. Collaboration among different branches and units of an organisation
7. To develop the Organizational culture.
8. To Improve the Quality of Work Life
9. To develop the commitment among the employees.
10. To increase the job satisfaction of an employee.

HRD MATRIX

The HRD Matrix shows the interrelationships between HRD instruments, processes, outcomes and organizational effectiveness as shown

1. **HRD instruments:** These include performance appraisal, counseling, role analysis, potential development, training, communication policies, job rotation, rewards, job enrichment programmes, etc. These instruments may vary depending on the size of the organisation, the internal environment, the support and commitment of the top management, the competitive policies, etc.
2. **HRD processes:** The HRD instruments lead to the generation of HRD of processes like role clarity, performance planning, development climate, risk-taking, dynamism in employees. Such HRD processes should result in more competent, satisfied and committed people that would make the organization grow by contributing their by best to it.

3. **HRD Outcomes:** HRD instruments and processes make people more committed and satisfied, where they tend to give their best to the organization enthusiastically.
4. **Organisational effectiveness:** Dimensions: Such HRD outcomes influence the organizational effectiveness, which in turn, depends on a number of variables like environment, technology, competitors, etc.

TECHNIQUES OF HUMAN RESOURCE DEVELOPMENT

Techniques of human resources development are also called HRD methods, HRD instruments, HRD mechanisms or HRD subsystems which is illustrated in the Box No. 15.1 which are as follows:

Box 15.1

1. Performance Appraisal
2. Potential Appraisal
3. Career Planning
4. Career Development
5. Employee Training
6. Executive Development
7. Organizational Change
8. Organizational Development
9. Social and Cultural Programmes
10. Workers' Participation in Management
11. Quality Circles
12. Employees Counseling
13. Teamwork
14. Role Analysis
15. Communication Policies and Procedures
16. Monetary Rewards
17. Non-monetary Rewards
18. Employee Benefits and
19. Grievance Mechanism
20. Quality Work Life
21. Welfare Facilities
22. Employees Discipline
23. Management Participation in Trade Unions
24. Social Security Measures.
25. Sound HRD Policies & Programmes

THE FUNCTIONS OF HRD MANAGERS

HRD Managers or departments play a crucial role in the organisation. A wide range of functions are enlisted in the Box No. 15.2

Box 15.2

1. Role Analysis
2. Human Resource Planning
3. Recruitment
4. Selection
5. Placement
6. Induction and Orientation
7. Performance Appraisal
8. Training
9. Management Development
10. Career Planning and Development
11. Organisation Development
12. Employee Counseling
13. Teamwork
14. Communication Policies
15. Grievance Mechanism
16. Employee Discipline
17. Quality Cirlces
18. Quality Work Life
19. Worker's Participation Management
20. Human Resources Accounting.

HRD TASKS OF LINE MANAGER

Appraiasal	*Training and Career*
1. To identify key performance areas of each employee. 2. To help employee in goal-setting. 3. To understand employee's difficulties and provide support. 4. To conduct timely appraisals.	1. To identify various competencies required by each employee for fulfilling his role. To identify promotion opportunities for each employee and the competencies required for promotion. 2. To communicate these needs to the HRD department. To help each employee develop his potential 3. To sponsor the employee for training.

5. To give feedback in a climate of openness and trust. 6. To hold counseling sessions and make employee feel success. 7. To suggest employee opportunities 8. To help career development activities.	4. To give feedback from the employee when he returns from training. To help those who do not have any further career opportunities. 5. To accept the reality without displeasure and plan the future. 6. To provide opportunities to the employee for putting his learning into practice. 7. To develop problem solving skills in the employees. 8. To give feedback to him about his potential

QUALITIES OF AN HRD MANAGER

According to Pareek and Rao, an HRD Manager must possess the following attributes.

Box 15.3

1. Knowledge of various types of performance appraisal systems and potential appraisal systems and ability to develop them.
2. Knowledge of various types of tests and measurements of behavior.
3. Ability to design and execute training programmes at various levels.
4. Knowledge of career planning and other personnel practices.
5. Knowledge of behavioral sciences.
6. Knowledge and skills in counseling
7. Understanding of overall organizational culture.
8. Knowledge of techniques in behavioral research.
9. Organizing ability
10. Systems development skills.
11. Initiative
12. Faith in human beings and their capabilities.
13. Positive attitude towards others.
14. Imagination and creativity.
15. Concern for excellence.
16. Concern for people and their development
17. Attitude for research and development work.
18. Friendly, sociable and affable.
19. Interest in learning new things.
20. Ability to work as team member.
21. Knowledge of potential appraisal
22. Knowledge of new trends of HRM

CASE STUDY

Mr. Karthikeyan after obtaining his B.E degree did a few odd job for two years and the completed his MBA degree from University of Madras in 2004. He went to Bangalore and began his career in computer industry as a software professional for a salary of ₹ 20,000. Then he did his post-graduate diploma in Computer Applications for one year and progressed to Systems Analyst and then Senior Manager of the electronic data processing department of a company. After four years, Mr. Karthikeyan did his MCA degree from University of Madras and became the Vice-President of Satyam Computers. At the age of 36, his 12 years climb up the executive ladder culminated in his being selected as CEO of the ₹ 2000, crore company where he was responsible for making strategic decisions. His annual salary grew upto ₹ One crore.

Mr. Karthikeyan could get so far so fast due to software industry boom, successful at whatever he undertook and his continuous upgradation of his skills and educational qualifications. He was a major force in developing software where he worked. His reputation for being highly organised is well known in the industry. He regularly handles telephone calls, e-mails, and reads a number of corporate up-dates and reports. Colleagues openly discuss about his ability to identify problems in a project and offer solid solutions.

Mr. Karthikeyan proudly admits that his professor at University of Madras helped him a lot in the form of counselling and mentoring which magnified his brightness and competency.

Questions

1. How did Mr. Karthikeyan's continuous development of his human resources aid his progress up the senior executive ladder?
2. What advice would you offer an aspiring manager about climbing the corporate ladder?

Appendix A

PROFILE OF SUCCESSFUL LEADERS

Dhirubhai Ambani

Achievements: Dhirubhai Ambani built India's largest private sector company. Created an equity cult in the Indian capital market. Reliance is the first Indian company to feature in Forbes 500 list

Dhirubhai Ambani was the most enterprising Indian entrepreneur. His life journey is reminiscent of the rags to riches story. He is remembered as the one who rewrote Indian corporate history and built a truly global corporate group.

Dhirubhai Ambani alias Dhirajlal Hirachand Ambani was born on December 28, 1932, at Chorwad, Gujarat, into a Modh family. His father was a school teacher. Dhirubhai Ambani started his entrepreneurial career by selling "bhajias" to pilgrims in Mount Gimar over the weekends.

After doing his matriculation at the age of 16, Dhirubhai moved to Aden, Yemen. He worked there as a gas-station attendant, and as a clerk in an oil company. He returned to India in 1958 with ₹ 50,000 and set up a textile trading company.

Assisted by his two sons, Mukesh and Anil, Dhirubhai Ambani built India's largest private sector company. Reliance India Limited, from a scratch. Over time his business has diversified into a core specialisation in petrochemicals with additional interests in telecommunications, innovative instruments like the convertible debenture. Reliance quickly became a favorite of the stock market in the 1980s.

In 1992, Reliance became the first Indian company to raise money in global markets, its high credit-taking in international markets limited only by India's sovereign rating. Reliance also became the first Indian company to feature in Forbes 500 list.

Dhirubhai Ambani was named the Indian Entrepreneur of the 20th Century by the Federation of Indian Chambers of Commerce and Industry (FICCI). A poll conducted by The Times of India in 2000 voted him "greatest creator of wealth in the century".

Dhirubhai Ambani died on July 6, 2002, at Mumbai.

Adi Godrej

Achievements: Chairman of Godrej Group

Adi Godrej is one of the icons of Indian Industry. He is the chairman of Godrcj Group. Adi Godrcj was born in a business family. His father's name was Burjorji Godrej and his mother's name was Jai Godrej. More than a century age, the Godrej's were into manufacturing locks and vegetable-based soaps. The Godrej products were among the first indigenously manufactured products to displace entrenched foreign brands.

Adi Godrej left India at the age of 17 to enroll at the Massachusetts Institute of Technology. Though he planned to study mechanical engineering but he later on switched to management. After his return to India, Adi Godrej joined the family business. He modernized and systematized management structures and implemented process improvements. Adi Godrej took the Godrej Group to great height during controlled economy era. After the liberalization process, Adi Godrej restructured company's policies to meet the challenges of globalisation. In the early 2000s, the Group completed a 10-year restructuring process through which each business became a stand-alone company with a CEO/COO from outside the Godrej family. Under Adi Godrej's leadership, the group is also involved in philanthropic activities. Godrej is major supporter of the World Wildlife Fund in India, it has developed a green business campus in the Vikhroli township of Mumbai, which includes a 150-acre mangrove forest and a school for the children of company employees.

Dr. K. Anji Reddy

Achievements: Founder-chairman of Dr Reddy's Group of Companies; Awarded with Padma Shri in 2001.

Dr. K. Anji Reddy is a pioneer in the pharmaceutical research in India and is founder-chairman of Dr Reddy's Group of Companies.

Dr Kallam Anji Reddy did his B.Sc in Pharmaceuticals and Fine chemicals from Bombay University and subsequently completed his PhD in Chemical Engineering from National Chemical Laboratory, Pune, in 1969. Dr. K. Anji Reddy served in PSU Indian Drugs and Pharmaceuticals Limited from 1969 to 1975. Dr. Reddy was the founder-Managing Director of Uniloids Ltd from 1976 to 1980 and Standard Organics Limited from 1980 to 1984.

In 1984, Dr. K. Anji Reddy founded Dr. Reddy's Laboratories and soon the company established new benchmarks in the Indian Pharmaceutical industry. Dr. Reddy's Laboratories transformed Indian bulk drug industry from import-dependent in mid-80s to self-reliant in mid-90s and finally into the export-oriented industry that it is presently. In 1993, Dr. Reddy's became the first company to take up drug discovery research in India and in April 2001 it became the first non-Japanese Asian pharmaceutical company to list on NYSE. By the end of fiscal year 2005, Dr. Reddy's Laboratories was India's second largest pharmaceutical company and the youngest among its peer group.

Presently, Dr. Reddy is a serving member of the Prime Minister's Council on Trade & Industry, Government of India, and has been nominated to the Board of National Institute of Pharmaceutical Education and Research (NIPER).

Dr. K. Anji Reddy is also a philanthropist. He is the founder-Chairman of Dr. Reddy's Foundation for Human & Social Development, a social arm of Dr. Reddy's, which acts as a catalyst of change to achieve sustainable development.

Dr. K. Anji Reddy has received many awards and honors. These include Sir PC Ray award (conferred twice, in 1984 and 1992); Federation of Asian Pharmaceutical Associations (FAPA)'s FAPA-Ishidate Award for Pharmaceutical Research in 1998; leading business magazine Business India voted him Businessman of the Year in 2001; CHEMTECH Foundation bestowed on him the Achiever of the Year award in the year 2000 and the 'Hall of Fame' award in 2005, for his Entrepreneurship, Leadership and thrust on Innovation; and in 2001, he was awarded the Padma Shri by the Government of India.

Azim Premji

Born: July 24, 1945

Achievements: Chairman of Wipro Technologies; Richest Indian for the past several years; Honored with Padma Bhushan in 2005.

Azim Premji is Chairman of Wipro Technologies, one of the largest software companies in India. He is an icon among Indian businessmen and his success story is a source of inspiration to a number of budding entrepreneurs.

Born on July 24, 1945, Azim Hashim Premji was studying Electrical Engineering from Stanford University, USA when due to the sudden demise of his father, he was called upon to handle the family business. Azim Premji took over the reins of family business in 1966 at the age of 21.

At the first annual general meeting of the company attended by Azeem Premji, a shareholder doubted Premji's ability to handle business at such a young age and publicly advised him to sell his shareholding and give it to a more mature management. This spurred Azim Premji and made him all the more determined to make Wipro a success story. And the rest is history.

When Azim Premji occupied the hot seat, Wipro dealt in hydrogenated cooking fats and later diversified to bakery fats, ethnic ingredient based toiletries, hair care soaps, baby toiletries, lighting products and hydraulic cylinders. Thereafter Premji made a focused shift from soaps to software.

Under Azim Premji's leadership Wipro has metamorphosed from a Rs.70 million company in hydrogenated cooking fats to a pioneer in providing integrated business, technology and process solutions on a global delivery platform. Today, Wipro Technologies is the largest independent R&D service provider in the world.

Azim Premji has several achievements to his credit. In 2000, Asiaweek magazine, voted Premji among the 20 most powerful men in the world. Azim Premji was among the 50 richest people in the world from 2001 to 2003 listed by Forbes. In April 2004, Times Magazine, rated him among the 100 most influential people in the world by Time magazine. He is also the richest Indian for the past several years. In 2005, Government of India honored Azim Premji with Padma Bhushan.

Bhai Mohan Singh

Born: December 30, 1917

Achievement: Founder of pharmaceutical giant Ranbaxy Laboratories Ltd; Awarded with Padma Shri

Bhai Mohan Singh can be called as the doyen of pharmaceutical industry in India. He is the founder of pharmaceutical giant Ranbaxy Laboratories Ltd.

Bhai Mohan Singh was born on December 30, 1917 in Rawalpindi district. His father Bhai Gyan Chand was a Hindu and his mother Sunder Dai was a Sikh. Bhai Mohan Singh began his business career in the construction business during the Second World War. His firm bagged a contract to build roads in the North East. After Partition, he left Rawalpindi and settled down in New Delhi.

Bhai Mohan Singh started business as a moneylender. Ranbaxy was started by his cousins Ranjit Singh and Gurbax Singh. Ranbaxy's name was a fusion of Ranjit and Gurbax's names. They were distributors for A. Shionogi, a Japanese pharmaceutical company manufacturing vitamins and anti-TB drugs. When Ranbaxy defaulted on a loan, Bhai Mohan Singh bought the company on August 1, 1952, for Rs 2.5 lakh.

Bhai Mohan Singh collaborated with Italian pharma company Lapetit Spa and later on bought it. Bhai Mohan Singh made his mark in the pharmaceuticals industry in the late 1960s when he launched his first superbrand, Calmpose.

Calmpose was an imitation of Roche's valium. But Roche had not patented it in India. In early 1970s when Indian adopted a regime of process patents in the Bhai Mohan Singh quickly realised that one could make any product in the world through reverse engineering. He established an R&D facility at Mohali and launched one blockbuster pill after the other, such as Roscillin, Cifran etc.

Ranbaxy Laboratories Ltd went public in 1973. At this time Bhai Mohan Singh introduced his eldest son Parvinder Singh in the company, who later on became the company's Managing Director in 1982. Bhai Mohan Singh also co-founded Max India with his youngest son, Analjit Singh.

With liberalisation differences arose between Bhai Mohan Singh and Parvinder Singh over the expansion and professionalisation strategy of Ranbaxy. Subsequently, in 1999 in a boardroom coup of sorts Bhai Mohan Singh was forced to bow down and Parvider took over the company. This broke Bhai Mohan Singh's spirit and he retired from active company affairs. He died on March 27, 2006.

Bhai Mohan Singh was a former vice president of the New Delhi Municipal Corporation (NDMC) and was awarded the Padma Shri for his contribution in civic matters. For his contribution to the industrial development of Punjab, the Punjab Government had named an Industrial Township near Ropar after Bhai Mohan Singh.

Karsanbhai Patel

Achievement: Man behind the hugely successful brand, Nirma.

Karsanbhai Patel is the man behind the hugely successful brand, Nirma. His' is a legendary rags to riches journey during which he shattered established business theories and rewrote new ones.

Karsanbhai Khodidas Patel (K.K. Patel) came from a humble farmer family from Mehsana, Gujarat. He worked as Lab Assistant in the Geology and Mining Department of the Government of Gujarat. In 1969, at the age of 25, Karsan Bhai Patel started a small-scale enterprise. He offered a quality detergent powder, using indigenous technology, at a third of the prevailing price, without compromising on the product. Karsanbhai named the detergent powder Nirma after daughter Nirupama.

At that time domestic detergent market was limited only to premium segment and was dominated by MNCs. Karsanbhai Patel started door-to-door selling of Nirma and priced it at ₹ 3 per kg. The next available cheapest brand in the market at that time was ₹13 per kg. Nirma revolutionized the whole detergent powder segment and in a short span of time created an entirely new market segment in the domestic detergent sector market. It gave the bigger established brands a run for their money and soon occupied the top market share. To add to all this, Nirma was made of an innovative formulation, which global detergent giants were later on compelled to emulate, it was phosphate free and hence environment friendly, and the process of manufacturing was labour intensive, which offered large scale employment.

Karsanbhai notched up one success after another. After establishing its leadership in economy-priced detergents, Nirma foray into the premium brand segment, in cakes and detergents was equally successful. It built up a 30% market share in the premium detergent segment and achieved a greater than 20% share in the premium soaps market.

Karsanbhai Patel has won many accolades on his way to success. The Federation of Association of Small Scale Industries of India, New Delhi, awarded him with the 'Udyog Ratna'. The Gujarat Chamber of Commerce felicitated him as an 'Outstanding Industrialist of the Eighties'. The Govt. of India twice appointed him Chairman of the Development Council for Oils, Soaps & Detergents.

Dr. Pratap Reddy

Achievement: Founder of the Apollo Hospital Group

Dr. Pratap Reddy is the founder of the Apollo Hospital Group, India's first corporate hospital group. He revolutionized the whole health care scenario of India and inspired others to follow the suit. Today, India has over 750 corporate hospitals all over the country.

Dr. Pratap Reddy came to India after serving as the Chief Resident of the Worcenter City Hospital in the US to start his practice in Madras with a modest earning of ₹ 100/- per day. The idea to establish Apollo Group of Hospitals came when Dr. Reddy lost a patient who couldn't make it to Texas for an open heart surgery. This inspired Dr. Pratap Reddy to create world-class medical infrastructure in India and make it more accessible and affordable to common people. Dr. Reddy's efforts bore fruit when he succeeded in setting up the first center of the Apollo Hospitals Group in Chennai in 1983.

Dr, Pratap Reddy soon followed this with India's first hospital consultancy body - the Indian Hospitals Corporation - and commissioned two more Tertiary Care Centers in India. Since its inception, Apollo has demonstrated that Indian skills are equivalent to the best centers in the world and has produced world-class results in the most complicated Cadaver Transplant. Today, the Apollo Hospitals Group has over 22 centers in major cities in India and a combined turnover of over US $ 100 million.

Dr Reddy is now spreading Apollo Hospitals Group to other parts of Asia. The group opened its first clinic in Dubai in March 1999 and is coming up with projects in Sri Lanka, Africa, Bangladesh, and Oman. Dr. Reddy is currently looking at secondary health centers in semi urban and smaller cities and has already identified 23 sites for the purpose.

Dr. Pratap Reddy's latest initiatives are "Med Varsity"-a virtual medical university providing total access to experts in the field of medicine anywhere in the world- and "MEDNET"-Hospital Systems Management package. Both the initiatives are expected to transform health care sector in India.

Shiv Nadar

Achievement: Chief Executive Officer of Hindustan Computers Limited (HCL), India's largest infotech çonglomerate

Shiv Nadar is the Chief Executive of Hindustan Computers Limited (HCL), India's largest infotech conglomerate. He figures in the Forbes list of Indian billionaires. Originally hailing from Moolaipozhi Village, Trichendur, Tutocorin District, Tamil Nadu, Shiv Nadar moved to Delhi in 1968. He worked as an engineer with DCM Ltd. But the entrepreneur in Shiv Nadar wanted to set up his own business. Therefore, he along with six of his colleagues launched a firm making office products like copiers.

In late 1970s, when IBM quit India, Shiv Nadar's HCL stepped in to fill the vacuum. In 1982, HCL came out with its first computer. Today, HCL derives 80% of its revenue from computers and office equipment. HCL has also been spreading its global reach. Its Singapore subsidiary, Far East Computers, achieved a breakthrough in imaging technology, which, among other applications, enables computers to read handwritten tax returns.

HCL has adopted innovative practices to achieve growth. In the U.S, a software subsidiary, HCL America, has reaped huge dividends by taking advantage of global time zones. Every morning, the company's Chennai office receives software assignments from the U.S, just after work stops there for the night. A team of Indian engineers, with salaries much lower than those of their American counterparts, complete the jobs and send them back in the evening.

In a short span of time, Shiv Nadar has reached pinnacle of success by his hardwork, vision, and entrepreneurial spirit.

Sunil Mittal

Achievement: Chairman and Managing Director of Bharti Group, India's largest GSM-based mobile phone service provider; IT Man of the Year Award 2002 from Dataquest and CEO of the Year, 2002 Award from World HRD Congress.

Sunil Mittal can be called as originator of cellular phone revolution in India. He is the founder, Chairman and Managing Director of Bharti Group and runs India's largest GSM-based mobile phone service.

Sunil Bharti Mittal's father was an M.P. Sunil did not followed his father's footsteps. After graduating from Punjab University in 1970s, he set up a small bicycle business in Ludhiana in partnership with his friend. By 1979, Sunil Mittal realized that his ambitions could not be fulfilled in Ludhiana, so he moved out to Mumbai from Ludhiana.

He spent a few years in Mumbai and in 1982, Sunil Mittal started a full-fledged business selling portable generators imported from Japan. This gave him a chance to acquaint himself with the nitty-gritty's of marketing and advertising. His business was running smoothly but later on the government banned the import of generators as two Indian companies were awarded licenses to manufacture generators locally.

In 1986, Sunil Bharti Mittal incorporated Bharti Telecom Limited (BTL) and entered into a technical tie up with Siemens AG of Germany for manufacture of electronic push button phones. Gradually he expanded his business and by early 1990s, Sunil Mittal was making fax machines, cordless phones and other telecom gear.

In 1992, when the Indian government was awarding licenses for mobile phone services for the first time, Sunil Mittal clinched Delhi cellular license in collaboration with French telecom group Vivendi. In 1995, Sunil Mittal founded Bharti Cellular Limited (BCL) to offer cellular services under the brand name AirTel. Soon, Bharti became the first telecom company to cross the 2-million mobile subscriber mark. Bharti Cellular Limited also rolled out India's first private national as well as international long-distance service under the brand name India One. In 2001, BCL entered into a joint venture with Singapore Telecom International for a $650-million submarine cable project, India's first ever undersea cable link connecting Chennai in India and Singapore.

Today, Sunil Mittal runs a successful empire with a market capitalization of approximately $ 2 billion and employing over 5,000 people. He has been honored with several awards. Sunil Bharti Mittal was chosen as one of the top entrepreneurs in the world for the year 2000 and amongst 'Stars of Asia', by 'Business Week'. He also received IT Man of the Year Award 2002 from Dataquest and CEO Of the Year, 2002 Award (World HRD Congress).

Sameer Gehlaut of India Bulls

India Bulls is one of the top business groups in India founded by Sameer Gehlaut, Saurabh Mittal and Rajiv Rattan in the year 2000 as India Bulls securities Ltd and later diversified into Finance, Real Estate and Power sectors. Sameer has been the chairman of the group since its inception. The Group had grown successfully under his leadership and is recognized as 'Business Superbrand' by the brand council. Gehlaut is listed as India's youngest self made billionaire.

Sameer Gehlaut has been the chairman of India bulls Group since inception. He is also the chairman of major India bulls companies: India bulls Power, India bulls Housing Finance & India bulls Real Estate. Under his leadership, India bulls Group has grown in scale and size to a business house with strong businesses in various sectors.

Mr Gehlaut started India bulls Group after working briefly with Halliburton before returning to India. Mr Gehlaut received a B.Tech degree in Mechanical Engineering from Indian Institute of Technology, Delhi

Young entrepreneur Sameer Gehlaut established India bulls in 2000, after acquiring Orbis Securities, a stock brokerage company in Delhi. The group started its operations from a small office near Hauz Khas bus terminal in Delhi. The office had a tin roof and two computers. In fact the same office also gave birth to another company, Classteacher Learning Systems which is a leading education company today. Class teacher was founded by Rohit Pande and Sameer Buti who were also classmates at IIT, Delhi. Sameer Gehlaut completed his Mechanical Engineering from IIT Delhi in 1995 .He worked for Halliburton in the United States. He came back to India to start an earth moving and mining business, which is presently run by his family.

India bulls were the pioneers in the online brokerage business segment. The company had a young management team and were able to raise money from time to time. Its investors included LN Mittal and Farallon Capital. In September 2004 the company came out with its IPO.

They also entered into new business segments. The group's business interests include real estate, consumer finance, mortgages, retail and power. They have a market capitalization of more than ₹ 25000 crores. We can recall that Indiabulls acquired 7.8 acres (32,000 m^2) of land from NTC for ₹ 441.75 crore, this was the Elphinstone Mills land in Lower Parel, Mumbai. They also acquired 11 acre ₹ (45,000 m^2) of the Land from NTC for ₹ 276.6 crore, this was the land of Jupiter Mills in Lower Parel, Mumbai.

India bulls entered into a joint venture with Sogecap for its foray into the Life insurance business. Sogecap is the Life insurance subsidiary of the French company Societe Generate.

Kishore Biyani,
Future Group

Kishore Biyani is the founder and the Group CEO of the Future Group and the Managing Director of Pantaloons Retail. The Future Group is a $1 billion company with its core business in the Retail sector. Kishore Biyani talks about the success story of Pantaloons, Big Bazar and Central Mall in his book 'It happened in India' which hit the book stores in the recent past.

Kishore Biyani is the Group CEO of Future Group, is one of India's leading business houses with multiple businesses in the consumption space. Future Group's main businesses include, retail, capital and investment advisory services, consumer finance, insurance, brand development, retail media and logistics.

Kishore Biyani founded Pantaloons in 1997, followed by a number of retail formats including Big Bazaar, Central, Food Bazaar, Brand Factory and Home Town. The group's flagship company. Pantaloon Retail along with its subsidiaries now cater to almost the entire consumption basket of a wide cross-section of Indian consumers. In the past 12 months, the group's retail formats attracted over 200 million customers. Headquartered in Mumbai, Future Group operates through 9 million square feet of retail space, in over 120 cities and rural centres across India and employs over 25,000 people.

The group's recent foray into capital services is led through Future Capital Holdings, focusing on asset management and consumer credit. It provides investment advisory services to assets worth over $ 1 billion and operates a consumer finance arm. Future Money.

Other group companies include, Future General, the group's insurance venture in partnership with Italy's General Group, Future Brands, a brand development and IPR company, Future Logistics, providing logistics and distribution solutions to group companies and business partners and Future Media, a retail media initiative.

Future Group's joint venture partners include, US-based stationery products retailers, Staples, French womenswear retailer, Etam, UK-based Lee Cooper, Middle East-based Axiom Communications and India-based Blue Foods, Liberty Shoes, Talwalkars' and Asian Electronics.

A staunch believer in the group's corporate credo, 'Rewrite Rules, Retain Values,' Kishore Biyani considers Indianness as the core value driving the group. He recently authored the book, 'It Happened In India,' which is now being translated in a number of Indian langauges.

Kishore Biyani was born in August 1961 and is married to Sangita Biyani. They live in Mumbai and have two daughters, Ashni and Avni.

Gautam Adani,
Adani Group

Gautam Adani is the founder and chairman of the Adani Group, a leading conglomerate company with total asset value of$12 billion. The Adani Group has more than 50 companies under it. The core businesses of the group are Energy, Commodities Trading, Real Estate, Oil and gas, Mundra Port operations, Natural gas distribution, edible oil manufacturing, mining and logistics. Gautam Adani is an university dropout and started working as a diamond sorter for a few hundred rupees. In 1988, he set up an import-export company called Adani Enterprises.

He was born in a Gujarati Jain family to, Shantaben and Shantilal Adani who had migrated from the town of Tharad in northern Gujarat in search of a livelihood. Adani has seven siblings the eldest being Mansukhbhai Adani. Gautam is married to Priti Adani, who is a dentist and heads Adani Foundation as a Managing Trustee. They have two sons. Karan Adani who is 23 years old and is currently pursuing his BS in Management from Purdue University, USA; Jeet Adani, their younger son is 13 years old.

At a young age of 18, he went to Mumbai with only a few hundred rupees and worked as a diamond sorter at Mahindra Bros. After 2 years he set up his own diamond brokerage outfit at Zaveri Bazaar. His elder brother Mansukhbhai, bought a plastics unit in Ahmedabad in 1981 and wanted Gautam to run it.

Adani returned to Ahmedabad and this was the beginning of Adani's journey into global trading by beginning to import Polyvinyl Chloride (PVC) which is a key raw material for manufacturing plastics. The Adani Group had a quiet beginning, but Adani used his skills of persuasion to get beneficial land allotment policies and guidelines from the bureaucracy. Adani's entrepreneurial and ambitious vision along with rigorous hard work made the Adani Group one of the fastest growing professionally owned enterprises in India.

Maintenance of world-class quality standards and a customer focused approach helped the Adani Group to achieve revenues of INR 262 billion by 2009

Sunil Bharti Mittal, Bharti Enterprises

Sunil Mittal is the founder, chairman and group CEO of Bharti Enterprises, India's largest mobile phone service company with operations across 19 countries in Asia and Africa. Sunil Mittal was one of the first Indian entrepreneurs to identify the mobile telecom business as a major growth area. Bharti Cellular Services is known popularly as AirTel. The Indian Government honoured him with the Padma Bhushan Award, the third highest civilian award in the year 2007.

Sunil Bharti Mittal is the Founder, Chairman and Group CEO of Bharti Enterprises and the Chairman of Bharti Airtel. Bharti Enterprises is one of India's leading business groups with interests in telecom, retail, realty, financial services and agri-products. Bharti Airtel is the flagship company of Bharti Enterprises, which is among the leading global telecom company with operations in India, South-Asia and Africa. Bharti has joint ventures with several global leaders: Singtel, Wal-Mart, AXA and Del Monte.

Sunil started his career at 18 after graduating from Punjab University in India in 1976 and founded Bharti. Today, at 55, he heads a successful enterprise which employs over 30,000 people.

Sunil has been recognized with the Padma Bhushan, one of India's highest civilian awards. He has also been conferred the LalBahadurShastri National Award for 2009. He is a member of the Prime Minister's Council on Trade & Industry. Sunil has served as the President of the Confederation of Indian Industry (CII), the premier industry body in India (2007-08). He also serves on the Board of Directors of Unilever PLC, Unilever NV and SoftBank, Japan.

Sunil has been awarded the INSEAD Business Leader for the World Award 2011 and the NDTV Profit Business Leadership Award 2011 for "Corporate Conscience". He has earlier received the Global Economy Prize 2009 by The Kiel Institute, Germany and the US-India Business Council also honored him with the 'Global Vision' Award 2008. Sunil has received the GSM Association Chairman's Award for 2008. In 2006, he was chosen Asia Businessman of the Year by Fortune and Asia Pacific CEO of the Year by Frost & Sullivan. He has been named Business Leader of the Year by several important media houses, including The Economic Times, Business Standard, and NDTV. Sunil was the Ernst &Young Entrepreneur of the Year in 2004. He is also a member of the Academy of Distinguished Entrepreneurs, Babson College, Wellesley, Massachusetts.

Sunil was the Co-Chair of the World Economic Forum at Davos in 2007 and is a member of its International Business Council. He is a member of several premier international bodies – Board of Trustees of the Carnegie Endowment for International Peace, Reuters Editorial Advisory Board, Singapore's Research, Innovation and Enterprise Council, Telecom Board of the International Telecommunication Union (ITU), the leading UN Agency and also a Commissioner of the Broadband Commission at ITU. He is a member of the India-US CEO Forum, the India- UK CEO Forum and India Japan Business Leaders Forum. He is also the Co-Chair of the India- Africa Business Council and the India-Sri Lanka CEO Forum, appointed by the Prime Minister of India.

Sunil is associated with several academic institutions - member of the Executive Board of the Indian School of Business; member of the Governing Body of London Business School, member of Harvard University's Global Advisory Council and the Dean's Advisory Board of Harvard Business School.

Sunil has been conferred with the degree of Doctor of Civil Law (HonorisCausa) by Newcastle University, UK, Doctor of Laws (HonorisCausa) by the University of Leeds, UK, Doctor of Science (HonorisCausa) by the Indian Institute of Technology (Kharagpur) and Doctor of Science (HonorisCausa) by the GovindBallabh Pant University of Agriculture & Technology. He is an Honorary Fellow of The Institution of Electronics and Telecommunication Engineers. He is an alumnus of Harvard Business School, USA.

Sunil believes that a responsible corporate has a duty to give back to the community in which it operates. This belief has resulted in Bharti Foundation, which is operating 254 schools catering to over 38,000 under-privileged children in rural India. Sunil was ranked among the Top 25 Philanthropists in the World in 2009 by the Barren's Magazine. He is also a Member of the Board of Trustees of Qatar's Education Above All Foundation, an initiative of Her Highness SheikhaMozabint Nasser.

Deep Kalra founded the online travel agency in 2000, that operated out of a small office space in Delhi. MakeMyTrip.com today has offices in 20 cities across India and 2 international offices in the USA. MakeMyTrip launched its website in 2005. In it's very first year of operations it became the largest e-commerce company.

Deep Kalra, Makemytrip.com

The past decade has witnessed a humongous behavioral change among Indian travelers. And the change was induced by MakeMytrip.

Started with the aim to empower the Indian traveler with instant booking and comprehensive choices, it has made online travel booking a common practice among Indians who until lately were inclined to research online while they only trusted traditional modes of payment for making payments.

Founded by Deep Kalra, an MBA from Indian Institute of Management, in a small office in Okhla, Delhi, MakeMyTrip started its journey in the US-India travel market in 2000 and its Indian operations in 2005. It offers its customers a bouquet of travel services and products with international and domestic airline tickets, Indian railway tickets, domestic bus tickets, international and domestic hotel reservations, car rentals, international and domestic holiday packages, and much more.

Just about a decade since its inception, the online travel agency has captured an enviable chunk of 48 percent in the online travel market. Today it is one of the most preferred names in the industry with one out of every twelve domestic flights in India booked via it. Currently, it has offices in 20 cities across India and two international offices in New York and San Francisco, in addition to several franchise locations.

While the core proposition of best deals to its customers at their convenience has helped the enterprise grab adequate attention, what has truly made the initiative a phenomenal success in the industry is the series of conscious and deliberate steps taken at the right time by the management. For instance, the enterprise's decision to grow the high-margin non-air business by offering holidays and online hotel bookings beyond just selling air-tickets has been crucial in maintaining the growth rate. Kalra says, "While the initial growth driver for MakeMyTrip was air tickets category, we could foresee that the ridiculously low costs were not sustainable for airlines in the long run. Therefore, we also made efforts to grow the non-air business."

Again, its decision to not market itself in India but exclusively target the NRIs and the US-India travel sector initially has paid off well."By focusing solely on the NRI market, we managed to conserve precious marketing dollars while our competitors burned their fingers in a premature online market," he tells us.

However, the Indian domestic market was soon ready to bring home the experience of buying tickets online. MakeMyTrip decided to launch its Indian operation in 2005. Kalra says, "We decided to launch in India with our own money. We had around ₹ 2 crore in the bank and we thought that we should do it." But ultimately, they didn't deploy their own money and instead went for private equity. "We realized that in the long run, India was going to be a hot market and all the big players would be investing in online travel which would make it important for us to focus on technology and build the brand to sustain us," says the content entrepreneur.

N.R. Narayana Murthy

Narayana Murthy began his career with Patni Computer Systems in Pune. In 1981, Narayana Murthy founded Infosys with six other software professionals. In 1987, Infosys opened its first international office in U.S.A.

With the liberalization of Indian economy in 1990s, Infosys grew rapidly. In 1993, the company came up with its IPO. In 1995, Infosys set up development centers across cities in India and in 1996, it set up its first officc in Europe in Milton Keynes, UK. In 1999, Infosys became the first Indian company to be listed on NASDAQ. Today (in 2006), Infosys has a turnover of more than $ 2billion and has employee strength of over 50,000. In 2002, Infosys was ranked No. 1 in the "Best Employers in India 2002" survey conducted by Hewitt and in the Business World's survey of "India's Most Respected Company." Conducted in the same year.

Nagavara Ramarao Narayana Murthy is the co-founder and chief adviser of India's best known software firm, Infosys Technologies Ltd. Even after stepping down as the CEO of the company in 2002, Murthy still continues to be among admired business men. He is among the advisory and board members of many reputed universities like Harvard, Stanford, and Yale, is the IT adviser to several Asian countries.

Tulsi Tanti

Achievement: Chairman of Suzlon Energy Ltd,

Ranks among top 10 richest men of India.

Tuisi Tanti is the Chairman of Suzlon Energy Ltd, a company dealing in wind energy. He is one of those first time entrepreneurs who saw potential in an inchoate idea, ventured into it, and made it big. Today, he ranks among top 10 richest men of India.

A commerce graduate and a diploma holder in mechanical engineering, Tulsi Tanti originally hails from Gujarat and is presently based in Pune, Maharashtra. Tulsi Tanti was earlier into textiles. He started his textile business in Gujarat. But he found that the prospects stunted due to infrastructural bottlenecks. The biggest of them all was the cost and unavailability of power, which formed a high proportion of operating expenses of textile industry.

In 1990, Tulsi Tanti invested in two windmills and realized its huge potential. In 1995, he formed Suzlon and gradually quit textiles. Suzlon Energy is the sixth largest wind energy company in the world and the largest in Asia. It is presently building what will be among the world's largest wind parks of its kind at 1,000 MW capacity.

Suzlon is currently concentrating on global expansion drive. It recently acquired Hansen Transmissions, a Belgian maker of wind-turbine gearboxes. Suzlon is also building a rotor-blade factory in Minnesota and has invested $60m in a factory in Tianjin, China. Tulsi Tanti is poised to make India a wind-power export hub.

Verghese Kurien

Born: November 26, 1921

Died: September 9, 2012

Achievements: Known as the "Father of the White Revolution" in India; Winner of Ramon Magsaysay Award; Awarded with Padma Shri (1965), Padma Bhushan (1966), and Padma Vibhushan (1999).

Dr. Verghese Kurien is better known as the "Father of the White Revolution" in India. He is also called as the Milkman of India. Dr. Varghese Kurien was the architect behind the success of the largest dairy development program in the world, christened as Operation Flood. He was the chairman of the Gujarat Co-operative Milk Market Milk Marketing Federation Ltd. (GCMMF) and his name was synonymous with the Amul brand.

Born on November 26, 1921 in Kozhikode, Kerala, Dr. Verghese Kurien graduated with Physics from Loyola College, Madras in 1940. Subsequently, he did his B.E. (Mechanical) from Madras University and went to USA on a government scholarship to do his Masters in Mechanical Engineering from Michigan State University. In between, he completed special studies in engineering at the Tata Iron and Steel Company Institute at Jamshedpur, Jharkhand, in February 1946 and underwent nine months of specialized training in dairy engineering at the National Dairy Research Institute of Bangalore.

Dr. Verghese Kurien returned from America in 1948 and joined the Dairy Department of the Government of India. In May 1949, he was posted as Dairy Engineer at the Government Research Creamery, a small milk-powder factory, in Anand, Gujarat. Around this time, the newly formed cooperative dairy, Kaira District Cooperative Milk Producers' Union Limited (KDCMPUL), was engaged in the battle of survival with the privately owned Poison Dairy, a giant in its field. Enthused by the challenge. Dr. Verghese Kurien left his government job and volunteered to help Shri Tribhuvandas Patel, Chairman of KDCMPUL, to set up a processing plant. This led to the birth ofAMUL and the rest is history.

In 1965, the then Prime Minister Lal Bahadur Shastri created the National Dairy Development Board (NDDB) under the leadership ofDr. Verghese Kurien to replicate the success story of Amul throughout the country. In 1973, Dr. Kurien set up GCMMF (Gujarat Cooperative Milk Marketing Federation) to market the products produced by the dairies. Under Dr. Kurien's stewardship, India became the largest producer of milk in the world. Dr. Kurien breathed his last on September 9, 2012, after a brief illness, in Nadiad, Anand, Gujarat. He was 90 years old.

During his illustrious career, Dr. Verghese Kurien won many accolades and awards. These include: Ramon Magsaysay Award for Community Leadership (1963), Padma Shri (1965), Padma Bhushan (1966), Krishi Ratna Award (1986), Wateler Peace Prize Award of Carnegie Foundation (1986), World Food Prize Laureate (1989), International Person of the Year (1993) by the World Dairy Expo, Madison, Wisconsin, USA, and Padma Vibhushan (1999).

Raunaq Singh

Born: 1922

Achievement: Founder of Raunaq Group; Elected as a member of the Executive Board of the International Chamber of Commerce, Paris.

Raunaq Singh was one of the earliest entrepreneurs of independent India who made it big. He was the founder of Raunaq group. The Raunaq Group's major companies include Apollo Tyres Ltd, Bharat Gears Ltd, Bharat Steel Tubes Ltd, Raunaq International Ltd, Menarini Raunaq Pharma Ltd, and Raunaq Automotive Components Ltd. Raunaq Singh was born in 1922. After initial struggle he went on to become a powerful figure in corporate India. At one point of time in his life he could afford only one paisa a day for meals and when he retired his group was employing 9000 people on his payroll.

Raunaq Singh was a great advocate of economic liberalization and globalization of the Indian business. He worked tirelessly to put the Indian industry on the global map. He held several key leadership positions in Industry & Trade Associations. These included President Federation of Indian Chambers of Commerce & Industry (FICCI), President The Associated Chambers of Commerce and Industry of India (ASSOCHAM), Chairman Engineering Export Promotion Council (EEPC), Chairman Automotive Tyre Manufacturers Association, and President Federation of Indian Export Organization. Raunaq Singh won several awards for his entrepreneurship. He was often referred as "Mr. Exporter", because of his inclination for exports and export promotion for Indian Industry. Raunaq Singh also won international recognition for his entrepreneurial skills, was elected as a member of the Executive Board of the International Chamber of Commerce, Paris for a three-year term.

Raunaq Singh died on September 30, 2002.

M.S. Oberoi

Born: August 15, 1898

Ahievement: Founder of the Oberoi Group of Hotels; Honored with Padma Bhushan in 2001.

M.S. Oberoi can be aptly termed as the father of the Indian hotel industry. Rai Bahadur Mohan Singh Oberoi was among the first to recognize the potential of the tourism industry, its ability to contribute to India's economic growth and generate direct and indirect employment. I (e worked tirelessly to put Indian hotel industry on global tourism map.

M.S. Oberoi was born on August 15, 1898, in the erstwhile undivided Punjab, now in Pakistan. He did his early schooling in Rawalpindi and completed his graduation From Lahore. In 1922, to escape the epidemic of Plague, he came to Shimla, and got a job of front desk clerk, at The Cecil Hotel at a salary of ₹ 50 per month. M.S. Oberoi was a quick learner and shouldered many additional responsibilities along with the job of desk clerk. M. S. Oberoi's diligence prompted Mr. Clarke to request Mohan Singh Oberoi to assist him when he acquired Clarkes Hotel. At the Clarkes Hotel, M.S. Oberoi gained firsthand experience in all aspects of hotel operations.

In 1934, M.S. Oberoi acquired The Clarkes Hotel from his mentor, by mortgaging his wife's jewelry and all his assets. In 1938, he signed a lease to takeover operations of the five hundred room Grand Hotel in Calcutta, which was up for sale following a cholera epidemic. In 1943, Rai Bahadur Mohan Singh Oberoi, acquired the controlling interest in the Associated Hotels of India (AHI) which owned the Cecil, and Corstophans in Shimla, the Maidens and the Imperial in Delhi, and a hotel each in Lahore, Murree, Rawalpindi and Peshawar. He thus became the first Indian to run the largest and finest hotel chain.

Dr. Kiran Mazumdar Shaw

She is the Chairman and the Managing Director of Biocon Limited a biotechnology company which is based in Banagalore, India. She became India's richest woman in the year 2004. The company was started by her in a garage in 1978 with just ₹ 10000 in which the process was to extract an enzyme from papaya.Despite many hurdles her company is the biggest bio-pharmaceutical firm in India. According to forbes she was ranked 80 on the worlds-100-most-powerful-women-2012 list.

Dr. Kiran Mazumdar-Shaw has entered the elite ranks of the Indian business world as India's richest woman. Born on 23 March, 1953, she is the Chairman & Managing Director of Biocon Ltd. She did her schooling from Bangalore and graduated in Zoology from Bangalore University in 1973, after which she moved on to Ballarat University in Melbourne, Australia. She became India's first woman Brew Master and started off as a trainee brewer in Carlton & United Beverages in 1974, following which she worked in various positions in Kolkata and Vadodara. She collaborated with Biocon Biochemicals Limited, Ireland, to found Biocon India in 1978. Initially, she faced many problems, but she was not the one to give up. Her firm has grown to be the biggest biopharmaceutical firm in India today. Though her business interests keep her occupied, she has found time to write a book titled 'Ale and Arty'. She tied the knot with John Shaw, in 1998, who was working as the managing director of Madura Coats. After their marriage, John Shaw quit Madura Coat and joined Biocon.

A very active social activist, she has been involved in various projects like the Bangalore Agenda Task Force (BATF). She was awarded the MV Memorial Award, given in honour of the great engineer and visionary Sir M Vishwesharaiah. Apart from this, she was awarded the Wharton Infosys Business Transformation Award in 2006, the Padma Bhushan in 2005, the Lifetime Achievement Award from the Indian Chamber of Commerce in 2005, the Ernst & Young Entrepreneur of the Year Award in Healthcare & Life Sciences Category in 2002 besides the Padma Shri in 1989.

Dr. Kiran Majumdar-Shaw has held several honorary and advisory positions. Among them, she was the Chairperson and Mission Leader of the Confederation of Indian Industry's National Task Force on Biotechnology, a member of the Prime Minister's Council on Trede & Industry in India, Member, Board of Science Foundation, Ireland , Member, Board of Governors, IIM Bangalore and many others. In doing so, she has set an example for other Indian women to follow.

Indra Nooyi

The 57 year old Indian women entrepreneur is the current Chairman and Chief Executive officer of PepsiCo which is the 2nd largest food and beverage business in terms of net revenue. Since 20012Λwhen she was appointed as the CFO and the president the company's revenue has risen 72 and the net profits have increase. She was ranked fourth on the 2008 and 2009 list on the worlds-100-most-powerful-women list.

Indra Krishnamurthy Nooyi was born on 28 October 1955 in the south Indian city of Madras, now Chennai. After graduating from Madras Christian College with Maths, Physics and Chemistry as subjects she did her Masters in Finance and Marketing from Indian Institute of Management, Calcutta. Her first job was with ABB and then she joined Johnson and Johnson (J&J) in Mumbai. While with J&J, she was closely associated with the launch of the sanitary napkin "Stayfree".

As a typical tycoon of the business from her acumen she has predicted the slowdown in the popularity of aerated soft drinks in the markets worldwide. This enhanced her position in the business world where for a woman it is very difficult to leave any mark on the corner room office of the big conglomerate. She is the one who has meticulously planned for the foray of Pepsi into the sport drinks market in association with Gatorade. Her quick decision making ability and sticking to the work until it gets accomplished has made Enrieo to comment, "If she gets an idea, she goes after it. There's no stopping her".

There is no doubt that her firmness and go getting attitude has won her laurels and has helped her to build a strong foundation in the career graph to reach the top echelon in the organization where many people aspire to reach. To become the Chief Executive Officer of a Multinational company, perhaps the first Indian to reach to this level has been a both tough and exciting experience. Indra has said that being a woman, immigrant and her color made it thrice difficult for her to reach her destination. The only mantra which she followed during the course of time was working hard twice as the male counterpart.

When it was announced that Indra Nooyi was going to replace Steve Reinemund as CEO of PepsiCo, it lit up fire in every mediocre soul that if she can achieve this insurmountable hierarchy nothing is impossible for a determined and strong willed person. The only thing required is perseverance. Indra Nooyi's story lays emphasis on true values of life. Although she faced many hurdles while reaching the highest peak in international level, she walks with pride holding the dignity and honour of her most loved country, India.

While growing up with her sister, Indra Nooyi's mother encouraged them to deliver a speech every night about what they wanted to be. After the speech the winner would get a piece of chocolate. This activity installed confidence and ambition in their little hearts, which helped them to pursue greater heights in the later parts of their life. When she moved to US for higher studies with little money, while studying in Connecticut she worked was a receptionist from midnight to sunrise. With that money she bought herself a western unit of US$ 50 for an interview at Yale, where she had just completed her masters.

Sulajja Firodia Motwani

Sulajja is the Joint MD of Kinect Engineering Ltd. She has done her MBA from Carnegie Mellon University, USA. The company has shown tremendous expansion since she joined. She has done someA tremendousA work by providing facilities to the poor. She has also been recognized for her outstanding business accomplishments. She was ranked number one among the top 25 business leaders by a poll conducted by Fortune India. She is a role model for the young Indian woman entrepreneurs.

Sulajja Firodia Motwani – the woman with kinetic energy

Sulajja Firodia Motwani, Joint Managing Director of Kinetic Engineering Ltd could be labeled without any doubt as "woman who means business". An MBA from Carnegie Mellon University, USA, she started her career at BARRA international, a leading investment analytic firm in California. 4 years of her experience at BARRA helped her learn the practical details of business execution. She came back to India and took over her family business.

Kinetic engineering ltd has shown a tremendous expansion during her reign. The company which had focused on the production ofgearless scooters has now shifted to various other projects with the company's tie-ups with reputed groups such as Mahindra & Mahindra, Hyosung motors, Italjet Moto etc. Responsible for the overall developmental activities of the company, Sulajja plays a vital role in designing and implementing new strategies for the company. Throughout these years she has been able to maintain a perfect balance between her professional and personal life. Her husband Mahesh Motwani is the managing director of Kinetic communications limited.

As a part of Kinetic's corporate social responsibility initiatives, they run a project called "swapnabhoomi" in Parbhani district of Maharashtra where they have adopted a cluster of 150 villages and is provided inputs for sanitation, literacy, vocational guidance, water conservation, irrigation, women's empowerment, village industries etc. These villages can aspire to be called ideal villages. In addition, they run a special program for rehabilitation of leprosy affected persons. Their new initiative is a foundation that assists the war wounded, ex-servicemen and war widows and offers them an opportunity for earning livelihood as they are no longer able to serve in the army or have lost the family members. They are offered an opportunity to set up authorized sales and service stations for Kinetic.

She has been felicitated with many awards. FICCI award for the empowerment of physically challenged, NCPEPD-Shell Helen Keller award for her social activities. Sulajja has won the Young Super achiever award given by Business Today in 2003. India today presented her the title for business "face of the millennium". Fortune India has placed her among the 25 business leaders of the next century in a poll of industrialists. On the increasing number of women entrepreneurs in India, she feels, "there are many opportunities for entrepreneurs today. This coupled with increased education levels among urban women, and a desire for double income in families, will certainly see a huge spurt in women entrepreneurship".

Priya Paul

Priya Paul is a woman entrepreneur who currently is the Chairperson of The Park Hotels. She joined the company soon after she finished her studies in the US and worked under her father at a tender age of 22. The HospitalityA IndustryA has recognized her efforts and she has consistentlyA receivedA many awards. Her chain of hotels is considered as one of Best Hotels Worldwide among 101 hotels in 2003.

Priya Paul, President of the Park Hotels and a Director of the Apeejay Surrendra Group, is among the few 'born to sweet delight', as William Blake would put it. And rightly so, as today she is a part of the hospitality industry where sweetness counts. Despite her tough job, this elegant lady exudes complete calm. "I have been learning yoga and meditation for the past five years from a teacher, Tripta Bhanot," replies the charming lady when questioned about it.

Armed with a bachelor's degree in economics from Wellesley College, USA, she started her career as the Marketing Manager of The Park in 1988. She soon climbed the ladder, being promoted to Acting General Manager and was finally given the chair of Director, Apeejay Surrendra Group, and President, The Park, in 1990.Armed with a bachelor's degree in economics from Wellesley College, USA, she started her career as the Marketing Manager of The Park in 1988. She soon climbed the ladder, being promoted to Acting General Manager and was finally given the chair of Director, Apeejay Surrendra Group, and President, The Park, in 1990. Does spirituality play an integral part in her professional life? "I stopped the formal training for yoga and meditation six months ago as I realized that spirituality is within you. My spirituality is something very personal and private for me. It's not something that I really want to share... Coming to meditation, it has helped me professionally by enabling me to distance myself from the chaos all around," she replies.

Priya is also Vice-President, the Hotel Association of India, and a founder member of World Travel Tourism Council (Asia chapter). Then, she's a member of the Young President's Organization, a member of the PATA Environment and Eco-tourism Committee and a trustee of "My family has always been involved in philanthropy. We have set up a number of trusts and institu India Foundation of the Arts.tions. I feel it is important for every individual, every company and corporate to contribute to society in whatever way. And I am not only talking about donating money. We have set up a number of schools in West Bengal and tube well projects in our tea plantations at Assam," she elucidates. "I got together with some friends to set up the Seed Shop at The Park, Delhi, three years ago as I had felt a certain need in the market for a one-stop shop for organic products, for natural products. But we have created this with the urban market in mind. It has done reasonably well and we are hoping to expand that. We are planning to put it on the Net. Our site is under construction."

What did she feel about the revival of New Age in the country? "I don't think there is any revival as such. It is in the English language that you find this more written about. Where the country is concerned, all these things have always existed. I was in Hardwar, India, recently. People had traveled there for a yajna 12 years ago and the culmination of this was two weeks ago. On Karthik Poornima there were some six million people there. These people have never had a revival, a New Age. For them it's a way of life. This has always been going on... Maybe worldwide there's a revival."

Neelam Dhawan

Neelam Dhawan is the Managing director of HP India. She worked with Microsoft India and handles the sales and marketing group. She has been a technology legend. She started her career in 1996 with HCL and then went on to join IBM as a Vice President where she was also on the board.It's been four years since she is working with Hewlett-Packard and we are sure she is going to take the company to new heights. Neelam Dhawan is the Managing Director of Hewlett-Packard India. She has countrywide responsibility for revenues and profitability and ensuring the greatest leverage from HP's Services, Personal Systems and Imaging & Printing businesses.

With a portfolio that extends to offshore activities, BPO, Software Engineering, Research and IT Services, Neelam is focused on shaping the company's overall business agenda and leading its strategy and corporate development efforts to make HP the most admired company in India.

Previously, Neelam was the Managing Director of Microsoft India, a position she held from 2005 to 2008. During her tenure, she sharpened Microsoft's strategic focus and improved its operating efficiency and execution, as well as its financial performance and customer focus. Prior to this assignment, Neelam held a variety of successful leadership positions in leading Indian IT companies, including HCL and IBM.

Neelam holds a bachelor's degree in Economics from St. Stephen's College, New Delhi, and a Masters in Business Administration from the Faculty of Management Studies, Delhi University.

Mallika Srinivasan

Mallika Srinivasan is the CEO OF Tafe Motor and Tractors Limited. As per Fortune list 2012 of 50 most powerful businesswomen she is ranked second.

Mallika Srinivasan one of most powerful CEO of Indian Business, Director of 4225 crore amalgamations group Tafe. She is Economic Time business women of the year 2006. Daughter of Sivalsilam, Chairman of Amalgamations Group, She joined the group in 1986. She modernized firm in all aspects and make $ 660 million company to US $20 million in 1986, It holds the second largest market share.

Mallika from the Industrialist family started her career as General Manager of Tafe - Tractors and Farm Equipment . When she entered the family business its turnover was 85cr and her hard work dedication made it reach 4225 company, running forward to rich heights of business. Under her guidance the business expanded its other sectors like engineering plastics, automotive batteries, panel instruments etc . And even runs hospitals, schools and charitable trusts. Her company made alliance with Massey Ferguson (A part of Ago). She is the president of Tractor Manufacturers Associations, Madras Management Association, And was the first lady as Madras Chamber of Commerce and Industry. Member of governing body of Indian School of Business

Sudha Murthy

She is one of my personal favourites as I have many of her books which she has written as an author. She currently is the Chairperson in Infosys Foundation. She has participated in rural development efforts and has also built several orphanages. She became the first female engineer to be hired by TELCO. She met Narayana Murthy while they were employed and then the two got married.

In her early days, Sudha Murthy was a computer scientist and an engineer. She was born in the year 1950 in the district of Shiggaon in Kamataka.

Sudha Murty scored the highest marks in SSLC (Xth grade) in 1966 from New Education Society Girls English School, Hubli.

Sudha Murthy did her engineering degree from BVB College of Engineering in Hubli. Placed as a topper in the state of Karnataka, she went on to get a medal from the CM for her accomplishment. After completing her Masters in the subject of Computer Science from HSc, Bangalore, she repeated her feat and topped her class, to receive yet another medal from the Engineers Institute.

Sudha was the first computer engineer employed by the company Tata Motors. She also initiated a bold move to introduce computer and library facilities in all schools in Kamataka. She taught computer science and started writing fiction with her first book 'Dollar Sose'. This book was written in Kannada and later translated to English, and it was even converted into a television serial in 2001 titled 'Dollar Bahu'.

Career

- Worked at TELCO as a Development Engineer in Pune, Mumbai and Jamshedpur and later joined Walchand Group of Industries at Pune as Senior Systems Analyst.
- Involved in the development of Infosys Technologies Ltd., in various capacities & worked as HoD for Computer Science in a reputed college of Bangalore University
- In 1996, started Infosys Foundation & till date has been the Trustee of Infosys Foundation & a Visiting Professor at the PG Center of a reputed college of Bangalore University
- Written and published 13 books - out of which, two are travellogues, two technical books, six novels and three educative books.

Appendix B

HOW TO ANALYSE CASE STUDY

Case is an intensive study of the actual business situations, events and problems happening in the industries. It is a method of analyzing real life situations.It is a systematic gathering of adequate information about business situation. It is a form of Qualitative and Quantitative analysis and careful observations of business situations or problems. Case is an in-depth and detailed study of the real life situation as a whole.Thus case presents facts,events and organizational circumstances surrounding particularly in managerial situations.

A case describes the actual working of business situation of a company, or a business situation at the time of it was conducted. It can be eye-witnessed narrative of a real life business situation, covering all the aspects of managerial decisions and executive actions against the back-ground of the environment and industry situations within which it operates. Cases may be written or oral on various functional areas to highlight certain problems. Cases may be general management which underscores policy decisions.

Objectives of the Case:

1. To increase the understanding of the students of what manager should do and should not do in guiding a business to success.
2. To increase the communication skills in conducting strategic analysis in a variety of situations happening in the industries.
3. To provide the student valuable practice in diagnosing strategic issues and strategic alternatives with the help of **SWOT** analysis.
4. To enhance the student's sense of business judgement based on changing scenario of the business.
5. To provide the students an indepth exposure to a variety of companies and industries to gain actual business experiences.

GUIDELINES TO ANALYSE CASE

There is no particular formula for analyzing case and no basic pattern which can be passed on. Each situation must be handled in a new and unique way. However, the following general steps may be applied to analyse the case.

1. For the first reading, carefully grasp the problem or situation and identify what kind of information it contains.
2. For the second reading, take time to proceed and study the tables, exhibits, figures to make notes of your own on important factors of case is given.

3. Try to answer the questions based on facts, events and situations of the case.
4. Identify the strategy. Objectives and achievements of the company.
5. Identify the strengths, weakness, opportunities and threats to the company.
6. What was the environmental setting with in the industry or the strategies consistent with the environmental strengths?
7. Identify the inconsistency, if any what was the impact on the industry.
8. Try to identify the problems involved and identify the possible solutions.
9. Apply appropriate management techniques to the solution of the problem. What are the alternatives available and which is the best.
10. Suggest the best alternative among the available alternatives finally to implement it in the industry for better results.